# A Story in Stones

Portugal's influence on culture and
architecture in the Highlands of Ethiopia
1493-1634

by J.J. Hespeler-Boultbee

Foreword by
**Richard Pankhurst**

**CCB Publishing**
British Columbia, Canada

A Story in Stones: Portugal's influence on culture and architecture in the Highlands of Ethiopia 1493-1634

Copyright ©2011 by J.J. Hespeler-Boultbee
ISBN-13   978-1-926585-98-7
Second Edition

Library and Archives Canada Cataloguing in Publication

Hespeler-Boultbee, J. J. (John Jeremy), 1935-
A story in stones: Portugal's influence on culture and architecture in the highlands of Ethiopia, 1493-1634 / by J. J. Hespeler-Boultbee ; foreword by Richard Pankhurst. – 2nd ed.

Includes bibliographical references and index.
ISBN 978-1-926585-98-7
Also available in electronic format.

1. Architecture--Ethiopia--Portuguese influences.
2. Ethiopia-- Civilization--Portuguese influences.
3. Ethiopia--History--1490-1889.
4. Portugal--Civilization--16th century.
5. Portugal--Civilization-- 17th century.  I. Title.

DT384.H48 2011    963'.00469    C2011-900642-1

Extreme care has been taken to ensure that all information presented in this book is accurate and up to date at the time of publishing. Neither the author nor the publisher can be held responsible for any errors or omissions. Additionally, neither is any liability assumed for damages resulting from the use of the information contained herein.

All rights reserved. No part of this publication may be reproduced, stored in a retrieval system or transmitted in any form or by any means, electronic, mechanical, photocopying, recording or otherwise without the express written permission of the publisher. Printed in the United States of America and the United Kingdom.

Photo credits: All photos contained herein are copyright J.J. Hespeler-Boultbee except:
Photos of Selassie Gemb (Washa) courtesy of Tim and Kim Otte de Hoop
Archival photos used in *Kwer'ata re'esu* section
Illustration credits: All illustrations contained herein are copyright J.J. Hespeler-Boultbee except:
Illustration of landscape at Abbay Gish Fasil courtesy of Anne Marsh Evans

Publisher:    CCB Publishing
              British Columbia, Canada
              www.ccbpublishing.com

## Dedication

This edition of *A Story in Stones* is affectionately dedicated
to my Lake Tana family

St. George, the patron saint of Ethiopia

*"By ways untrod I walked with God, by parched and bitter path;*
*In deserts dim I talked with Him, and learned to know His Wrath."*
                                                        *- Robert Service*

## Monarchs During Portuguese-Ethiopian Contact, 1493-1634

| **Portugal** | | **Ethiopia** | |
|---|---|---|---|
| Afonso V | 1438-1481 | Eskendar | 1478-1495 |
| João II | 1481-1495 | Naod | 1495-1508 |
| Manuel I | 1496-1521 | Lebna Dengal | 1508-1540 |
| João III | 1521-1557 | Galawdewos | 1540-1559 |
| Sebastião | 1557-1578 | Minas | 1559-1563 |
| Henrique | 1578-1580 | Sartsa Dengal | 1563-1596 |
| Filipe I de Castile | 1580-1598 | Ya'qob | 1596-1603 |
| Filipe II de Castile | 1598-1621 | Za Dengal | 1603-1604 |
| Filipe III de Castile | 1621-1640 | Ya'qob | 1604-1607 |
| | | Sussenyos | 1607-1632 |
| | | Fasiladas | 1632-1667 |

Note: See full chronology on page 183.

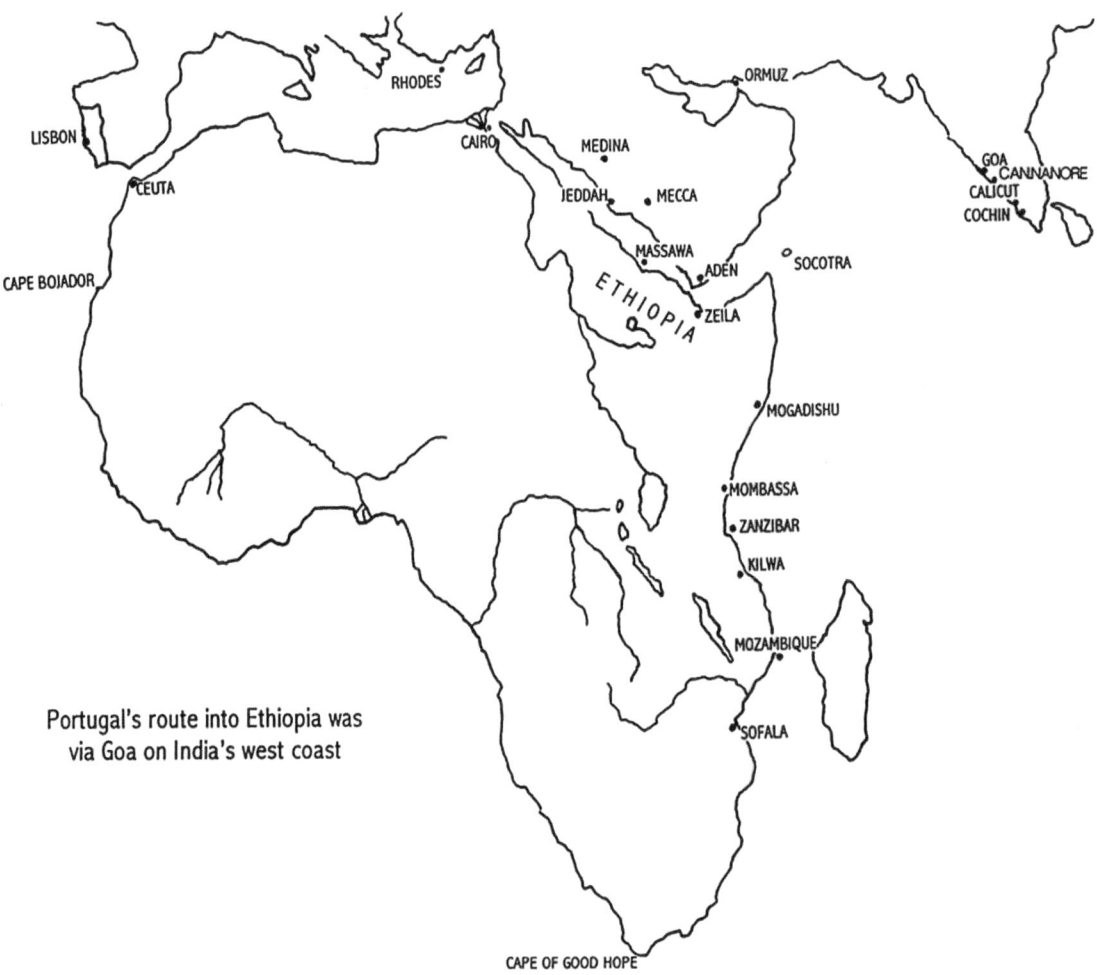

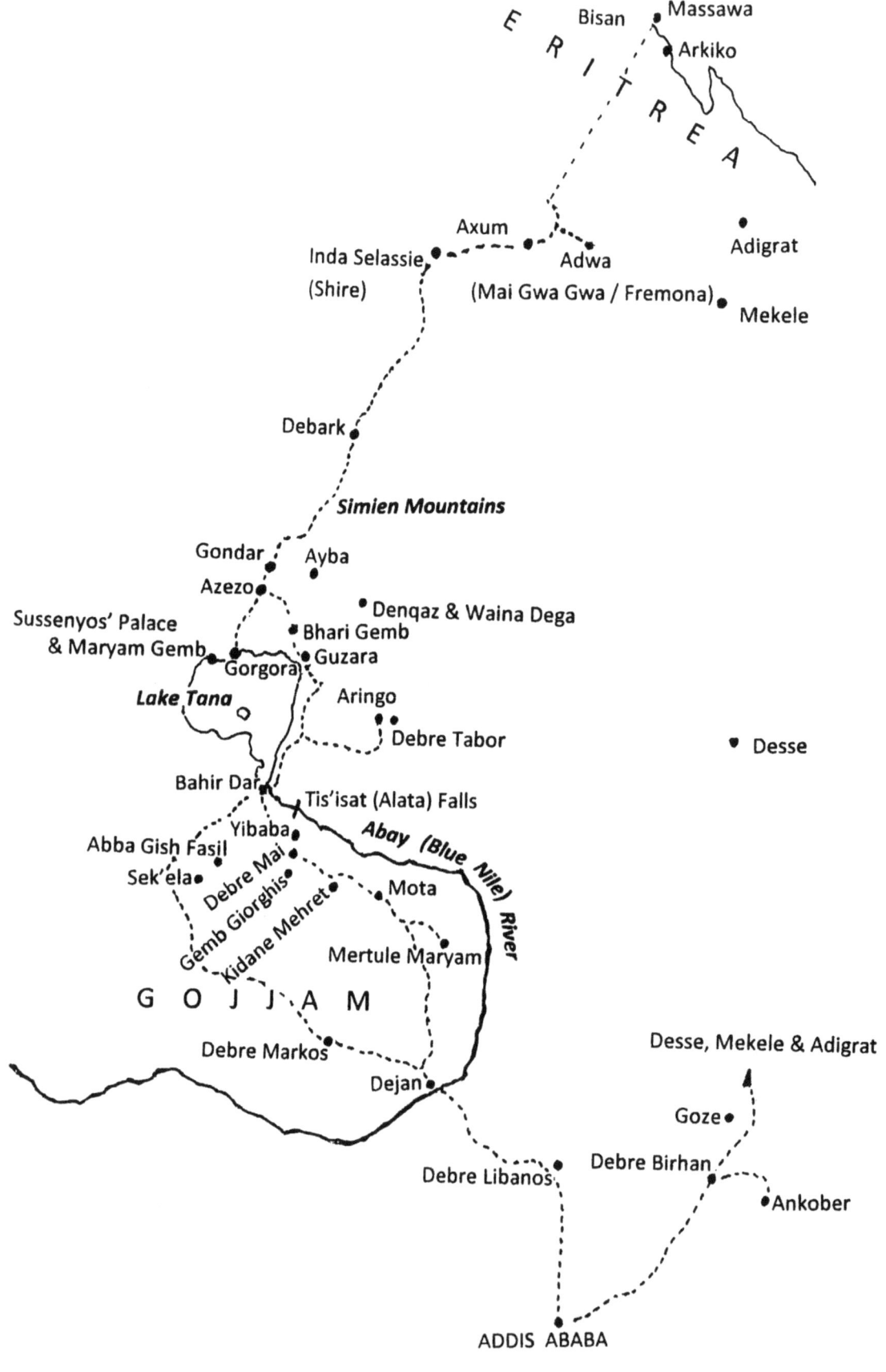

# Contents

| | | |
|---|---|---|
| Monarchs During Portuguese-Ethiopian Contact | ................ | 5 |
| Maps:   1) Portugal's Route into Ethiopia | ................ | 6 |
| 2) Detail of Ethiopia | ................ | 7 |
| Foreword by Richard Pankhurst | ................ | 12 |
| Preface by Dr. Tsehai Jemberu | ................ | 14 |
| Acknowledgements | ................ | 16 |
| Author's Note to the Current Edition | ................ | 19 |
| **Introduction** | ................ | 21 |
| Voyage of Discovery | ................ | 22 |
| Understanding the Social History | ................ | 23 |
| Examining the Record | ................ | 24 |
| Past and Present | ................ | 25 |
| Enter the Portuguese | ................ | 26 |
| Continuing the Research | ................ | 28 |
| **Part I – The Story** | ................ | 30 |
| Portugal and Pêro da Covilhã | ................ | 31 |
| Confrontation: Islam and Christianity | ................ | 37 |
| Prester John | ................ | 38 |
| Da Covilhã's Letter | ................ | 39 |
| Highland Court | ................ | 41 |
| The Portuguese in the Indian Ocean | ................ | 43 |
| Ahmad Grag'n | ................ | 45 |
| In Search of Paradise | ................ | 47 |
| The Exasperating "Dom" João Bermudez | ................ | 49 |
| Emperor Galawdewos | ................ | 51 |
| The Jesuits | ................ | 52 |
| Emperor Minas | ................ | 53 |
| Rebellion | ................ | 54 |
| Heresy: Rome's Rebuttal | ................ | 55 |
| Pêro Páez | ................ | 56 |
| Emperor Sussenyos Converts to the Church of Rome | ................ | 57 |
| "Our sun has been eclipsed…" | ................ | 59 |
| **Part II – The Stones** | ................ | 62 |
| Portugal's Cultural and Architectural Influences | ................ | 63 |
| Before Setting Out | ................ | 64 |
| Ankober: Assessing the Ancient Land | ................ | 65 |
| Examples of Typical Portuguese Stonework | ................ | 69 |
| Goze | ................ | 75 |
| The "Portuguese Bridge" on the Gur River | ................ | 78 |
| Mertule Maryam | ................ | 81 |
| The Church Museum | ................ | 90 |
| Alata Bridge at Tis'isat | ................ | 91 |

| | | |
|---|---|---|
| Páez house in the Compound of St. Giorghis Church at Bahir Dar | ................ | 94 |
| Kebran Gabriel, Entos Eyesu, Zege and Liblibo | ................ | 95 |
| The Lake's Grandest Monasteries | ................ | 97 |
| Gemb Kidane Mehret and Collala | ................ | 105 |
| Yibaba | ................ | 106 |
| Gemb Giorghis and Gemb Maryam | ................ | 108 |
| Shimbet Mikael | ................ | 110 |
| Residential Structures | ................ | 113 |
| Debre Tabor | ................ | 115 |
| Aringo | ................ | 116 |
| Guzara | ................ | 118 |
| Bhary Gemb | ................ | 121 |
| Teklahaimanot Church Complex at Azezo | ................ | 123 |
| The Winter Palace of Geneta Yesus at Azezo | ................ | 124 |
| Gondar's "Chicken House" | ................ | 125 |
| Fasil Bridge Over the Angreb River | ................ | 126 |
| Gondar's Castle Bridges | ................ | 127 |
| Old Quarters of Gondar and Gorgora | ................ | 128 |
| Gondar's Six-Castle Compound | ................ | 132 |
| Kusquaum, Fasil's Bath and Tomb of Zobel | ................ | 141 |
| Denqaz and Waina Dega | ................ | 142 |
| Gobatit Bridge Over the Angreb River | ................ | 147 |
| Defeche Kidane Mehret | ................ | 149 |
| Desit Giorghis | ................ | 150 |
| The Palace of Emperor Sussenyos and Maryam Gemb Church | ................ | 152 |
| Sek'ela and Abba Gish Fasil | ................ | 155 |
| Mai Gwa Gwa or Fremona | ................ | 157 |
| Cobblestones | ................ | 159 |
| Amba Wehni | ................ | 160 |
| Selassie Gemb (Washa), Sabara Dildiy, Ayba, Galawdewos church | ................ | 161 |
| Other references | ................ | 163 |
| **Sundry Commentary** | ................ | 164 |
| Denial | ................ | 165 |
| - Histories | ................ | 166 |
| - Objectivity/Subjectivity | ................ | 168 |
| - Stonework | ................ | 168 |
| - Flux | ................ | 169 |
| - Recap | ................ | 170 |
| The Wars with Ahmad Grag'n | ................ | 172 |
| Legacy | ................ | 173 |
| Kwer'ata Re'esu | ................ | 177 |

| | | |
|---|---|---|
| **Select Bibliography** | .................. | 180 |
| **Chronology** | .................. | 183 |
| **Glossary** | .................. | 194 |
| **Index** | .................. | 196 |
| **About the Author** | .................. | 203 |

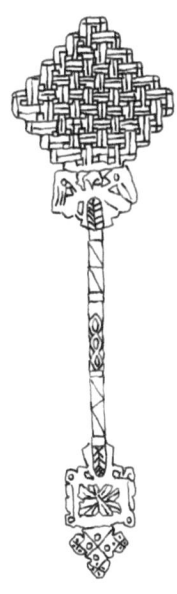

# Foreword
# by Richard Pankhurst

Ethiopia, known to medieval Europe as the Kingdom of Prester John, was at the time of its first contacts with Portugal in the sixteenth and seventeenth centuries, a Christian kingdom situated in Africa between the Red Sea and the Blue Nile. The realm traced its origins to the ancient Axumite Empire, which had risen to prominence further north, near the Red Sea, around the time of the birth of Christ. A great commercial kingdom, it had produced its own currency and had adopted Christianity as its state religion as early as about 330 AD. This conversion had been occasioned through contacts with Christians from Syria. The result of this was that the Ethiopians and their religious establishment became linked with Alexandria, the see of St. Mark and the Eastern Orthodox family of churches rather than, as in the case of the Portuguese, with Rome, the see of St. Peter and the western, Roman Catholic Church.

Ethiopia, at the time of its historic contacts with Portugal, may be likened in many ways to a European feudal monarchy. It was ruled, except in times of rebellion or civil war, by powerful emperors. They exercised considerable control over both the nobles and the peasantry, and claimed descent, through King Solomon of Jerusalem and the Ethiopian Queen of Sheba, from the Biblical Kings of Israel. The country's Metropolitan, or head of its church, known as the Abun, was invariably a Copt, chosen from among the monks of Egypt.

Despite these and other differences, Ethiopia and Portugal, in the sixteenth and seventeenth centuries, developed important though, in the final analysis, impermanent diplomatic, military, religious and cultural ties.

A Portuguese diplomatic embassy, led first by Duarte Galvão (who died en route to Ethiopia) and later by Rodrigo de Lima, visited the country in the 1520's. The mission's chaplain, Francisco Álvares, wrote the first and one of the most detailed accounts of Ethiopia ever penned. It is well worthy of study, even after almost half a millennium.

Immediately after the departure of the Portuguese embassy, the Ethiopian Christian state was overrun, and threatened with extinction, by its Muslim neighbours. The Christian kingdom was, however, duly saved through the intervention of a Portuguese expeditionary force led by Cristóvão da Gama, son of the famous Vasco. The Muslim leader, Imam Ahmad Ibn Ibrahim, known as Grag'n the Left-Handed, was killed in battle in 1543, after which the Christian state was speedily restored.

Memories of this momentous Portuguese involvement in Ethiopia inspired Ignatius Loyola, founder of the Society of Jesus, to take a keen interest in the country, and in its conversion to the Roman Catholic faith. A first Jesuit mission, composed largely of Portuguese, arrived in the country in 1557, and other missionaries followed in subsequent decades. One of their leaders, Pêro Páez, himself a Spaniard, was so successful that he converted two successive emperors, Za Dengal (ruled 1603-1604) and Sussenyos (ruled 1607-1632). The latter's attempts to convert his subjects to Roman Catholicism were, however, deeply resented, both by the Orthodox priesthood, and by the nobles and populace at large. Many rebellions followed. Sussenyos found himself obliged to restore the traditional Ethiopian faith after which he abdicated, in 1632, in favour of his son, Fasiladas. The new emperor proceeded to banish the Jesuits and other Roman Catholics from his empire, and it rapidly reverted to the old Orthodox faith.

Páez, an able missionary and a persuasive diplomat, was also a notable builder. He constructed many edifices for Emperor Sussenyos, notably at Gorgora and Denqaz, situated respectively north and northeast of Lake Tana. He, and several other Jesuits, most notably the Portuguese, Manuel de Almeida, and the latter's compatriot, Manuel Barradas, also wrote comprehensive studies of Ethiopia and its people.

Emperor Fasiladas subsequently established his capital at Gondar, an important settlement on the trade routes to both Sudan and the Red Sea. Probably making use of Portuguese builders, Indian craftsmen who had come from the sub-continent with the Jesuits, or Ethiopians who had trained with them, he built the first of a number of castles at Gondar, which have made the city famous to this day.

*

The main features of Ethio-Portuguese history as outlined above are well known, and have been the subject of numerous studies. Fieldwork on the subject, and in particular on the remains of Portuguese architecture in Ethiopia, and on Portuguese influence on indigenous Ethiopian architecture, has, however, been noticeable by its absence.

We are therefore deeply indebted to Jeremy Hespeler-Boultbee, himself an artist, art and architectural historian and master builder, as well as a bookish scholar, for his initiative in studying Portuguese, Portuguese-Indian or Ethio-Portuguese buildings in Ethiopia, and thus opening an entirely new field of Ethio-Portuguese studies. It is to be hoped that his on-going investigations, which are fascinating in themselves, will also encourage other scholars, both Ethiopian and Portuguese, to meet the challenge of probing further into other aspects of Ethio-Portuguese historical and cultural studies.

It is further to be hoped that the publication of Jeremy Hespeler-Boultbee's researches will serve as an inspiration for joint Ethio-Portuguese work for the preservation and restoration of historic monuments and other buildings in Ethiopia; and that Portuguese, emulating the courage and resourcefulness of their sixteenth and seventeenth century forebears, will co-operate with Ethiopian counterparts in saving Ethiopian antique structures, many of which – though by no means all! – have been recognized by UNESCO as part of the world's cultural heritage.

RP
Institute of Ethiopian Studies
Addis Ababa University

# Preface
## by Dr. Tsehai Jemberu

**Addressing This Book's Critics**

The task of any historian, among other techniques, is to search for evidence which is mostly scarce, disfigured or destroyed through the 'activities' of time and thus have lost their form and content, and have become unrecognizable to the untrained eye. After examining each 'data' and reflecting and comparing with the settings of the time as well as after evaluating what earlier historians have said, the historian would then interpret or reinterpret and assign meaning or 'discover' what has happened during that era – the causes, the happenings and the consequences. Historians, as all humans, are not omniscient, are engulfed with emotions, perspectives, biases and the like. A good historian guards his findings against his/her internal feelings as much as s/he can.

That is what Mr. J.J. Hespeler-Boultbee did in the first edition of his enlightening book *A Story in Stones*. He searched for his 'data' – the stones – carefully examined them, and provided us with his interpretations which resulted in the partial history of Ethiopian masonry during XV to XVII centuries. Mr. Hespeler-Boultbee has paid dearly in researching this work. He has traversed the difficult highland terrains for many years to the extent of risking his health and life. With sheer personal dedication, he was able to study not only the intact structures but also the ruined and forgotten ones, and even the 'remnants' of once graceful buildings – stones scattered far and wide where a peasant farmer, unaware, removed them to clear his farmland or use some to build his house; stones a shepherd boy threw at some unwanted animals; stones an idler carried to place under a tree where he could rest his head under its shade. With his remarkably sharp and learned eyes he marked some of these stones, analysed the styles in which they were shaped, the patterns they were placed one on another and 'discovered' some part of Ethiopian History! And then, he told us that the building designs of the time had Portuguese origin.

I worked with Mr. Hespeler-Boultbee for about two years while he was teaching at Bahir Dar University. I found him to be an accomplished mason and a dedicated historian with an ardent interest towards contributing something to human knowledge. I believe that he has no ill intention against any group of people except for telling what his findings told him.

I observed that some of my fellow colleagues were too critical of his assertions – too prejudiced towards Europe as the source of African civilisation – to put it modestly! I have strong reservations on this stance. Firstly, he did not say all structures, but rather most of the buildings of the highlands built during some 300 years of our history. Secondly, most of the outcries heard were too emotionally charged and not supported by counter evidence. Thirdly, though he has put forth many assumptions, he also has the stones – his evidence – within his hands. Fourthly, he has invited others with better equipment and skills to test and investigate the same.

Contrary to these critical colleagues, I believe this book has a lot of significance to Ethiopian history. The knowledge that Ethiopians were not living inside small shacks as we see them today, but used to reside in lavish stone mansions, should make us raise our heads higher. The story that the country was a haven to poor Europeans during some era (just as we do now – immigrating to the west in search of a better life) indicates that this used to be a truly advanced civilisation – more than what other historians tell us about the country. The Europeans came to Ethiopia not to displace some 'primitive' people (as they did in America or Australia) but in search of a better life! He sounded the alarm bells alerting us to not only try and preserve the existing known sites, but also to save the ones under destruction, many of which are essentially unknown! And even, maybe, to collect the scattered stones and rebuild?

He did not say the buildings are not Ethiopian, but that most have Portuguese origins in design; built by Ethiopian engineers – some of whom could be descendants of earlier Portuguese migrants. *So what?* We are presently constructing buildings, some of which have designs taken from Europe, Asia or Latin America. Some of the engineers could be Americans, or Chinese, or Congolese. But nobody has doubted that these buildings are Ethiopian. The same logic applies to Gondar or Mertule Maryam. Mr. Hespeler-Boultbee has put this interdependence and inter-learning of knowledge and skills intelligently into his book. Maybe the Ethiopians learned the trade from Portugal and added something of their own. The Portuguese learned it from some Africans (maybe Ethiopians!) and added something of their own. And so on! No people are *pure* by blood. Neither is there knowledge that is *pure* and created by one single population group. We were in one global world then, and still are today – mixing and learning from each other.

Finally, I would like to offer my humble (and probably naïve and simple) advice to my Ethiopian historians. Mr. Hespeler-Boultbee may be right, partly right or totally wrong. But he has forwarded many ideas and hunches concerning a part of our history. Since any piece of research poses more questions than answers, it is therefore left for us to investigate further. He has enlightened us and provided many new avenues to explore, so let's pick up the proverbial baton and carry forth to continue this important area of research.

For those colleagues mentioned earlier, the stones are located in your backyard – not thousands of miles away as they were for Mr. Hespeler-Boultbee. Let us continue to be proud Ethiopians by proving our long history of civilization with hard evidence instead of myths and hearsay.

Respectfully,
Dr. Tsehai Jemberu
Former President, Bahir Dar University

## Acknowledgements

The specific content of these pages, based on both fieldwork and research, is a personal thesis from which some of my many and various mentors and learnéd colleagues will have varying opinions. Comment on this point is made in a later section. As Prof. Pankhurst has mentioned it is hoped that this work will serve to encourage other Ethio-Portuguese scholars, archaeologists and architects to explore further this unique area of research.

First a quick word of background:

My introduction to the Ethiopian Highlands had nothing to do with architecture. My initial trip there was made in order to follow through on a line of investigation concerning the Portuguese diplomat-discoverer-explorer-spy and soldier, Pêro da Covilhã.

His was the story I was chasing at the beginning, and it is a story that will always intrigue if only because we can never know its entirety. What is known I recount in these pages. The course of my involvement with Ethiopia was to change, to expand, considerably. In my first connections with Addis Ababa University I was directed to Prof. Richard Pankhurst, a man whose reputation as an historian and scholar concerning every aspect of Ethiopian life is paramount. It was Prof. Pankhurst who introduced me to the facilities of the Institute of Ethiopian Studies at the university. He also insisted I meet and talk with Dr. Merid Wolde Aregay, since retired but at the time of my first arrival in Ethiopia the chairman of the university's Department of History, and a specialist in that period of his country's story that related specifically to Portugal's years of contact.

It was Dr. Merid who recognized the utility of my own qualifications as historian, architectural historian, designer/sculptor and, quite coincidentally, as a builder and stonemason who had spent some twelve years restoring old and traditional houses in Portugal.

"You can identify, so go and identify!" was Dr. Merid's stern demand of me. In this way he initiated my extraordinary odyssey through the Ethiopian Highlands.

So to Drs. Pankhurst and Merid I feel I owe a deep debt of gratitude for their involvement in opening up a field of interest that I am sure will remain with me the rest of my days. It is by now, not surprisingly, an interest that goes far beyond the mere one hundred and forty years of Portugal's involvement in the Highlands. Ethiopia's story goes back some three thousand years. Anywhere along that time-line one may pick up a loose thread and follow it to the dawn of pre-history.

At Portugal's venerable University of Évora I feel a special vote of thanks is due to numerous colleagues and scholars whose contributions of time, patience and assistance were always generous and helpful, particularly in relation to the data and slide bank facilities required for the Portuguese edition of this work. Although I was the photographer who took each shot exhibited in its pages, many of the resulting slides are now used as reference material in the university's research organization, CIDEHUS-UE. I would like, therefore, to acknowledge this and my debt of thanks to both the research organization and the university itself for their generous co-operation. I would especially single out Dr. Rui Manuel Namorado Rosa, then chairman of the university's Conselho Directivo, who benefited me with long hours of his wise counsel; likewise, Dr. Filipe Themudo Barata, good-natured and long-suffering chairman of the Department of History; and Dr. Helder Fonseca, the director of CIDEHUS-UE (*Centro de Investigação e Desenvolvimento em Ciências*

*Humanas e Sociais de Universidade de Évora* – Research and Development Centre in Human and Social Sciences of the University of Évora).

Drª Valentina de Castro, also of CIDEHUS-UE, has contributed her time and effort most graciously, and it would be remiss of me not to single her out for special thanks.

Drª Isabel Castro Henriques, Department of African Studies, and Drª Luísa Leal de Faria, Department of History, both of the Faculdade de Letras, Universidade de Lisboa, contributed critical and constructive suggestions, for which I am thankful.

Dr. João Pedro Garcia, director, Serviço Internacional, Fundação Calouste Gulbenkian, has been especially helpful with generous funding through the facilities of the foundation, particularly during the early stages of this work.

Fernanda Durão Ferreira has been a delightful and knowledgeable colleague in research, and the observations and commentary in her essay entitled *O Estilo Gondar*, especially in regard to Guzara castle, have been enlightening and most helpful.

Tim and Kim Otte de Hoop, who hail from Holland, but live and work at Gorgora, at the north end of Lake Tana, have done and continue to do most useful research work on many different aspects pertaining to the theme of this study. Many details contained in this second English language edition are due entirely to their doggedness, particularly the photographs of Selassie Gemb (Washa).

In addition, there are others to whom I would wish to express my gratitude:

In Ethiopia: Dr. Abdussamad H. Ahmad; Abenet Nurbeza Terega; Ahmad Zekaria; Alebachew Tiruneh; Alemayehu Gebrehiwot; Alemie Temesgen; Assefa Taye; Assefa Wubne; Awoel (Danny) Hagos Murhusel; Babi Giamberi; Brook Tessema; Chanyalew Medhin; Dr. Stanislaw Chojnacki; Degife Gebresadik; Endalamaw Sahilu; Ephrem Giorghis; Fasil Ayehu; Fasil Giorghis; Frehiwot Takele Kassa; Fikreyesus Zewdu; Genet Wolde Tsadek; Getnet Yigsaw Nigusie; Sister Laura Girotto; Kifle Shirga Nijnepo; Judith McDonald; Retta Telila; Sami Bequele; Shimelash Bequele; Sisay Tarekegne; Tadele Fantahun; Zewdu Abebe.

Dr. Tsehai Jemberu, for seven imaginative and insightful years the president of Bahir Dar University, deserves a special mention here. Always cheerful and open to ideas, there can be nothing for me to add to what he has written so eloquently and with such kindness in the preface of this edition – except for my expression of deep gratitude for his unfailing assistance and friendship.

In the Introduction there are two small drawings – one of a girl's head, the other of a priest – which are my own renderings of drawings done much earlier by Jill Last in the Ethiopian Tourism Commission's book of indigenous costumes. She has credited them as being copied from the photographs of others. No matter the source, her depictions in that publication are educational and absolutely stunning.

In Portugal: Abdissa Birratu Gamada; António Bossa Borralho; José Bustorf; Nitah Camotim; Carmo de Castro; Brad Cherry; Dr. Pedro Miguel Dias Duarte; Ole Eistrup; Diogo Fialho; Jorge Cunha Freire; António Eloy Garcia; António Guerra; Luís Leote de Rego; Maria Clara Lourenço; José Maria and Teresa Machado; Dr. Luís Martins; Nuno Moquenco; Drª Teresa Pinto Correia; Francisco "Sapo" Ramos; Glória Ribeiro; Alison Roberts; the brothers Domingos Maria and Luís Mário Ruivo Pica; Mário Francisco Ferreira Serrano; Andrew Shore; António Filipe Sousa; Agostinho Peres Valério.

In Germany: Prof. Dr. Dr. Erwin Klein of the University of Berlin, has proven a stalwart ally and wise counsellor. Many thanks, also, to Drs. Andreu Martínez d'Alòs-Moner and Wolbert Smidt of Hamburg University.

In Spain: José Carlos Gonzalez Fernandez of Málaga has provided generous support, assistance and advice.

In England: Girma Moges, architect, read the original manuscript and contributed most useful commentary.

In Canada: Michelle Biggins, Ron de Boer, Steve Bognor, Klaus Bohn, Dr. Michael Gervers, Teresa Hallatt, John and Helen Harrison, Dan Hilts, Mick Lowe, Mike Merritt, Archdeacon Christopher Pratt, Paul Rabinovitch, Dee-Anne Reed, Rev. Scott Sinclair, Dr. Allan Stone, Don van Schepen, Jim Van Wyck, and Jane Wood.

Anne Marsh Evans, well known and respected artist of Meaford, Ontario, penned one of the many drawings in the book. See page 155 for her image of the three horseback riders on the mountain road to Abba Gish Fasil. Never having been there, she nonetheless captured the essence of the scene most admirably from my description, and for this I both thank her and express my highest regard for her artistry.

In the United States of America: Dr. La Verle Berry, Library of Congress, Washington.

My son, Michael, far more adept with a computer than I could ever hope to be, put in long and tedious hours scanning and arranging all the artwork in the book – photographs and drawings. For this I happily express my indebtedness to him for both his ability and patience.

I would like to note my special thanks to the membership of the Rotary Club of Owen Sound, Ontario, for the interest its membership so generously demonstrated in my overall involvement in matters Ethiopian, and their own involvement in specific charitable donations to Ethiopia. Similarly, in Victoria, the Anglican Diocese of British Columbia has demonstrated its commitment and generosity, for which I register the gratitude of both myself and innumerable underprivileged children in Ethiopia.

I would like to express my warmest appreciation and *abraços* to the publisher of the earlier Portuguese edition of this book, João Osório de Castro. Himself an historian and playwright of note, he took a great interest in this project from its inception.

Though, for brevity, numerous services and supports received from all those listed are not necessarily specified, I am confident each one knows full well why I would want to include his or her name, and to express my deepest and most sincere thanks. A work such as this would not have been brought to fruition without the assistance and support of so many dear friends and colleagues.

JJH-B

## Author's Note to the Current Edition

This work was originally published by ELO in Portugal in 1999, under the title: *Uma História em Pedras – Vestígios Portugueses na Etiópia, 1493-1634.*

As I was at the time closely involved with research at the university in Évora it was natural, as well as a courtesy to my colleagues in the History Department and at CIDEHUS-UE, that the findings of my work should initially be published in Portuguese. This was fine for those people who wished to examine the data solely from a Portuguese perspective. It was of little use to scholars wishing to tackle the same story from an Ethiopian standpoint, for by far the greater majority of them work in either their own Ethiopian language, or else in English, the principal lingua franca for postgraduate study in Ethiopia.

In preparing this English language edition some ten years after the earlier one in Portuguese, four years after the original English language edition, it has been necessary to take a number of things into consideration, not least of which is the cost of bringing out a book that, in its Portuguese version, contained some eighty colour photographs. So a number of pen and ink drawings are included. Some were executed on site, others were worked up much later from photographs. In several instances, I do believe, the drawings highlight details within the text that were not so sharply defined in the photographs. The exercise has given me a great deal of pleasure and afforded me the chance to add an even more personal touch to the design concept of the book.

After having been closely, and recently, associated with the pedagogical university at Bahir Dar for a period of nearly two years, I have assumed a deal of responsibility in taking a stance diametrically opposed to that of some of my colleagues at that institution. The resulting essay, Denial, is newly incorporated into this edition of *A Story in Stones*, and will be found towards the end of the book, in a section entitled Sundry Commentary which did not appear in earlier editions of this work. The opinion and data contained in these essays will be found within the body of the text itself, for the most part, but the essays are useful summaries casting light on different perspectives of the overall theme. The last of the commentaries, concerning the *kwer'ata re'esu*, is a curious story which serves to present a Portuguese element to the Ethiopian story. It has a modern twist to it.

For twelve years I worked on the restoration of old farm buildings in Portugal. For an even longer period of time I operated a ceramic studio at my home. I found both pursuits highly creative – very similarly connected (at least to my way of reasoning) through the natural sculptural sense I have possessed since earliest childhood.

I lived in Portugal for many years, and had been emotionally involved with the place for at least a dozen years prior to moving there. One way or another I have spent a good deal of my life imbibing the history and culture of the place. Following up on a line of research so linked with the country's historical era of greatness was not, and still is not, an altogether alien pursuit for someone like me. Even after so many years I am long resigned to my status among the Portuguese as *entrangeiro*. Most certainly I am also a foreigner – *ferenghi* – to the Ethiopians among whom I have lived and worked. After such protracted absence from my own land I suppose it should come as no great surprise that I even feel a bit foreign in Canada, too.

However classified, and for the benefit of whomever, there is a sense of release in coming home to the English language with the contents and information contained in this work.

Rendering Ethiopian words, and particularly proper names, into Indo-European script has always presented a challenge. Every writer entering the Semitic language area of Ethiopia appears to struggle with the problem, whether attempting to render into English, French, Portuguese, or some other.

Thus, for example, the emperor who reigned between 1607 and 1632 is variously consigned to the written page as Susenious, Susenyos, Susneyos, Sousneyos, Sunsenios, etc.

Which is correct?

Try it, says an Amharic-speaking friend: SUn-<u>SUn</u>-YuS.

I bend my ear to a language very foreign to my culture, and what I am sure I really hear is SUnS-<u>SEN</u>-y-OS.

Likewise I have had similar difficulties with Sartsa Dengal, Debre Libanos, Galawdewos, Giorghis, Teklahaimanot, Tewedros, and scores of other place and personal names.

So, while acknowledging that the new Encyclopedia Aethiopica is attempting to standardize such spellings, a definitive system is to date incomplete. Thus I plumb for a simple consistency rather than an academic accuracy that may not be yet fully developed. I do this with the unreserved willingness to go along with agreed spellings once they are established.


JJH-B
Victoria, British Columbia, Canada

# Introduction

There is strong historical and design evidence, amounting to something considerably greater than mere coincidence, that the so-called "Gondarine" architecture of the Ethiopian Highlands had a Portuguese building methodology, imprint and culture as its strongest foundation. Much of this foundation, but by no means all of it, was imported by Jesuit missionaries around the middle of the XVI and the beginning of the XVII centuries. The initial building program stretched throughout the relatively short period of time that the Portuguese were active in the Ethiopian Highlands. It culminated in a conscious and extended method of construction that continued far beyond the time, in 1634, when the last of the Portuguese religious was caught and either expelled or executed. There was no special secret to the methodology. For the Portuguese it was a matter of common knowledge and so much of it, maybe most of it, was subsequently taught to local artisans.

Since many of the Portuguese who settled these Highlands married local women, it is perhaps more significant that this methodology was passed down from father to son in the manner of the paternal Portuguese artisan tradition that exists even today. Within a generation the offspring of these first builders were Ethiopian Highlanders and, also in line with paternal inclinations, great numbers of them had adopted the Roman Catholicism of their fathers. The folkloric building skills they learned were only a slightly more rustic version of the same Catholic traditions that, in Metropolitan Portugal itself, gave rise to the splendours of what was later to become known as the "Manueline" architecture of that general period.

This work is by no means the first study of Portugal's early Renaissance contact with Ethiopia; something that turned out to be, in point of fact, the first major encounter between a dominant European Christian culture and a large and highly developed African Christian culture. It is, I believe, the first time that the extraordinary story of this contact is being re-told in conjunction with a description of contemporary architectural vestige, using that vestige in order to winkle out significant aspects of the story. This treatment tends to cast the whole saga in a different light. While the entry of the Portuguese was fired initially by curiosity, and not a small degree of hesitancy on the part of both Portuguese and Ethiopians, there can be little doubt that a later influx of Europeans, by far the greater part Portuguese, had every intention of staying and settling. The idea of colonizing had not yet come into vogue, but that is more or less what the influx represented. This is readily apparent by the size and extent of the building program.

Some of this program has been duly recorded; a more significant proportion of it appears not to have been or, if ever it was, has not yet come under close scrutiny. At this juncture one is forced to leave the discussion open-ended. A great deal of Ethiopia's ecclesiastical documentation has been lost or mislaid. As almost every Ethiopian hill seems to have a church perched on its crown, so almost every church in the country has an archive – of sorts. Cataloguing such an abundance of material as is contained in them has barely begun. While some records were kept in Ethiopia, and written down in Ge'ez, Tigrinha or Amharic, yet other records exist, kept by the Roman Catholic missionaries and other individuals who entered the country and either wrote treatises, or sometimes just letters home. Such references if and where they exist might be expected to be found in a variety of European languages, and in any number of different locales. It is anybody's guess as to how many more such writings, if and when they come to light, might divulge information that can specifically expand our knowledge concerning any particular historical structure. One way or another, as can be readily assumed, any comprehensive search of vestige, or documentation referring to it, has proven and will continue to be a painstaking process.

Almost all Portuguese historians and academics spoken to concerning this stone vestige are surprised to hear that it is so vast, and they appear more astonished yet to see illustrative evidence of it. However, they certainly acknowledge recognition of the evidence.

Architectural vestiges of Portugal's history in Africa are scattered over a wide area of Ethiopia's Highlands, for the most part in the provinces of Gojjam, Gondar and Tigray. In the main these are abandoned sites and in a state of ruin and decay. There are, in those distant regions, examples of practically everything that the Portuguese were capable of building at the time: palaces, castles, churches, monasteries, religious residences, bridges and simple residential and farm houses and outbuildings. These regions contain, in fact, the largest collection of Portuguese style architecture anywhere in Africa or, arguably, in any part of the world outside Metropolitan Portugal itself and Brazil.

**Voyage of Discovery**

What follows is a synthesis of numerous exploratory journeys into Ethiopia's Highlands. During the first two expeditions, in February-March, and again in October-November, 1996, an extensive array of architectural vestige described in this work was re-discovered. It had been left behind as a result of the Portuguese presence in those Highland regions between the years 1493 and 1634. Subsequent journeys uncovered yet more.

Though recorded, the story which makes up the initial section of this book has grown cold to the point where, today, it has become almost totally disassociated with the remains of its stone or architectural reality scattered as ruins across a broad stretch of the Ethiopian Highlands. Furthermore, it is almost as though this story, long ago, had been deliberately dropped from regular historical curricula and conveniently put out of mind, by both Ethiopians and Portuguese.

Why?

Within Ethiopia, it is principally because of a necessary preoccupation with survival; but also it is due to national pride.

An almost mystical silence has developed around the stone structures that stand today. Questioned on this, it quickly becomes clear that most local Ethiopians themselves have indeed long forgotten the origins of these landmarks. In many cases this has been due to the constant pressures of their own acute problems. Year-in and year-out over the centuries, their attentions had been concentrated by the demands of forging an elemental livelihood. When a man's family is hungry and he must spend the greater part of a day hunched over a digging stick, his wife perhaps lumbering home heavy clay pots of water on her back, the importance of the finer historical details of any culture would tend to fade. Nevertheless, in those few instances where rumours filter through to locals as to the European origin of structures under the shadow of which they have passed their entire lives, as like as not there is an understandable but angry denial. I have heard it many times: "The-Europeans-never-gave-us-anything-but-problems" kind of response, coupled with, "Are you Europeans incapable of crediting us Ethiopians with the ability to build such things ourselves? We were building in stone long before the arrival of the Portuguese!"

The discussion requires patience.

## Understanding the Social History

The truth is that many of these structures were indeed built by Ethiopians and, in some noteworthy cases, after the departure of the Portuguese. In this regard, though, it is important to remember the fact alluded to above: that the Portuguese mixed liberally with the local population; were, indeed, completely absorbed by it. They fled or died out, to be sure, but they left their considerable skills behind them to the benefit of their children and grandchildren, and this to such extent that, even today, certain undeniable Portuguese structural and decorative traits can be detected in the modern folk building of the region.

In Portugal the seeming obliviousness surrounding these achievements has been due to a variety of different circumstances, though the foremost of them, as with the Ethiopians, is essentially a sort of nationalistic pride.

Within the country itself there is actually sparse documentation of Portugal's Ethiopian involvement, and for two reasons. Firstly, it had not taken very long for the Portuguese to realize that Ethiopia was really something of a red herring for them; that their true commerce-dominated interests lay elsewhere in the Indian Ocean and Far Eastern Spice Islands. Secondly, Portugal's disastrous effort at converting Orthodox Christian Ethiopia to the Church of Rome ultimately became an acute national embarrassment. The Jesuit missionaries' ignominious expulsion from the Ethiopian Highlands in 1634 had become yet another national calamity of major proportions, for there had been others. Earlier, in 1578, the resounding defeat of Portugal's elite army and nobility at the Battle of Alcácer Quibir, in Morocco, and the death in this debacle of young Dom Sebastião, Portugal's boy king, had stunned the country, draining it of both purpose and will. It was as a result of this that Portugal had inevitably fallen under Spanish domination, remaining so for sixty years, and conclusively heralding the end of Portugal's years of overseas dominance. The subsequent rise of Holland's, Britain's and France's global ambitions, to say nothing of Spain's, had given Portugal plenty to worry about, so that an ecclesiastical failure in Africa, though painfully close, was an eminently forgettable item.

And so the whole sorry affair conveniently faded into the mists of history.

The glory bits remained: Pêro da Covilhã's amazing journey, Padre Francisco Álvares' account of the first Portuguese diplomatic embassy, Cristóvão da Gama's heroic little army and its swashbuckling defeat of Islam in the Highlands. Such stories entered the lexicon of gallant Portuguese saga, and have been told and retold over the intervening years to dress an otherwise rather shabby national self-image. Other names, João Bermudez, André de Oviedo, Pêro Páez, Afonso Mendes, classed as "successes" or "heroes" on one side of the historical divide, are quite definitely viewed as "failures" or "anti-heroes" on the other, as we shall see.

The fact that communities had arisen and flourished, that missionaries had struggled manfully, succeeded or failed, that individuals had laboured on the land, built themselves houses and married, or not, raised their families, interbred and ploughed and mixed themselves so thoroughly into the land that they became, through time, a part of that land – all this faded very quickly, and has remained very obscure until today. Indeed it is not in the least unusual, even now, to encounter highly knowledgeable historians who express surprise at learning the Portuguese had ever set foot on Ethiopian turf, let alone penetrated to the country's hinterlands.

However, it is possible to determine from the architectural remnants scattered across these lands precisely where the Portuguese had been and, by extension, to use the stones that are the sole survivors of that presence to reveal something of the story attached to them. Due to certain unique peculiarities in Portuguese building methods, the architectural forms, even the stones themselves – the ways in which they are cut, or not, and put together, with or without mortar – constitute a valuable source "archive" that can corroborate or deny detail already contained within known documentary archival material. They can augment it, even create it, where there is no written chronicle.

One thing has become amusingly clear, particularly to an historical investigator who is neither Portuguese nor Ethiopian: when addressing a Portuguese on these matters, the assumption is that it is an element of Portuguese history that is being discussed. Similarly, talking on the same matters to an Ethiopian, it is presumed Ethiopian history is under consideration. Unfortunately two stubborn and proud people on opposite sides of the same argument will likely thump their chests till Doomsday and balk at giving ground. The obvious point this reinforces is that history is universal, that everyone will have a hand in it no matter where they are – British diplomats in New York, Chinese living in Tierra del Fuego, or Laplanders wandering the Great Karroo. The only arbitration, in the end, is sweet reason and the inevitable acceptance of the fact that history belongs to all mankind, crosses borders without so much as a nod and is, of itself, mankind's greatest mixer. People may be proud of their history if they so choose, but they can never claim it entirely unto themselves.

**Examining the Record**

This presentation will examine the ancient relics, and try to piece them together with something of the story that surrounds them. The tale is as fascinating as history itself can conjure, but until now has remained disconnected from its stone ruins for almost five hundred years at least in part because of the sheer inaccessibility of the region. Even within that remote and difficult place, many of the sites themselves are isolated and hard to reach. The populations living closest to them today no longer remember the origins of the relics that stand silently in the midst of their agricultural fields or beside their mud-hut villages. In many cases there are no roads. The great amnesia exists also in Lisbon and other centres where records were kept, or not, and in any case, until recent years, in a state of disorder that defied easy access.

Of course there are some records. Many, many things have been written down. Royal and religious chronicles were kept, and many of these do indeed survive – in Lisbon or at the Vatican, in Addis Ababa and, in too many cases, in individual and appallingly inadequate church "museums," the "archives" referred to above, scattered about the Christian Highlands of Ethiopia, or in individual Portuguese libraries. However, no part of Africa ever went through a period of history equivalent to Europe's Enlightenment, nor indeed its Industrial Revolution, and this has meant, inevitably, that information was never diffused in quite the same way, or in the same quantity, as it was in Europe. What might have been known to a few scholars or monks, or even a royal court, was not necessarily known to the populace at large, so that a collective amnesia is not altogether incomprehensible. Today more than ninety percent of Ethiopia's population is agriculturally based. People tied to the toil of the land are not generally concerned with the academic pursuits of historians or scholars. The scale of the hardships facing a rural peasantry is just too burdensome. In the five hundred years since the Portuguese started living and working among the Ethiopians there has been plenty of incentive and opportunity to obliterate the past.

**Past and Present**

Ethiopia is a desperately poor country. It is a harsh, forbidding and difficult landscape, its terrain seemingly thrown together at the whimsy of wild gods. For centuries the Highland region has remained virtually an impenetrable mass of towering rock and plummeting ravine. Even in modern times transportation throughout the nation is a nightmare concern for politicians, administrators, engineers, road builders and communications personnel. On this account alone a topography such as Ethiopia's would present any government with an extraordinary array of intricate and multi-faceted administrative problems. Add to this compound the elements of ignorance and poverty on a gigantic scale, the attendant cultural resistance to change and modernity nurtured by three millenniums of often traumatic history, and it is possible to begin understanding some of the underlying fabric of one of the most complex and fascinatingly beautiful countries on earth.

This is not the correct forum to give a detailed account of Ethiopia's long history, any more than it is to describe its geology, but one might usefully have a rudimentary picture in one's mind. Its history stretches back into eras long preceding human record, and in consequence Ethiopia is one of the oldest nations on earth. These are facts that surprise many people who tend not to juggle with the rationale and concepts of time. The Ethiopian Orthodox Church, founded in 347 AD, is one of the oldest of the Christian church assemblies. The fact that it is older than the foundation of the Roman Catholic Church by seven centuries is likewise a surprise to some.

The word Ethiopia is derived from the ancient Greek term used to describe dark-skinned people. The Ethiopians themselves are thought to be descendents of indigenous tribes of "white men with dark skins" who merged with migrants filtering across the Red Sea from the southern Arabian peninsula in pre-Biblical times. Their principal languages are derived from old Sabaean, Semitic and Cushitic tongues.

The so-called Black Jews of Ethiopia, the Falashas, are unable to explain or date their origin but, in any case, it is known that their beliefs pre-date the Jerusalem Talmud. The remains of "Lucy," known to the Ethiopians as Dinquinesh, translated as "you are wonderful," and estimated at 3.2 million years, is believed to be one of the oldest human fossils yet discovered. These remains came from the desert wastes of the Afar Depression in northern Ethiopia/Eritrea.

Ethiopia's ancient coastal province, largely comprising what is now Eritrea, is the Land of Punt described in the hieroglyphs of the Egyptian pharaohs. Ethiopia claims the Queen of Sheba who, as the story goes in the Old Testament, travelled to Jerusalem and mated with King Solomon. Their son, Menelik, is considered the founder of the nation, and it was he, as the Ethiopians relate their history, who took the Ark of the Covenant from the temple at Jerusalem and brought it, by circuitous route, to Axum where it reputedly yet resides. Sceptics may place their tongue in cheek on hearing all this, but it is a foolish historian that dismisses myth and legend.

**Dom Alfonso V of Aragon**

In point of fact, the first recorded contact between a European power and Ethiopia dates to 1427 when Dom Alfonso V of Aragon received, at his court in Valencia, two emissaries sent by Emperor Yesaq (1414-1429). For several years the Christian church in Rome had been aware of the existence of a Christian church in Ethiopia, but there had been little interest in making contact due, in large part, to uncertain geographical knowledge, the difficulties presented by the vast wastelands of the Egyptian and Nubian deserts, and also to the hostility on the part of the Egyptian authorities who dominated Christian Alexandria.

Likewise the emperor in Ethiopia knew something about Europe, for Dom Alfonso's visitors were sent specifically to request a group of artisans to return with them to the Ethiopian Highlands. Alfonso obliged by sending a team of 13 men, but it appears that all of them perished on the journey. Again, in 1450, the Spaniard wrote a letter – this time to Emperor Zara Yaqob (1434-1468) – offering to send craftsmen providing the emperor guarantee safe passage. Apparently the letter never arrived.

When Portugal's first emissary arrived at the court of Emperor Eskendar, about 1493, he discovered that a few Greek and Armenian traders had managed to penetrate into the Highlands, mainly to the north of Shoa. They had been doing business here intermittently for a number of years. The Venetian painter, Niccoló Brancaleone, was also present, having been sent by the Venetian authorities to teach painting to the local Christians. He is thought to have arrived in the Highlands between 1480 and 1482, and for over forty years was a major influence on the development of Ethiopian iconography and church painting

**Enter the Portuguese**

It was just a little more than five hundred years ago that Ethiopia's massive and most beautiful Highlands opened up to the burningly inquisitive entry of the first of the Portuguese explorers. What was perhaps a hesitant and explorative entry at first became, after a few years, a somewhat stronger and more insistent flow. Other individuals followed the first lone adventurer. A few more years and what initially had been just a seepage of Renaissance European culture had become a fair torrent of both missionaries and soldier/settlers. Such are the vagaries of rumour that it took only a brief span of time for these same Highlands to become known as a Paradise on Earth, the sort of place where a man could live out his days in tranquility and relative peace. It was not only seen this way by a host of Jesuits and other mostly Portuguese religious, but also by the mariner flotsam of the Indian Ocean and Far Eastern trade routes, many of whom were intent on escaping something.

Here one must try to imagine the harsh life aboard the sailing ships of that era, the dreadful stinking and putrid conditions both on deck and below, the absence of safety, and the months at sea sometimes under tyrannical captaincy. At the same time one must bear in mind conditions on land, the impoverishment and the debtors' courts that were capable of making life a misery in homeland Europe; or perhaps some worse persecution brought about by both the just and unjust laws of the times. It was to the Ethiopian Highlands that a hodgepodge of idealists and castaways beat their paths, each individual trying to build a new life for himself and his newly acquired family. These people – all men – came alone, but in significant numbers. They mixed and they married. Along with their hopes and dreams of a new life they came to build their homes, their temples, their palaces.

What remained after the last of them had packed up and left, or died, was this silent story in stonework, lonely monuments to a far-off and ultimately rejected culture. The tangible evidence of a European fantasy that remained was swamped and then swept away by the far more robust demands of a fiercely proud indigenous population.

Ethiopia would present practically any scholar of any discipline with a lifetime of study. This presentation purports to examine events linked to only some one hundred and forty years of the country's history. Contact with Portugal began in 1492/3, when Pêro da Covilhã, that intrepid first adventurer, accomplished his Bunyanesque march across the coastal deserts into the Shoan Highlands. It ended definitively in 1634, the year that Portugal's Jesuit missionaries and other Roman Catholics were finally and unceremoniously hoofed out of the country, or else hounded down and executed, or in some other way forced into recanting their Catholic beliefs and resorting to the far more predominant Orthodoxy.

This is the point, perhaps, when it might be useful to comment upon an expanding demographic situation. It is impossible to relate specific figures or percentages, but certain historical trends are worthy of comment and consideration.

Where other European nations, long prior to their status as colonial powers, quickly adopted an attitude of exceptional superiority towards the indigenous peoples they encountered during the time of the early Discoveries, the Portuguese themselves tended not to do this. One could point to their adoption of slavery as an obvious rebuttal of this statement, but my own opinion (and that of many scholars) is that while one cannot through any exercise of reason deny slavery was a gross exploitation of human beings – and that, within the period of the history studied here, African human beings were the unwitting objects of this cruelty – by far the most predominant motive where the Portuguese were concerned was economic, not racial superiority.

Individuals within all colonial powers entered into mixed relationships, and in by far the greater number of cases such an act was widely condemned – on the grounds of superiority. This was the case in all countries – except Portugal. The mixing of the races in Brazil, and everywhere else that the Portuguese went ashore in these early years, is notable.

It was no different in the Highlands of Ethiopia. The Portuguese are a hardy people with a robust and zestful outlook on life, though no more so than the Ethiopians with whom they came in contact. Both parties to any personal relationship would have recognized the overriding compatibility of the two cultures, not least of which would have been the fact that both parties to it would have shared a similar Christian belief structure. The disciplines of their respective denominations notwithstanding, at the very least there would have been an acknowledgement of their common Christian base – a factor which would have tended to eliminate the importance of traits and customs, taboos, that could have been far more significant among parallel cultures or belief systems facing what might have been considered the complexity of inter-racial mixing.

The Portuguese found themselves wives in these Highland regions; concubinage and extra-marital relations were also widely practiced. Inevitably this led to large numbers of mixed-race children and the beginning of a demographic factor which, as this thesis will argue, would also have created the genesis of a cultural adaptation visible less in the physical bloodline features of the people themselves than in the products of their creative genius.

## Continuing the Research

No doubt in years to come it will be possible to add further detail, though probably in not such great a quantity that the mystery of the sites examined here will ever be totally revealed. This treatise can in no manner attempt to supply the definitive word on this fascinating investigative field, but perhaps will serve as the jump-off point for additional research at some future date. Anyone reading this will discover it is based on original field research combined with many years of study and practical experience in architectural design. A select bibliography is included towards the end of the book, and I believe that many of my findings are well supported in these writings. To do iron-clad justice to the subject it would be necessary to call into play a large array of essentially scientific expertise, an impossible imposition to place on the back of a lone scholar-explorer sifting through the Ethiopian Highlands.

Having viewed the **stones** of the architectural remains, I have attempted to connect them to the history, or the ***story***, as accurately and as intelligently as possible. Readers should approach this subject, as I have tried to, with an open mind, as though considering a hypothesis. They must accept that my historical base, factual in its essence, has been interlaced with several "what if" scenarios in an effort to make sense of the whole, and in anticipation that others will be prodded into digging deeper into this unusual area of study.

Proofs positive are wonderful and everybody loves to attain them. Sometimes they are comfortable, and there are those who are never so content as when conclusions are placed before them, Q.E.D. Scientists, lawyers and politicians love them.

One must not knock the scientist. Not too hard. He has his essential role to play and, in the end, we count on him. However, a scientist who attempts to work without employing intuition, even in such a case as when that intuition borders on fantasy, is not pushing science to its possible limit. Rather, he is limiting the boundaries of imaginative exploration. An historian, seeing himself as a scientist and who, out of hand, dismisses myth or intuition, is both fool and impostor and does his chosen science no justice.

The point here, and which I try to make throughout, is that if we do not posit ideas, particularly concerning dim history, how can we possibly seek alternatives, or perhaps that which might ultimately lead to proof? Thus the essential line in this work is to attempt to recount historical fact and accompany it with examples of quite sizeable portions of extant architectural vestige. This, in conjunction with some level of supposition, may serve to present a more complete picture of what was actually happening on the ground.

Opening this area of study has been totally absorbing. My sense of delight would be the more complete knowing that those who read these pages are also enjoying themselves. There always lurks the danger that when everything is proven scientific fact the sheer fun of an exercise might somehow evaporate.

# Part One

# The Story

## Portugal and Pêro da Covilhã

Portugal's most celebrated history is maritime, but one of the country's greatest and longest lasting exploits, and least known or understood, begins with the terrestrial exploits of Pêro da Covilhã. The mystical, predominantly mythical, story surrounds Portugal's search for the fabulous Christian king, Prester John – his earthly kingdom equated with the Garden of Eden. One's sense of historical caprice is tweaked when it is realized that in addition to the mystery that surrounds the story of Prester John and Pêro da Covilhã there is a certain irony, too. No one quite knows whatever became of the Portuguese soldier-explorer-diplomat. The last recorded sighting of him alive was in 1526, but there is no indication that this was actually the year of his death. He was born about 1460 so it is quite conceivable that he lived well beyond 1526 – another fifteen or twenty years; we simply do not know. We do not hear of him again, as if he had been swallowed up by the mists that waft across those vast Highlands.

And therein lies the historical irony.

Pêro da Covilhã's incredible forced march overland into the Ethiopian Highlands about the end of 1492, or beginning of 1493, marked the substantive beginning of Portugal's meteoric era of conquest and supremacy. Information he sent back to Lisbon would have contributed to the voyage which Vasco da Gama made only a few years later around Africa's southern cape and into the Indian Ocean. From that point on, Portugal's ships and military dominated the coastline of all Africa, Persia, India and beyond – all the way to Japan and the shores of China.

Let us move ahead for a moment to 1578, the date of Portugal's disastrous defeat on the battlefield of Alcácer Quibir, and the death of her king, Dom Sebastião. This is the year that most clearly marks the demise of Portugal's glorious prominence as the era's superpower. A cadaver purporting to be that of the king was eventually returned to Portugal from Morocco, and today rests in a tomb at Lisbon's São Jerónimos. However, there arose at the same time the romantic notion that it was not the young king who had been brought back. It was said, in fact, that he had just disappeared into the mists that covered the fields of that bloody Moroccan catastrophe, and took the greatness of his homeland with him.

It is intriguing to wonder what other historical events might be hidden by Africa's mists. There is irony, or at least the Humour of the Fates, in that both the man who marked the beginning of Portugal's greatness and the man who marked the end of it, should somehow have been consumed by African mists – even if the idea was only metaphor. Such things are tailored to tease the imaginations of scientifically minded historians who would prefer to tie things down neatly, put dates on them or encase them in stone sarcophagi.

Even today the psyche of the Portuguese is said, tongue-in-cheek admittedly, to be such that everyone in the country is still waiting, still longing, for the return of the lost warrior king. It is called *sebastianismo*. One thing that most definitely is not tongue-in-cheek is Portugal's continued close tie to Africa. It is an exceptional bond that is proving far stronger than any that existed up into the modern era of colonialism. It is a common saying that Portugal is an African country on the southern fringe of Europe. One could argue the precise geographical point, but sentimentally and in terms of the nation's view of itself it is a concept that should bear close scrutiny and be taken seriously.

And Pêro da Covilhã?

History has sidelined him. He did a great thing, to be sure, and he made it into the storybooks, but he never came home. Surely he died, but when? And where? Under what circumstances? The silence that surrounds him is so thick that one might almost conclude his homeland does not wish to know. Perhaps his passing into the gloaming and oblivion of the craggy land where he spent at least the last half of his life suits some dark and fatalistic purpose of his stock; that his homecoming, had he managed it, would ultimately have proved an embarrassment. In a seagoing era he was not a mariner, though he travelled on ships, and further than many a sailor. In any event, it was Vasco da Gama who swept around Africa's Cape of Good Hope in 1497. In August, 1499, it was da Gama who brought home to Lisbon the breathtaking news of his landfall on the Indian subcontinent. The razzmatazz of that cataclysmic event seems to have been more than sufficient to cast Pêro da Covilhã for all time into the shadows of history, although he had arrived in India fully a decade prior to da Gama. Da Covilhã did not sail with his own fleet, and perhaps his greatest achievement was accomplished on foot. Portugal's greatest achievements and her fame, in her past as well as from this moment forward, would be borne on the sea and in ships. The men that sailed these ships and the cargoes they carried home – this is what would waft Portugal to her hours of historical greatness.

Pêro da Covilhã conquered nothing, brought home no spices or gold. He and his legacy simply faded to an indistinguishable design on the pageantry wallpaper of Portugal's story, one of many spots reserved for those legions of heroes in any nation's annals whose accumulation of individual acts is usurped or discarded by those named to posterity, or for some other twist of kismet. There is no substantive memory of

Statue of Pêro da Covilhã in the *praça* of the city from which he took his name, Covilhã, in the Serra da Estrela, central Portugal

him in the country, nor even the city, in which he was born and which he left, even though there is a rather nondescript statue of him desperately attempting to revive his memory in the city of Covilhã in Central Portugal's Serra da Estrela. More than anything this statue seems to be a reminder that truly he had been, and remains, nondescript. Throughout Portugal, and for centuries, his story was destined to be told as a paraphrased introduction to the greater seaborne saga. However, knowing even the skeletal outline of his personal story permits a flavour of his achievement to filter through.

Strangely, though, da Covilhã's achievements do linger. Happily it is possible better to comprehend his place in the Ethiopian Highlands where he lived and settled than in Portugal, though even in Ethiopia he initiated no commercial enterprise. The European religious fanaticism that invaded Ethiopia's Highlands, a spiteful, insensitive phenomena with which da Covilhã had little in common, but which had attempted to barge its way down the path he had first paved with diplomatic care and finesse, eventually fell flat on its face. Yet it is da Covilhã's name that, metaphorically, is written first in the Highland's architectural elements that were piled into monuments of his homeland's presence there – even when very clearly the majority of them were erected by the hands of others long after he himself must have passed on.

He was born in Covilhã, the small city on the eastern side of Portugal's central mountain chain, Serra da Estrela, and was committed to noble service from the time of his childhood. There are scant details of these early years, but it would be an uncommon and exceptionally bright boy whose services would prove so favoured and sought-after, and for so long, by numbers of august households. Prince Henry the Navigator died in 1460; coincidentally it was also the year of Vasco da Gama's birth – the man who was to benefit most from da Covilhã's travels and observations.

Da Covilhã was quick, he was clever, and he was trusted. At the age of six he entered service as a page in the Seville household of the Duke of Medina-Sidonia, head of Spain's all-powerful Guzmán family. Then when he was around fifteen-years-old he returned to be with his parents in Lisbon, and was to serve the Portuguese royal court as junior squire to the king, Dom Afonso V (not to be confused with Dom Alfonso V of Aragon). He was with Afonso at Plasencia when Castile was claimed for Portugal, and as a young knight he took part in the Battle of Toro in 1476. He accompanied Afonso to France in an abortive quest to secure the backing of King Louis XI for the Castile claim. After Afonso died in 1481, he was appointed squire of the royal guard of Dom João II.

Dom João favoured da Covilhã and chose him to undertake important diplomatic missions to North Africa. On one occasion the young knight was ordered to convey messages of peace to the Moors and obtain for Portugal the trading monopoly of a valued carpet production. Another time he was sent to Fez to reclaim the remains of Portugal's Dom Fernando, the royal prince who had been taken hostage and who died in prison there in 1443 following his brother's, Prince Henry the Navigator's, disastrous attempt seven years previously to conquer Tangiers. History relates that in order to carry out this second mission, da Covilhã boldly captured seven members of the local potentate's family, finally exchanging them for the young prince's bones. On his way home he also bought horses for Prince Manuel, the Duke of Beja.

Though several years younger than the knight, Prince Manuel was also very much taken by da Covilhã's loyalty and abilities. The two of them formed a bond that was to last the duration of Manuel's life, though they were destined never to see one another again after da Covilhã had departed on his fateful mission to "India." Dom João II died three years after da Covilhã had left on his India mission; Dom Manuel had already ascended the Portuguese throne by the time Pêro had a chance to present his credentials at the exotic court of the Ethiopian emperors.

By 1487 Pêro da Covilhã had proven himself to be one of Dom João's most trusted and capable confidants, and it was in this year that he was chosen, along with three other young courtiers, to participate in major overland expeditions into Africa. An earlier small expedition had left just the year before. António de Lisboa and Pedro de Montaroyo had reached as far as Jerusalem and discovered they could go no further because neither of them knew how to speak Arabic. Both Pêro da Covilhã and his companion, Afonso de Paiva, could hold their own in fluent Arabic. Soldiers and trusted servants of their king, both were gentlemen of that age of chivalry when service to god and king would undoubtedly have been everything for which men of their standing and background might have chosen to live or die. Like most young adventurers of their age in any age, they almost certainly thought themselves blessed with immortality.

Da Covilhã was no fool. He would have known something of his future prospects had he chosen to remain in his homeland. Portugal has never offered very much to its unfavoured masses, and so much the less in the turbulent times of the late XV century. Famine, pestilence, poverty, superstition, bigotry and persecution – all these were the era's realities, and a man of Pêro's astuteness would have recognized these things, known how to stay in front of them. He is thought to have come from a minor noble family, or at least a family of some influence and standing. It is possible his family was considered "New Christian" – people of Jewish background who had renounced their religious heritage, perhaps a generation or two prior to da Covilhã's birth, in order to avoid the pogroms and harassment that flared constantly throughout Iberia. In fact New Christians were generally seen as Christians of convenience, ingratiating and untrustworthy self-servers, and thus selected for particularly merciless persecution.

Whatever the small print details of da Covilhã's background, and they remain essentially unknown, Dom João II was a most exacting and meticulous king. Many scholars past and present have considered him to have been a genius. After the failure of the Lisboa and Montaroyo expedition, a man of such calculating and gifted mind as João would have been especially attentive to any follow-up effort, careful indeed not to make the same mistake twice. He wanted the right team for the upcoming mission to India and Africa.

The historian, C.R. Boxer, has aptly described the three motors that drove the Portuguese in their Discoveries. One was religious fervour, the earnest desire to promote Christianity through missionary work, and so to seek Christian allies in the face of what was considered an Islamic threat. Finding the Christian king, Prester John, was at the top of the list. Another was sheer greed, the undoubted commercial benefits to be gained by diverting directly to Lisbon the spice trade from the controlling middlemen of the Mid East and Venice. The third, if not the most obviously important then at least the most creatively stimulating, was a burning curiosity to know more about the world beyond the bounds of European shores. Portugal was the first Renaissance superpower, and it fell to her lot to lead the way with fervour, greed and curiosity in varying proportions.

This "motor" analogy of Boxer's is useful. The Renaissance was nothing if not a great seeking, an alliance of means with the imperatives of extreme curiosity that created an essentially open and questing mindset. This very much describes Pêro da Covilhã. He lived his life without fanfare; he wrote his famous letter from Cairo, and likely translated a few others from Amharic into Portuguese, but he is not known to have written a manifesto of his views, or a memoir of his adventures. It is a pity, for he might have left a most valuable documentation of his life and times. It was more his style, it seems, to embark immediately upon setting a worthy example of his culture of origin, and the sophistication of the era in which he lived. Indeed he was a highly gifted linguist, able to speak Portuguese, Castilian Spanish, French, Italian, Arabic and at least several dialects of the Ethiopian Highlands. A man of such skill knows that language is not only the ability to use new words in translation, but to have the more complex knack of assuming the culture that surrounds them. This would indicate a degree of adaptability and tolerance that had much more to do with his own Renaissance needs, and the needs of those among whom he had come to live, than it did with the selfish aspirations and greed of the merchant class he ultimately chose not to represent – the Portuguese he chose not to rejoin; for he never returned to his homeland.

Pêro da Covilhã entered Ethiopia around the end of 1492, or beginning of 1493, in an effort to complete a diplomatic mission originally assigned to the man who was his companion for the first part of the journey, Afonso de Paiva.

At the instigation of Dom João II the two men had travelled to the southern end of the Red Sea where they separated, Paiva heading into the unknown deserts and mountains of Ethiopia to make contact with the legendary Christian king, Prester John; da Covilhã setting off for the coast of India to assess trading potential and sea routes. Having completed his assignment, as well as sailing down the east coast of Africa as far south as Sofala in Mozambique, da Covilhã returned to Cairo only to discover that Paiva had died.

Two Portuguese Jewish messengers had brought a letter addressed to both men from the Portuguese king in which the monarch had particularly emphasized the extreme importance of Paiva's mission finding Prester John. Although wishing to return to Portugal himself, da Covilhã turned about in order to fulfill his partner's task. He did so indirectly. First he delivered one of the messengers, a rabbi, to Ormuz, and then he ventured in disguise into both Mecca and Medina becoming, it is believed, the first Christian ever to do so.

To enter Ethiopia he landed at Zeila, at the southern end of the Red Sea, marched four hundred and fifty kilometres inland across a formidable desert, and succeeded in meeting up with Prester John and his court near Ankober, on the edge of the Highland escarpment. By any measure, da Covilhã had performed an amazing feat just by arriving. He was not to know it at the time, but he had chosen the most complex and difficult route into the zone. Most future entries were to be made via Massawa or Arkiko, further to the north.

He learned to speak the local language of Shoa, became a trusted advisor to the emperor on diplomatic and military matters, befriended the Dowager Empress Eleni, and was appointed governor/steward of her lands in Gojjam. He remained in the Highlands for the rest of his life, and what little is known of him is due to his having persuaded the Prester and Empress Eleni of the importance of opening up diplomatic relations with Portugal. From this point on, the Portuguese always referred to the emperors of Ethiopia as "the Prester." A Portuguese diplomatic mission arrived in the Highlands in 1520. Pêro da Covilhã was found very much alive, his story being recorded by the mission's chaplain, Padre Francisco Álvares.

Pêro da Covilhã was still alive when the mission left Ethiopia in 1526. He travelled to the coastal city of Massawa with its departing members, entrusting his Ethiopian-born son to the care of Rodrigo de Lima so that the young man could return to Portugal's court to be educated. The boy died on the way to Goa. There is no known recorded detail concerning Pêro da Covilhã following his trip to the coast. It is unknown whether or not he ever learned of his son's death.

Whatever his motive, he had initially and carefully prepared the ground for the Ethiopians to recognize the Portuguese as people to be trusted, as well as brothers in Christ. It would seem that in his contacts with the Ethiopian emperors, and especially with the Dowager Empress Eleni, da Covilhã had assiduously worked for the kind of understanding and equality between the two peoples that based their meeting on respect rather than domination, and that his efforts had been recognized, well received and accepted. The spirit of conquest, spurred by greed, which quickly overlapped this kind of chivalry in other regions of Portuguese activity never succeeded in the Highlands. The Ethiopians had a well-centred and clear comprehension of their own cultural and religious values and, though some wavered for a time, their judicious instincts appear to have alerted them to Portuguese deviousness. Apart from their souls, and we obliquely examine this point, the Ethiopians had nothing that the newcomers wanted so badly that it was necessary to exercise dominion and force to get it, even had it been possible. True, the Portuguese later contemplated using force to create converts, but the idea was never successfully implemented.

The Ethiopians genuinely offered themselves and their Christian beliefs. This was something that da Covilhã and the other earlier Portuguese who entered the Highlands could understand, after all, and that the Jesuits ultimately were to find impossible to refute or exploit. In the end it should be said that the Portuguese settler-soldiers came and built and merged and, in doing this, became Ethiopian and stayed. There was no conquest. Nothing was taken away. That which was unceremoniously hoofed out in 1634 had little or nothing to do with the earlier and enlightened glimmer of Renaissance thinking. What was expelled was a blind and intolerant fundamentalism, having a great deal more to do with religious greed and domination than Christian faith or charity. In a very real sense we find both greed and curiosity wrapping themselves in a religious cloak – and if we are able to see how these traits exist in our world today, there is no reason to believe the same miserable traits went unnoticed five hundred years ago. The conned always know when they have been conned, though sometimes too late. It is the pure arrogance and selfishness of the con involved with his con that prevents him from detecting his own stupidity.

One typical characteristic of the Portuguese, even today, presents a penchant for explaining itself in a manner which would seem to plead "The world has got us wrong... does not understand us." Indeed there is some justification for this. Portuguese history was for too long recounted by those who perceived and distorted it through a prism of exaggerated national grandeur. At home, in light of several centuries of colonial mismanagement and eventual colonial wars, this led to confusion. Abroad this attitude was seen as pretentious. Portuguese history is not widely understood even by many Portuguese themselves. In the world at large the tendency is to lump early Portuguese history into an Iberian catch-all, the events and thinking of the period of the Discoveries, for instance, very often confused as a simplistic pre-Columbian prelude to the louder and more robust period of Spanish conquest, domination and colonization.

Immediately on top of the initial Discoveries came the sweeping mercantilist "gold rush," the greed Boxer talks about so eloquently, of the Spanish, Dutch, British and French to be sure but, in the beginning and foremost, of the Portuguese themselves. Right at the start of the Discoveries, when the Pandora's Box was just being opened and there was a bright glow beaming through between the darkness of mediaeval Europe and the accumulating darkness of greedy acquisition and domination, there was a small space of idealism, a germ that persisted in a significant segment of the Portuguese psyche and ran concurrent with the greater movement that eventually swept it aside. It was a perceptible period of transition between Middle Age concepts of chivalry and the realpolitik of conquest and acquisition that came about with the Renaissance. It is the idealism of this psyche that inspired the first years of the Discoveries, lasting through to the time of Pêro da Covilhã and his clear integrity. It was an idealism that could not sustain itself, was quickly corrupted into a savage race to wealth and the power that grows from it, and ended in the twisted "moral correctness" of what grew from slavery into racism, and then the colonialism which lasted most overtly into the second half of the XX century. This idealistic glimmer accompanying the first flush of the Discoveries is worth examining, romantic though it may be, because it is this that really set the *questing* Portuguese apart no matter how much their efforts later became enmeshed in the nets of corruption and violence being cast about them, or by the sheer force of those who emerged from behind them to steal their limelight.

Portuguese history is deserving of wider attention and comprehension – by foreigners, no doubt, but also by the Portuguese themselves. For this idealistic glimmer is real, and it is what provides clues to the best of the Portuguese entity. Once sought it is quickly found; in reality it has existed throughout the country's history. Examining this glimmer might help to draw attention to, and define, the intersection of two key streams of thought and culture, one European the other African, at the point of their earliest convergence. It was happenstance that this convergence occurred at a salient moment in the histories of the two countries concerned, but no country's history exists in isolation. A man of the world like Pêro da Covilhã would have understood this.

Most histories of Ethiopia pinpoint 1541 and the arrival in the Highlands of Cristóvão da Gama's army, and the later Jesuit missionaries, as being the start of the "Portuguese era." Clearly the thesis put forward in these pages does not acknowledge this. The entry of Pêro da Covilhã nearly half a century earlier, his immediate contact and connection with the imperial court, and especially his friendship with the Dowager Empress Eleni, is of the utmost significance. It is of significance both in terms of its proactive contact in summoning the Portuguese to the Highlands, and also in terms of the initiation of a radical architecture that is visible today in the stone ruins of an active past. And it initiated a design influence that is still current.

**Confrontation: Islam and Christianity**

Several separate strands of religious history were developing at this point in time, but by far the most significant to the European Christians was the squeeze being put on them by Islam. Indeed, Islam had virtually surrounded Christianity. It was a process that had been going on for several centuries; the earlier Crusades had been nothing if not a major effort to push the Muslims back and, if at all possible, to deal them a death blow in order to reclaim Jerusalem. In this way Christendom would be hammering home, through symbolism and a *fait accompli*, the theological correctness of Christianity.

As far as was known in Portugal at the close of the XV century, when Europe was still emerging from the ignorance, darkness and superstition of the Middle Ages, the Christian world comprised a rather fragile line extending from Coptic Alexandrian Egypt around the eastern end of the Mediterranean into Syria and Anatolia and up into Armenia. Italy was a Christian stronghold, as was Iberia and parts of Britain and France. The Nestorians formed small isolated groupings stretching from Asia Minor into the sub-continent and on into the Tartar lands of China. Nubia, in what is now Sudan, was also Christian; so was Sana'a, in what is now Yemen. In the greater part of Europe, though, Christianity appeared to exist only in pockets. These farther areas of the faith were very distant indeed, and virtually unknown. To the mind of a western European even Constantinople was a confusion and a mystery. The city-states of the north had been converted to Christianity, as had been the Lowlands, Germany, Scandinavia, the Baltic and on into Russia. In between were gigantic expanses of dark forest and ignorance. To the eyes of the Portuguese, who constituted the superpower of the time, the heart of Christianity was the arc of civilization that stretched from the Vatican to Lisbon.

Islam's rapid expansion was viewed with alarm and venom. From its inception in the VII century it had spread like a brushfire creating its own momentum: north from Arabia into Palestine and Syria; west into Turkey and the underbelly of Europe, Bosnia and the Balkans; east onto the broad steppes of the former Soviet satellite countries. Unseen from a European vantage point, it had moved with ease across the Gulf regions and on into the sub-continent of India, then down into Indonesia and on into Southeast Asia. Islam hopped across into Africa as if the Red Sea was not there, then it swept down the seaboard of the Indian Ocean carried by Arab traders, and west across the deserts of Egypt and North Africa into the Maghreb. From there it worked its way south on the caravan routes leading into Mauritania and Chad, and north across the Strait of Gibraltar into Andalusia and southern Portugal. Here bitter wars were fought against Islam – crusades, in fact. What we came to call The Crusades is no more than a descriptive term for a series of wars considered, at the time, very much a riposte to the Antichrist. Formal history has numbered seven or nine of them, depending upon one's reference but, to be sure, there were many lesser crusades. The greatest of all Christian dreams had been to re-establish a Christian capital in Jerusalem, sullied in its capture by Syrian and Egyptian Arabs in 980. Though briefly re-conquered by Christendom on the eve of the XII century, Jerusalem was retaken by Saladin in 1187 and subsequently dominated by Islam.

**Prester John**

The Portuguese kings found their rationale in the expansion of Christianity. Tantalized and teased though their curiosities surely were in the quest for scientific knowledge and discovery, they were also avaricious and lusting for wealth to a point of phobia quite beyond the easy comprehension of a modern socially conscious observer. All sins were acceptable, it seemed, in the cause of Christian conversion; a good Catholic had only to confess his sins to receive absolution for the worst of them. Such self-serving liberalism left a lot of leeway for enthusiastic abuse. What a boon it would be to Christianity as a whole if the Christian world of Europe could ally itself with a Christian world as yet unknown on the other side of Islam. It would give the Muslims a hefty boot in their rear, and turn a profit into the bargain by diverting the routes from the eastern markets into the harbour at Lisbon. The whole wide world, it seemed, was Portugal's oyster.

For several hundred years there had existed stories about a great Christian king who lived somewhere beyond the farthest reaches of Islam. He first appeared in European legend in 1145, described as a Nestorian prince whose empire was far to the east, beyond Persia. He was thought to have been both priest and king, and was known to his subjects as Presbyter, or Prester, John. The name likely derived from, first, the Hebrew and, later, the Romanized transliteration of the Mongol title of a military leader, Kor-khan, easily twisted into "Yohanan," "Johannes," or "John." Having conquered Persia, the story went, this mighty king attempted to march his armies west to restore Jerusalem to Christianity, but he was unable to cross the Tigris River and so reluctantly turned back. Twenty years later, Europe was set a-buzz by the mysterious appearance of a letter from this "Prester John of the Indies" addressed to all the Princes of Europe, but to the Byzantine and Holy Roman emperors in particular. It was an obvious forgery but the public wanted to believe in it, so great was their fear of Islam and their hope for the salvation offered by an omnipotent Christian king.

The populace of the time was happy to believe the most astonishing things about this Prester John. It was readily accepted that he had access to enormous quantities of silver, gold and precious stones; that his kingdom was so wealthy it knew no begging; that food was abundant, and all manner of fantastic animals roamed at peace in a kingdom that spanned "The Four Indies." Its cities and towns reflected the highest civilization imaginable, and the Prester's forty-two adjutant lords had sworn to restore Jerusalem to its rightful Christian path. It was music to the ear of a besieged Christian. The simple European villager was only just then beginning to emerge from the darkness of his superstitions, and the stories that first greeted him and impressed him beyond measure were those of the extraordinary colour and glory of the Byzantine and Arab cultures. He did not at all wish to see himself as part of a Christian world that lagged behind these, so adopted the legend of Prester John with quite irrational enthusiasm.

But where was this great Christian king?

Marco Polo came up with an answer at the end of the XIII century, claiming he had been in contact with just such a king in the Tartar lands of Karakorum. Then he made the unpardonable mistake of informing all those who would listen to him that the Prester had died in a fierce battle with Ghenghis Khan. Nobody wanted to hear such a terrible tale. It demolished both hope and self-esteem.

In 1330 a Dominican friar, Jordanus, published a book telling the amazing tales of his years in Persia, and in it he recounted how the Emperor of Ethiopia was the same man who was known in Europe as Prester John. Later, in the middle of the century, a Spanish Franciscan published a book of geography that referred to Prester John as being the "patriarch of Nubia and Abyssinia." Suddenly the story was alive again, complete with all the exaggerated details of the letter of 1165. The one big difference was that it was now Ethiopia, or "Abyssinia," which was beginning to emerge on the world map and in the collective mind of Europe as the true Garden of Eden. It was located in the great mountainous regions of "India," somewhere south of Egypt, down the Red Sea.

To the mindset of early Renaissance Europe, anywhere east and south of Cairo was considered "India."

**Da Covilhã's Letter**

Pêro da Covilhã was a man of something less than thirty years old when he was chosen along with three other men, to form two essentially land-based exploratory teams to scout out Prester John. Da Covilhã was paired with Afonso de Paiva, and they were to proceed to the eastern end of the Mediterranean before heading south.

The other two, Gonçalo Eanes and Pêro da Évora, were to head directly south to regions of west Africa already frequented by Portuguese mariners on the Atlantic coast. They were instructed to turn north and east at that point to search for new lands, new riches and, of course, Prester John. A story originating on Africa's west coast had circulated concerning a great king called Ogané who lived in mountains far to the east. Could this be the Prester? Nobody knew quite what lay between the Portuguese coastal factories on the Atlantic side of the continent and Ethiopia, wherever that was. Eventually these two explorers were to find their path led to Timbuktu, Tucurol and home again.

Pêro da Covilhã and Afonso de Paiva had a totally different experience. The two of them travelled together to Rhodes, then south to Cairo masquerading all the while as Muslim honey merchants. From there they headed south in caravan with other traders, down the Sinai to the town of Tôr, and by boat south on the Red Sea to Suakin, then eventually on to Aden. Paiva's mission was to cross the Strait of Bab el Mandeb to the African mainland, make his way into the mountains to contact Prester John, then attempt to cross Africa to Benin where, hopefully, he would connect with the Portuguese at São Jorge da Mina and arrange transport home. In the event that crossing Africa might prove unfeasible the two adventurers agreed to meet back in Cairo in one year's time.

Even today a traveller would have to think long and hard before contemplating such a journey; but one must realize that in the period concerned there were no maps of any accuracy, and no concrete knowledge of the hardships one would encounter, doubtless much harder in those days than today, in crossing Africa from Ethiopia to Benin. If today, from a more knowledgeable modern viewpoint, we should be tempted to consider a journey like this to be a measure of antique ignorance, so must we also realize that such a thing is an indication of the fortitude and courage of the discoverers of the day. In fact there were, and still are, trade routes that criss-cross the continent, and it is entirely possible that the early Portuguese had some knowledge of them. We must not be too quick to condemn XV century travel offices as entirely foolish. As we shall see, Pêro da Covilhã himself undertook no less arduous an expedition than this, and succeeded. While Paiva was off scouting for Prester John, it fell to da Covilhã's lot to explore the "India coast" and report back to Lisbon with a full knowledge of its commercial possibilities.

We do not know what became of Afonso de Paiva other than that he died, and probably very soon after arriving on the African coast. Before discovering this sad fact, Pêro da Covilhã was to accomplish one of the most amazing journeys ever recorded concerning that historical era. Availing himself of only what Arab shipping plied those seas, he crossed from Aden to Goa on India's west coast, there initiating inquiries that gave him a clear idea of the spice trade, its origins, shipment and marketing. He subsequently made his way north into the Gulf of Persia and the island of Ormuz. From there he turned southwest, back towards the Horn, and sailed with these same Arab merchant seamen down the entire coast of East Africa as far as Sofala, near Beira, in Mozambique. The year 1490 saw him back in the Red Sea, heading north for his tentative rendezvous in Cairo with Afonso de Paiva. He was met instead by two Portuguese travellers, Rabbi Abraham of Beja, and José, a shoemaker from Lamego. These men brought the traveller a letter from Dom João, and it was also they who imparted the news, which they themselves had only learned upon their arrival in Cairo, that Afonso de Paiva had died.

Ignorant of Paiva's death, Dom João's letter beseeched the two young emissaries not to return home without having achieved their missions, and he stressed the importance of contacting Prester John. The king further requested Pêro da Covilhã to accompany Rabbi Abraham to Ormuz.

At this point Pêro da Covilhã had been anxious to return to Portugal. Nevertheless, there in Cairo and preparing to embark again with the rabbi, he penned a long and descriptive letter to his king in which he detailed everything he had been able to glean during his voyages concerning the commercial prospects of the rim of the Indian Ocean – and beyond. He now knew that it was possible to round the southern tip of Africa. This fact he learned definitively from the two men he met in Cairo, who had departed Lisbon following the return of Bartolomeu Dias' epic voyage round the Cape of Good Hope. They were thus able to inform da Covilhã how Dias had been successful in his bid to navigate the southern point of the African continent into the Indian Ocean. The great navigator had sailed from Lisbon towards the end of 1486, a few months prior to Pêro da Covilhã's own departure with Afonso de Paiva. It is more than likely, though, that da Covilhã would have deduced Dias' success when he himself sailed south along Africa's east coast on an Arab trading ship. News of the strange and terrifying sight of the Portuguese ships that had nosed their way north from the southern cape had flashed rapidly up and down the coastline by "bush telegraph," so that Dias' entry into the Indian Ocean was very quickly common knowledge.

The letter da Covilhã wrote to Dom João was given to José de Lamego to carry back with him. The actual document has never been found, but a detailed description of it does exist. As instructed, da Covilhã accompanied the rabbi to Ormuz and left him there to travel back to Portugal on his own, overland. Meanwhile da Covilhã himself returned by ship to the Red Sea and managed to make his famous expedition into the holy Islamic cities of Mecca and Medina. He was probably the first Christian ever to do so and live to tell about it. Sometime after this, he again turned about and made his way south in the Red Sea to the port of Zeila, located today in the northwest corner of

Somaliland. This would have been about the end of 1492, or beginning of 1493. He had been away from home for nearly six years.

There is considerable controversy concerning Pêro da Covilhã's letter to his king, and whether or not the document itself ever actually arrived. Leaving Lisbon in July, 1497, Vasco da Gama sailed directly into Calicut, which would seem to indicate that he knew where to go. He did not arrive there until May, 1498, though, and there has never been a satisfactory explanation for the nearly seven years separating de Lamego's return to Lisbon with the letter (or the information it contained) and da Gama's own embarkation. Nor has there been explanation for the fact that when da Gama did arrive in India, he brought considerable derision down upon his own head by presenting the local potentates with gifts of decidedly inferior quality. Presumably if da Gama had been aware of da Covilhã's letter he would have been better prepared to match the wealth and sophistication of his hosts. Another opinion that would help to explain this lapse, and one that has gained some favour because it is thought more accurately to depict the nature of da Gama's arrogant character, is that he simply did not give a damn about the diplomatic niceties required in the giving of suitable gifts. From the very beginning, conquest appears to have been his rather more paramount mindset.

**Highland Court**

Trekking inland from the Red Sea coast, da Covilhã was quick to establish contact with "Prester John" in the province of Shoa, an area encompassing the escarpment forming the eastern edge of the Ethiopian Highlands. Pêro was an accomplished linguist, and learned the language of Shoa in the time it took him to walk in from the coast. He learned, too, that the emperor's correct name was Eskendar. (Although each ruler had his own name, for many years after this first encounter the Portuguese came to refer to all Ethiopian emperors as "O Preste João," or simply "O Preste," as though it was a title rather than a name.) The emissary so impressed the monarch with his military prowess, his knowledge of geography, his diplomatic skills and languages, that he immediately became a favourite at court and a close consort of the emperor and his successors. Most importantly of all, he befriended the Dowager Empress Eleni, a child-queen to Eskendar's grandfather, Emperor Zara Ya'qob (d. 1468). Eleni was possibly the same age, or just a little older, than the Portuguese himself. A highly intelligent woman who survived her husband by more than half a century, she commanded the greatest love and respect of her people, and wielded immense power within the court as a counsellor to the emperors.

Eskendar was assassinated some two years after da Covilhã had made contact with the royal court. Emperor Naod (1495-1508), succeeded to the throne upon the death of his half brother, and continued to favour both Eleni and the Portuguese emissary.

Without launching into a lengthy thesis on Ethiopia's religions, it would nonetheless be useful at this stage to make a brief examination of what Pêro da Covilhã discovered when he arrived in the Highlands. The single greatest reason why he was so sure he had found the court of Prester John was precisely because he had discovered this new world to be Christian. His mandate, after all, was to seek in these regions for the greatest of all Christian kings.

Christianity was being practiced in the area of the Axumite empire as early as 330 AD. The formation of the Ethiopian Orthodox Church came with the conversion of the then royal household in 347 AD, some seven hundred years prior to the schism of the Byzantine and Roman doxologies that brought about the establishment of the Roman Catholic Church we know today. The Ethiopian

Orthodox Church sprung directly from the Coptic Church of Alexandria, and is therefore one of the oldest Christian assemblies. To this day it has remained little changed.

The story of Ethiopia's church is well documented. Christian teaching was first brought to the Axumite empire by Frumentius who, as a boy, had been travelling with family and friends from Alexandria south along the Eritrean coast. Local militias had captured the ship and slaughtered everybody aboard, but he and his young friend, Aedesius, were spared and were taken to the king at Axum as slaves. Both boys were Coptic Christians, and their manner so impressed the king, Ezana, that he permitted himself to be converted by Frumentius, and in turn he decreed that Christianity would thenceforth become the religion of all areas of his Highland kingdom. Returning to Alexandria after some years to plead with Bishop Athanasius to supply the Highlands with a worthy church leader, Frumentius himself was named, and appointed to become the new church's first Abun, or patriarch. From that very early time the head of the Ethiopian church was traditionally selected from among the elders of the Alexandrian Copts, a practice that continued until early in the XX century. This new church thus came into being about two hundred years prior to the Christian conversion of Nubia, and it enjoyed considerably greater fortune than its lowland Nile co-religionists. The first of the Islamic invasions of the lowland regions began in 652 AD and concluded with the capitulation of the Christians following the Mamluk assaults of the XIV century. The Highland church, though bitterly attacked by lowland Muslims a century later, was able to resist. It did so, as we shall see, with the assistance of a Portuguese army.

That historic intervention was still some way into the future when, at the end of 1492 or early in 1493, da Covilhã marched westwards from the Red Sea and into the Christian Highlands to meet Prester John. In no way did he come as a missionary, though, and his first assignment at the royal court was as a soldier. His assessment of the emperor's armies was that, though numerous, they would prove to be a poor match in any confrontation with a well-constituted and disciplined enemy. Weaponry was poor and tactics were almost non-existent. There was far too little discipline, and this laxity was coupled with too much posturing and preening on the battlefield itself. Da Covilhã settled into training the army anew and, in time, his organizational skills were rewarded. He was granted lands in the province of Gojjam, a massive territory nestled on the inside bulge of the Blue Nile River, northwest of Shoa, in area not very much smaller than all of mainland Portugal. These lands were probably assigned to him in *gult*, a system of royal patronage not entirely unassociated with the idea of feudalism inasmuch as the tenant would have been required to repay the owner with produce from the land. When required, he would also have been responsible for furnishing manpower for the military.

Empress Eleni presided over large tracts of land in Gojjam, and there is a strong possibility that da Covilhã's grant was in fact a stewardship of her holdings. In any event, it is in the eastern section of Gojjam that one finds the ruined palace and church of Mertule Maryam. Legends told often enough seem to take on a validity of their own, and though they abound in this area any truths concealed in them are extremely difficult, if not impossible, to verify. Mertule Maryam's visible ruins are undoubtedly of Portuguese origin, which is not to say that they could not have been built upon far older foundations. While much is known concerning the extant ruins, much more yet awaits the detailed scientific assessment of modern archaeology. In talks with locals, priests and elders, I heard the claim that the complex structure was built under the direction of Empress Eleni's "European advisor" – who could have been none other than Pêro da Covilhã - and that it was used by both himself and Eleni as their provincial headquarters. Parts of the structure appear to date from the earliest years of the XVI century, while other sections, the Jesuit history of which is well recorded, date from the early XVII century. Also on record is the request by the empress for da

Covilhã to go there and oversee the building of an altar in the chapel. Other stories present da Covilhã as lover to Eleni; yet others present Eleni as true mother to Emperor Lebna Dengal (1508-1540), sired by the Portuguese himself. Accepted history is that the empress died childless; there are no records proving otherwise. We shall probably never know the full details of the relationship between Eleni and da Covilhã; history has a delightful way of hiding burning tittle-tattle behind obscure rumour. There can be no doubt, however, that they had a very close relationship.

It is known that Pêro da Covilhã married a local girl, and that the union produced at least one son. The boy was twenty-three in 1526, the year the Portuguese diplomatic mission left the Highlands, and da Covilhã attempted to send him back to Portugal entrusted to the personal care of Ambassador Rodrigo de Lima. The idea was that the young fellow was to receive an education at court in Lisbon. Sadly, though, he died on the journey to Goa. Details of this were recorded by Padre Francisco Álvares, the embassy's chaplain, who had maintained careful notes of all aspects of the mission since its arrival in 1520, and who later published the most far ranging account of life in the Highlands that has come down to us today.

This embassy was the result of efforts initiated and encouraged by Empress Eleni, and it is impossible to believe that she thought to do this without consulting closely with Pêro da Covilhã. How would she otherwise have known, even, of Portugal's existence, let alone its superpower status? Emperor Lebna Dengal was a boy of eleven when he came to the throne in 1508. It was Eleni who acted as his regent until he came of age, but it was Pêro da Covilhã who acted as her chief counsellor and proved a strong factor working in the background. By the time the embassy arrived, Lebna Dengal was a young man and had assumed his imperial duties. He was a stubborn and proud person whose curiosity concerning these foreigners had been piqued by Eleni and da Covilhã, but who did not take kindly to advice of any sort – particularly, it would appear, in diplomatic or military affairs. Both the dowager empress and her Portuguese advisor are believed to have had an extremely difficult time cajoling and guiding the young emperor into making intelligent decisions.

**The Portuguese in the Indian Ocean**

Sir James Bruce, the Scottish historian who spent several years in Ethiopia in the XVIII century, has claimed in his writings that the Islamic-Christian confrontation in the Highlands began when Lebna Dengal ascended to the throne as a boy in 1508, with Eleni acting as his regent until 1515. Other historians place the date a little later. When one pieces together various events with the benefit of hindsight it would seem that Bruce was probably not far off in his estimate.

By 1508 the Portuguese navy was very active and disruptive throughout the Indian Ocean. In the year immediately following da Gama's return to Lisbon in 1499, Pedro Álvares Cabral had been assigned by Dom Manuel I (1495-1521) to take a major expedition of thirteen ships to India for the express purpose of establishing a fortified trading post at Calicut. It was on this ill-fated voyage, a wide arc through the south Atlantic to take best advantage of currents and winds, that Cabral landed on the coast of what is now Brazil and claimed it for the Portuguese crown. Disaster awaited the fleet a month later as it rounded the Cape of Good Hope in a storm. Four ships were lost with all hands, including Bartolomeu Dias, but the rest continued on and landed at Calicut in September, 1500.

The local Muslim ruler received Cabral well, but disputes soon arose with Muslim merchants who, in December, 1500, incited a large force of Hindus to attack the Portuguese trading post. Most of the defenders were killed before reinforcements could come to their aid from the ships anchored in the harbour. Cabral's response was severe. He bombarded the city, then captured ten Muslim ships and executed everybody aboard them. Later sailing south to Cochin he was agreeably received, managed to take aboard his ships a quantity of spices and completed loading his cargo at Carangolos and Cannanore before sailing for home in January, 1501. Two more ships were lost on the return, but the remainder made it to Lisbon by June of that year.

Vasco da Gama's second voyage to India began in January, 1502. Its purpose was punitive and to establish, without doubt, Portugal's hegemony throughout the Indian Ocean. On his arrival in Indian waters he laid in wait for an Arab merchant ship. He boarded her off Goa, seized the cargo, then locked the crew and some three hundred innocent passengers, including women and children, below decks. He then set the ship afire. There were no survivors. He followed this with a second massacre of Hindu fishermen at Calicut, and bombarded the city's port. Later yet, when he learned that a friendly gesture from the ruler of Cochin was actually an attempt to entrap him, da Gama attacked Arab shipping off the coast and put them all to flight.

By October 1503 Vasco da Gama was back in Lisbon, but the pattern of stern Portuguese control had been established and it was to increase and continue relentlessly. By 1508, the very year Lebna Dengal became emperor of Ethiopia as a boy, confrontation was hardly anything out of the ordinary. The next year the Portuguese routed the Muslim fleet off the coast of Diu.

Goa on India's west coast was conquered by Afonso de Albuquerque in 1510. It was a good port, and a good trading centre, and very soon became the headquarters of Portugal's eastern vice kingdom. It was also the Indian Ocean embarkation port of entry into the Ethiopian Highlands.

In 1513 Turkish military and naval forces in the Red Sea were strong enough to withstand Afonso de Albuquerque's attempt to sack Aden, but they were not able to prevent him from entering the Red Sea and chasing the Egyptian-Gujarati fleet away from the Eritrean coast of Ethiopia.

Perhaps Ethiopia's emperor could have pointed a finger of blame at Portugal for shaking the hornet's nest, and undoubtedly he did just that. Blaming them would have made little difference by now, though. Other dynamics were also forcing a confrontation between Muslim lowlands and Christian Highlands, so that the Portuguese element in the entire fracas, though significant, was only a part of the problem. By 1515, when the young Ethiopian Emperor Lebna Dengal took control of his throne, he had already been forced into a running war, a dire situation that avoided resolution for the remainder of his life.

In 1517 the Muslim Turks conquered Egypt itself, and Syria, and their strength grew significantly up and down the Red Sea coasts. This enabled them, three years later, to create strong links with the Islamic seaboard regions of Ethiopia and to encourage the local population to come out in open revolt against the domination and rule of the emperor in the Christian Highlands. The Islamic point of view was clear: if Christian Portugal could attack the Turks and their Islamic allies anywhere throughout the enormous area of the Indian Ocean or Red Sea, then there was every justification, to say nothing of good tactics, in promoting coastal Islam to turn on Portugal's Christian allies in the high hinterland.

In 1509 Empress Eleni had sent an Armenian confidant and diplomat named Matthew to Portugal to try to convince Dom Manuel I to open relations between the two countries. She understood the Muslim threat very clearly, and turned to Portugal because she recognized the utility of a strong Christian friend. Naturally, she would have been encouraged to this opinion through her proximity to Pêro da Covilhã. Unfortunately Matthew was not well received. He was held in suspicion because if he was truly a representative of Ethiopia, why was he not an Ethiopian? Badly treated by people who should have been his courtly hosts, he made slow headway, and it was not until 1520 that he was able to re-enter Ethiopia with the diplomatic embassy of Rodrigo de Lima.

It was a fractious embassy at best. Initially and badly planned in Goa, its fundamentals had actually been hastily assembled by the Portuguese governor of India, Diogo de Sequeira, while he was sitting with his ships at Arkiko on the Eritrean coast. Personality clashes nearly tore the group asunder. After the embassy had reached the Highland court it was the Ethiopian emperor himself who felt obliged, on several occasions, to intervene in the various wranglings of his guests. Time and again he was called upon to soothe frayed Portuguese tempers, or to listen to opposing viewpoints. It did not create a good impression, and Lebna Dengal clearly decided he had best not ask the Portuguese for anything. He wanted their quality armaments, but he could hardly have been convinced that more of these quarrelsome people would be of substantial benefit to him. He saw these foreigners, in general terms, as brash and arrogant people, overly and individually ambitious and self-serving. These were traits of character that tended to run counter to the retiring and natural humility of the Christian Highlanders. One may imagine he must have felt some relief when the embassy left in 1526, but by this time his problems with the coastal Muslims, which had been increasing in intensity every year, had built to a crescendo. An efficient Portuguese Embassy might have been able to secure military assistance for him. Such a fractious mission could only have been a distraction, though, and it no doubt contributed to the overall opinion that it was best for the emperor to fight his own battles without being sidetracked by such amicable irritations.

## Ahmad Grag'n

The coastal Islamic armies were under the command of the vizier of Adal, Ahmad Ibn Ibrahim el Ghazi, known more familiarly as Ahmad Grag'n the Left-Handed, a giant of a man who possessed a penchant for brutality matching his evil disposition and terrifying reputation. A cavalry officer, he had risen to eminence by deposing the local sultan and having a pliant emir installed in his place. In no time it was Grag'n himself who wielded full powers over the combined armies of Adal and their ancient enemies, the Somalis.

In 1529 Grag'n resoundingly defeated Lebna Dengal's numerically superior army at the Battle of Shembra Kuré, and he swarmed over the Highlands. Here, for the next dozen years, Grag'n destroyed every Christian church and monastery he could find, along with whatever treasured artefacts they contained. Razing town after town, he enforced conversion to Islam at sword point, and killed any and all who hesitated or resisted. For the Christians, the Ethiopian Orthodox Church itself, and all subsequent historical record, it was a disaster of enormous proportions. Quantities of the most treasured cultural and religious objects, writings and icons, were obliterated. The Ethiopian armies were dismembered, scattered and demoralized so completely that their elements turned and fled before an Islamic assault rather than attempt to re-group and fight on.

Empress Eleni had died in 1523, pleading till the end that Lebna Dengal request Portuguese military assistance. Always a headstrong man inclined to pigheaded pride and not just a little suspicious of the Portuguese, Lebna Dengal resisted this idea until after his defeat at Shembra Kuré and even further humiliations culminating in a major setback at Amba Geshan in 1533. Now he put through his request. The Portuguese military was almost as slow to respond as their embassy had been before it, and it failed to appear until 1541. By this time Lebna Dengal had died and been replaced on the throne by his eighteen-year-old son, Galawdewos.

Had he still been alive, Pêro da Covilhã by now would have been a venerable man indeed, over eighty-years-old. Possibly he was already long dead, but not necessarily. Whether he was or not, something of his cavalier spirit, that glimmer of the true knight, was still very much alive in Cristóvão da Gama, the twenty-four-year-old commander of the Portuguese force that landed at Massawa in June of 1541.

Son of the great admiral, Vasco, and younger brother to Estevão da Gama, the newly-appointed governor of Portuguese India, Cristóvão immediately summoned Ahmad Grag'n to battle despite the fact that he only had four hundred men to throw into the fight. While these were all handpicked warriors, sworn to defend Christianity or die, and armed with the finest steel and musketry known at the time, Ahmad Grag'n fielded an army of several thousand men and willingly obliged the young upstart.

Miguel de Castanhoso, who landed at Massawa with Cristóvão and was possibly the only Portuguese ever to return to his homeland following that expedition, has left us a thrilling account of this entire episode.

Ahmad Grag'n was not only beaten in his first battle with the Portuguese, but in the second as well. At the third major encounter, however, Cristóvão was captured. He was humiliated, tortured and finally beheaded by Ahmad Grag'n himself. Far from sapping the morale of the Portuguese this act served to rile them. Those still able to fight now joined forces with the young Emperor Galawdewos. At the Battle of Waina Dega in 1543, high in the mountains to the northeast of Lake Tana, Ahmad Grag'n was finally out-manoeuvred and killed, his armies chased from the Highlands. The small Portuguese contingent, reinforced from Massawa, and able to provide modern backbone, weapons and tactical skills to Galawdewos' Christian forces, was instrumental in stopping the continued destruction of Highland communities. In a very significant sense the Portuguese really did play a decisive role in the salvation of Ethiopian Christianity. The irony here is that, at the outset of Portugal's mission into the Highlands, it had been hoped that Prester John would rally the European armies of all Christendom behind his own to drive Islam into the sea. As it turned out the Prester's armies were so weak that they could not even defend themselves, and required a Portuguese band of four hundred stalwarts to accomplish a task the emperor's thousands of warriors could not. After this the myth of an omnipotent Prester John was utterly destroyed once and for all.

This was not the conclusion of hostilities between the Islamic and Christian forces. The Muslims were pushed from the Highlands, but they remained strong and bellicose in the coastal lowlands. Their Turkish naval allies were still a force to be reckoned with on the Red Sea. The only road home for the Portuguese who had penetrated into the Highlands was back across a hostile landscape, and out through a hostile sea. Some attempted it, but most of them failed and fled back into the Highlands to seek the shelter now offered by Galawdewos. They were welcomed and held in high honour, not least because the young emperor was now having trouble with the encroachment of the Galla tribesmen from the south. These were a fierce warrior people going through a period of rapid expansion, and who were themselves also suffering persecution at the hands of the Somalis further to their south. Seeking new lands, the Galla were taking advantage of the weak position now displayed by the Highland Christians, and were moving into areas softened up over the long period of Muslim invasions. Once again Portuguese arms and fighting skills were desperately required to come to the assistance of the Ethiopian emperor.

As one might expect, Portuguese military leadership in Ethiopia had dissipated after the death of Cristóvão da Gama. What was left comprised an individualistic and ragged lot of well-armed and rowdy adventurers whose numbers were occasionally beefed up by replenishments of yet more boisterous cutthroats drifting up from the coast. Some of these men were guards accompanying missionaries as they entered the Highlands, and were always on the lookout for ways to enrich themselves. On the one hand Galawdewos was truly grateful to the Portuguese soldiers who had helped him in the defeat of Ahmad Grag'n, and he was happy to grant them lands and special privileges. Nevertheless, while it was clear that he both wanted and needed the guns and expertise these warriors could provide he was also coming to mistrust them. Several of these mercenaries had offered their services to rival princes and warlords critical of Galawdewos and later, of his brother and successor, Minas. Galawdewos was shrewd enough to recognize that the surest way to placate such a dangerous contingent was to coddle it, and so he continued to shower the Portuguese with his largesse. This situation changed quite dramatically when Minas came to power some years later.

**In Search of Paradise**

An overview of this period will clearly show, interestingly, that although Portugal was the Renaissance "superpower," the power was not actually all that super. The country's navy and military forces were dominant in the region of the Indian Ocean and elsewhere; but even at that time, with a population in the homeland of less than one-and-a-half million souls, the country could in no way be described as populous. There were severe limits to the control of all areas over which Portugal claimed suzerainty. The country had enormous difficulties in finding the manpower to crew its sizeable fleet. In those days Portugal's swashbuckling seamen caused consternation in every port they entered. On the high seas the blackguards who manned the ships, the swiftest and most modern navy afloat, showed virtually no restraint in attacking and plundering any vessel that sailed under another nation's flag. In point of fact it was only in the next century that this appalling behaviour came to be recognized as "piracy."

Every Portuguese ship had a Portuguese commander. Very often the majority of the ship's complement comprised a motley gathering of dockside heavies recruited or shanghaied from everywhere up and down the coast from Guinea all the way around Africa to the Horn, Arabia, India, Malacca, the Philippines, Japan and China. These people, whether Portuguese noblemen, Greek, German, Armenian or Italian merchant adventurers, riff-raff and flotsam on the run from lord only knows what governors, slavers or crimes, all went by the generic "Portuguese" if they served on a Portuguese ship, or in any way championed or worked for the Portuguese cause.

The navy and sea going was not a sure profession in those days. If a man kept going to sea for years on end, his chances of survival diminished greatly. A deck hand would be lucky to live four years. Many of these men could never "go home." No matter where they came from, they were faced with a long list of miseries. They had toothless hag wives and bawling children to make impossible demands upon them when survival itself was anything but certain. Famine, plague and disease were rife, debtors' courts were ready to cast them into rat-infested dungeons and there was the Inquisition in Christian Europe. Stout ropes were waiting to hang any number of them.

Despite the fact that Prester John was clearly not the magnificent warrior-priest-king he was initially thought to be, the idea of Paradise persisted. Word had spread that high in the hinterland of a place called "Abyssinia" there was a Christian emperor who asked no questions. He ruled over a land of lakes and streams and a temperate climate, where there were forests and game a-plenty. A man could pluck his easy living from the trees, sow his crops, build himself a house and settle down to raise a family with the most beautiful women in the world. Every sailor's dream. Every ruffian's refuge. All he had to do was get there.

These were the "Portuguese" who came to Ethiopia, and while many of them truly were Portuguese, many of them were not. Italians, Greeks, Arabs, Indians – to the indigenous people of the Highlands, all of them were "Portuguese."

Among them Portuguese nationals were dominant, of course, and they brought their considerable skills with them. In their lives prior to sailing into the Indian Ocean they had been farmers or fishermen, soldiers, artisans or merchants. In addition they were also builders. Theirs was a nation of builders. Architecture, grand or folksy, was their national and natural artistic bent. Their nation was one of the leading lights of the Renaissance, and the cultural expression of the era in Portugal was primarily architectural.

It did not take the Portuguese very long to discover that there was little commercial potential for them in Ethiopia. If the object of a man's endeavour was to get rich, there were much easier pickings in India and the Spice Islands. Sailing around the southern end of Africa, the eastern coastal ports of the continent made navigational good sense. Mozambique Island in particular became an important way station for shipping going in either direction. In other ports up and down the coast – Kilwa, Zanzibar, Mombassa, Mogadishu, even Socotra which was abandoned very early on – Portuguese engineers and builders erected substantial fortifications that still stand today, for each had its particular importance in terms of defence, trade or provisioning.

Ethiopia was somewhat off the beaten track. Massawa or Arkiko, even Zeila further south, were not on the route of sail. Moreover, Portugal never dominated the Red Sea, the ports of which were principally controlled by unfriendly Muslims. Great care was needed at all times. Portuguese ships sailed past Aden courageously enough, but as like as not there would be a Turkish patrol to defeat, out-manoeuvre or avoid. In any case there were difficult winds to navigate in this narrow seaway. A captain had to pick the right season for getting in and getting out again.

Arkiko, on the mainland a short distance south of the island port of Massawa, was especially favoured by Portuguese captains sneaking up to the coast to drop off people or cargo. If one goes there today, it is easy to see why, though nothing of the old town has been left standing following Eritrea's modern war of independence. At Arkiko, the sea is shallow for several hundred metres out from the beach, and a man could easily wade from a boat to the dry land, or be carried in by shallow-draft rowboat. This fact alone would enable an experienced sea captain lying well off, to hoist sail and speed away should he spy trouble on shore, thus at least saving his ship if not whatever it was he had just dropped off. For those coming ashore, though, Arkiko possessed other obvious advantages over Massawa. On the mainland behind Massawa there is a level stretch of desert terrain several kilometres wide. There is no cover whatsoever. Should a Muslim shore patrol on fast ponies or camels happen to see a group of people heading inland, it would be an easy matter to chase them down and cut them off. The hinterland behind Arkiko, on the other hand, comprises a range of rugged dunes and hills. In minutes, a clandestine landing party could take refuge in this harsh landscape, and would stand much more of a fighting chance of making it past the hostile Muslim coastal strip to the relative safety of the Christian Highlands.

Commercially, the Portuguese had an easy choice to make. Ethiopia was a dud. On the other hand, there were Christians in those remote Highlands. If one could get past the Islamic barrier that stretched along the coastal regions, one was home free, so to speak, and headed for Paradise. This fact did not escape the attentions of the thousands of freebooters, mercenaries, fugitives and adventurers who attempted to carve their individual paths to Paradise, perhaps each with the idea in mind that here was the one place on earth where life could be started anew. Neither did it escape the attentions of the Roman Catholic Church, the initial aims of which would have been twofold: to establish a firm Christian ally against Islam, and to provide fertile ground for Roman Catholic proselytizing.

The reality of the first of these was quickly apparent. As we have seen, rather than Portugal being able to count on Ethiopia's great fighting machine, it was the Ethiopians who required Portuguese assistance, a fact that came lumbered with all the negatives of a gigantic monetary drain. The Portuguese and the Good Lord Himself seem to have had a clear understanding on that issue: despite numerous requests over the years, no troops. Cristóvão da Gama was to prove the exception, not the rule. Missionaries, that was a different matter altogether. These people, the Ethiopian Highlanders, were clearly good souls and they even called themselves Christians, but their Orthodoxy – ah, that was a pity. So erroneous, the notion of Christ's singleness of nature, the Trinity united as one, the concept of two Sabbaths.

Heretical, actually. They would have to be taught.

**The Exasperating "Dom" João Bermudez**

At first Roman Catholicism appears to have inched its way unobtrusively into the Highlands. Then the inching evolved into a gush, and the gush inevitably into an intolerable onslaught.

Pêro da Covilhã was the first. Nevertheless, it really does appear he arrived in the Highlands as Christian tolerant enough in the practice of his faith to avoid drawing down on his head the resentment of his hosts. If, indeed, he was the mastermind behind the construction of the palace and chapel at Mertule Maryam, indications would seem to point to a curiously innocent mix of the Roman Catholic and Orthodox strains of Christian expression. There is a distinct possibility that it really was a genuinely Christian brand of liberalism. Its mere Christianity would have been sufficient to the spiritual and devotional needs of either congregation. Such philosophy would fit quite comfortably within the thesis of a Renaissance glimmer of openness and tolerance. In these Highlands da Covilhã appears to have been an example of its archetype.

If such was the case this idyllic formula came under threat very soon, for the Portuguese Embassy was to arrive in the fall of 1520. From that point on, despite the benign tolerance of the embassy's pastor, Padre Francisco Álvares, the imperial court of the Highlands was destined to become inextricably entangled with the machinations of both Rome's and Lisbon's concepts of correct godliness.

At the same time there is really no evidence that either the royal court or the elders of the Ethiopian Orthodox Church initially met this new form of Christian expression with anything other than open Christian tolerance and generosity. At first there had been a high point achieved in these matters by the lay example of Pêro da Covilhã and the religious example of Padre Francisco. Though on numerous occasions the padre had been invited to say mass and explain his liturgy to the emperor, doing so with a deal of imagination and kindly flair, it was mostly downhill from there. From that point on it is not really much of an exaggeration to say that Roman Catholicism in Ethiopia moved off at a disastrous pace. Despite its opportunities and even some successes, in the end it fared little better than to stumble to a predictable demise three decades into the XVII century.

This tragic saga of errors can be said to have started with João Bermudez, or "*Mestre* João," as he preferred to style himself before promoting himself to "Dom." He was the embassy barber which, to give the edge to such seemingly low rank, meant that he was surgeon-bleeder, a sort of XVI century diplomatic medical officer. To qualify his position yet further, nobody in his right mind in today's world would seriously contemplate committing himself to the care of such ignorance. From all accounts coming to us from his contemporaries it seems that even then *Mestre* João, for all the abilities he possessed as a barber, was considered by many as little more than buffoon.

Being accredited to the embassy, João Bermudez was well connected at the Ethiopian imperial court, and it does appear that he performed a few useful medical functions; enough, at any rate, to give a moderately favourable impression to Emperor Lebna Dengal. When the embassy departed Ethiopia in 1526, *Mestre* João elected to remain in service at the court.

With his back to the wall at the height of the Islamic invasion, in 1535 the emperor appears to have relied on the services of the exceptionally ambitious Bermudez (it's Bermudez himself who claims in his own writings the emperor appointed him to the rank of patriarch of the Ethiopian Orthodox Church). Championing such lofty new position for himself, and with the knowledge of the emperor, the former barber set off on a special mission to Lisbon seeking military aid. According to Bermudez the emperor had entrusted him to the post because there was no patriarch at the time, the old one having died. No doubt Lebna Dengal felt that *Mestre*, now *"Dom,"* João would be able to exercise some authority in Portugal. To be on the safe side, and to the emperor's credit, the envoy was dispatched in company with a highly trusted and capable Ethiopian advisor, Saga Zaab, a man whose attributes included a competent fluency in the Portuguese language.

Bermudez arrived with pomp in Lisbon, and succeeded in achieving little except irritating the court of Dom João III. Before leaving for Goa again in 1538, he badgered both the Portuguese king and Pope Paul III for an official recognition of the title to which he claimed he had been named by the Ethiopian emperor. Although he made expansive claims for himself, in point of fact later correspondence of both the king and the pope make it clear that the man was considered a garrulous impostor. Be that as it may, he was accompanying Estevão da Gama's fleet, still calling himself patriarch, when it sailed into the Red Sea bound for Massawa in 1541. This was the same fleet that bore Cristóvão da Gama and the small army that, two years later, was destined to put Islam to flight from the Highlands.

Bermudez was a braggart and an ass, but he saw himself as the leader of a great church, and he never let those around him overlook what he considered to be his rightful claim to the dignity due his office. Today we would possibly laugh him off as a stuffed shirt, but unfortunately he was also dangerous.

The story of the stay in Massawa is a shocking one, even in the retelling of it nearly five centuries later. Estevão chose to leave the fleet's heavier and slower ships behind in port while he and his young brother, Cristóvão, set off to the northern end of the Red Sea to raid Turkish shipping near Suez. The ships remaining at Massawa lay at anchor under the command of Manuel da Gama, Estevão's kinsman. It was known that the mainland beyond the islands of Massawa was heavily patrolled by Muslims, so Manuel ordered the crews of the larger ships to remain aboard their vessels, only to go ashore with his specific permission. He lacked something of the da Gama flair for authority, however. In addition, Bermudez, the patriarch who had also been left behind at Massawa, began to goad the Portuguese soldiers, claiming his Highland patriarchate to be a wonder-filled Paradise. Such a great cause these brave men would be fighting! What a terrible shame, to be kept waiting behind in the insufferable heat of Massawa when there was a valiant Christian fight to be fought!

A group of some eighty restless Portuguese warriors, bored and anxious to prove their fighting skills, their heads filled with the patriarch's nonsense, managed to jump ship and make their way to the mainland. Once on land they contacted a guide who promised to lead them to join the friendly forces of the Christian emperor. It was a trap. The men were ambushed by Muslim soldiers, and all but one were killed. This one made good his escape and managed to find his way to the coast and back to the ships, bringing the terrible news to his commander. Manuel da Gama, infuriated that his strict orders had been so flagrantly disobeyed, ordered the man hanged along with four others he accused of also being party to the escapade.

Unfortunately Bermudez was not one of them, otherwise a good deal more of the man's mischief might have been avoided.

**Emperor Galawdewos**

Lebna Dengal died in 1540, and his young son, Galawdewos, thus became emperor in command of the Christian forces struggling to hold off the relentless invasions of Ahmad Grag'n. Upon the return of Estevão's fleet from the northern reaches of the Red Sea, a small army of four hundred handpicked soldiers was placed under the command of Cristóvão da Gama, and they immediately set off into the Highlands for their first battle with the Muslim leader at Amba Sanayt. This they won handily.

The patriarch, Bermudez, reported to his new emperor and in short order became as much of a nuisance in the court of Emperor Galawdewos as he had been at the court of Dom João III in Lisbon. He was, he claimed, the appointed patriarch of the Ethiopian Orthodox Church, raised to that position by the emperor's own father. He insisted that Galawdewos was bound to accept his divine command. It was God's intention that the Ethiopian Orthodox Church place itself under the authority of the Roman Catholic pope, the Vicar of Christ's "True Church."

Galawdewos was unimpressed. While at first he had simply found João Bermudez tedious, he was now roused to anger, and more determined than ever to see to the appointment of a new Abun to lead the Orthodox faithful. He banished Bermudez from his court, sending him into Tigray; Abun Yosab arrived in the Highlands from Coptic Alexandria in 1548. In truth, Galawdewos' position was awkward. He did not wish to offend the Portuguese because he had come to count on them in his war with Islam, and he genuinely got along well with most of them. A correspondence ensued with the king in Portugal concerning this wretched barber, and it would appear that Dom João III gave his full support to the emperor. In the end no one wanted to assume responsibility for Bermudez, or give him credence, and the young Ethiopian monarch was successful in sidelining him completely.

For all his contempt of the so-called Portuguese patriarch, Galawdewos was tolerant and accommodating towards the Portuguese as a whole. He also appeared to have no special problem with their brand of Christianity. He got along well with the soldiers, especially, welcoming them into his court, granting them lands, favours and creating special places for them in the columns of his guards. Even so, he always made it clear that he had no intention of ever switching his religious denomination.

This, along with the difficulties of communication between Ethiopia's Highlands and Goa, or Lisbon, or Rome, created confusions and misunderstandings – in Goa, Lisbon and Rome. The Portuguese king, in fact, received two letters that he specifically interpreted, erroneously as it happened, as requests by Galawdewos for a patriarch ordained by Rome. With neither Rome nor Lisbon paying the least attention to the claims of João Bermudez, and completely unaware that a Coptic Abun had already been appointed, a Roman Catholic prelate was duly named in 1554 – João Nunes Barreto. His bishop and intended successor was to be André de Oviedo.

**The Jesuits**

In 1555 the Church of Rome in its infinite wisdom decided to assign the task of mission work in Ethiopia to the Society of Jesus, the Jesuits. This religious order was noted for its teaching skills, and as well for its devotion to Rome as to Christ. Portuguese missionary participation would predominate because Portugal was the superpower of the region and because, according to the Treaty of Tordesillas signed between Portugal and Spain with the pope's blessing in 1494, Ethiopia fell within that half of the world under Portugal's mandate. Portugal was already "in" Ethiopia, moreover, ideally placed in Goa to police such a responsibility on behalf of Rome. Ignatius Loyola had initiated the Jesuit order in 1534, and by the close of the following decade Francis Xavier had made a substantial name for both the order and himself through his missionary enthusiasm in the Far East and Goa. So while Barreto and Oviedo were still in Lisbon awaiting papal documents to take up their posts in Ethiopia, two messengers were sent from Goa to the court of the Highland emperor to make preparations for the arrival of these religious leaders. One of these messengers was Gonçalo Rodrigues, a priest. The other was named Diogo Dias. Rodrigues was the first of many Jesuits to arrive in Ethiopia over the following years.

True to form, João Bermudez had escaped from his banishment in Tigray, and he succeeded in meeting Rodrigues and Dias upon their arrival. Truculent, sour and vindictive at being pushed out of the way by both Ethiopians and Portuguese, Bermudez continued to stir up trouble. First of all he informed the Portuguese delegates that Barreto and Oviedo would not be welcome because Galawdewos had already arranged for a new patriarch to come from Alexandria. He told them that only the force of arms would convince the stubborn young emperor to switch his allegiance from the Ethiopian Orthodox Church to the Church of Rome, but that if the emperor could be made to see the error of his ways, the entire Christian population would come over. Rodrigues and Dias were convinced, but nonetheless sought an audience with the emperor and explained their reasons for coming. The emperor was at last able to announce in a face-to-face confrontation that he had no intention of abandoning his traditional church, and that he had never requested a patriarch to be appointed in either Lisbon or Rome. As a gesture, and to avoid offending the Portuguese king, he said that Barreto and Oviedo would be welcome if they came solely to minister to the Portuguese residents of the Highlands.

Padre Gonçalo Rodrigues and Diogo Dias returned to Goa disappointed, angry and unconvinced by the arguments of Galawdewos. Bermudez went with them. Barreto and Oviedo duly arrived in Goa in September, 1556, and there ensued a meeting of the Council of India to which Rodrigues and Bermudez were invited to give their opinions – that nothing short of a sizeable military force could ensure the conversion of the Highlands to the Church of Rome.

Fortunately, cooler heads prevailed. The viceroy at Goa expressed his unwillingness to employ military might in such a cause, and in any event he could not spare the troops in numbers sufficient to make a difference. Ultimately it was decided that Barreto would remain in Goa, while Oviedo and five other Jesuits would make their way to the Ethiopian court to see if they could be a little more persuasive. They arrived in the Highlands in June, 1557.

Galawdewos received Oviedo with courtesy, and at the Jesuit's request the emperor arranged a series of public debates between the Jesuit missionaries and the Orthodox priests. These were held periodically over many days, and occasionally the emperor himself would join in the argument. However he and the Orthodox defenders were intransigent. Debate ranged about theological questions as to the very nature of the Christian god, a subject that had driven the eastern and western churches asunder and kept them bitterly divided since the XI century. Till today there has not appeared a resolution to this problem, so there was never any real likelihood that these informal gatherings in the presence of the Ethiopian emperor were going to be able to dispose of the issue definitively.

Oviedo understood this, and then proceeded to do a remarkably foolish thing. In the hope of frightening the emperor into a different and more agreeable frame of mind, he became angry and stormed out of the court. In February, 1559, Oviedo published a manifesto in which he denounced the Orthodox faith as a false doctrine and forbade Roman Catholics to have any close association with followers of Orthodoxy.

Such behaviour was unacceptable to both Ethiopian nobility and the Orthodox clergy, although the emperor himself appears to have been charitably forgiving. The public at large came to view the Jesuits, and Roman Catholics in general, with considerable alarm, and to suspect that their unreasonable demands would eventually entail the support of some kind of military force. Before any further developments could take place, Galawdewos, still fairly congenial towards the Portuguese, and with some of his favourites among them at his side, was killed in a skirmish with an Adel raiding party in 1559. His brother Minas replaced him on the throne as the next emperor.

**Emperor Minas**

Thus the impact left on the Orthodox community firstly by Bermudez and secondly by Oviedo was, in balance, negative. Bermudez had left Ethiopia for good, never to return. In the years in which he had assumed himself to be patriarch of all the Christians in Ethiopia he had succeeded in alienating and antagonizing almost everyone with whom he had come in contact, so that the general impression left for the Orthodox to consider was that all members of the Roman Catholic faith, particularly the missionaries and priests, were arrogant and intolerant. They were referred to openly within Orthodox communities as the messengers of Lucifer. Once back in Lisbon João Bermudez published his memoirs (1565), making sure that he was seen as the hero of Portugal's civilizing Roman Catholic mission in unruly Ethiopia. He concluded his days as a storyteller at the court of Dom Sebastião. The young monarch would listen intently as the old rogue recounted tall tales of illustrious Portuguese deeds on that heathen African continent. It was the sort of propaganda, unfortunately, that no doubt assisted the unstable young king in making his decision to lead the noble armies of Portugal to disaster at Alcácer Quibir in 1578.

Emperor Minas was no friend to Oviedo and the Portuguese. He looked upon Roman Catholicism with an intolerant, unforgiving and fierce loathing. Immediately upon assuming the throne he revoked all religious privileges that had been granted to the Roman Catholics by his brother. Ethiopians were forbidden to take part in the mass in Roman Catholic churches. Jesuit missionaries were forbidden to preach in public. When Oviedo had the temerity to complain he was banished from the court.

Minas was harsh, and he took a great dislike to the changes in society that were wrought after the wars with Ahmad Grag'n, especially those changes which appeared to infringe upon the dignity and authority of the emperor. He set about instituting reforms that he thought would restore certain traditions, but immediately ran foul of the nobles and provincial governors. Rebellion broke out in 1560 in the northern province of Tigray under the leadership of governor Azmach Yeshaq. Oviedo had sided with the governor, persuading the Portuguese soldiers in the country to join against the emperor and, at the same time, appealing for further Portuguese troops to be sent from India. The additional soldiers never materialized. In July, 1561, Minas attacked in the north and defeated Yeshaq's army. Yeshaq himself managed to escape, and many of the Portuguese who had been fighting against Minas were taken prisoner. Oviedo was kept under close surveillance at court, permitted to minister only to these prisoners. The privileges of the Portuguese soldiers had already been severely curtailed; now their lands were confiscated as well.

Yeshaq regrouped his forces. He abandoned hope of receiving aid from Portuguese India, and instead signed a pact with the Turks at Massawa to rejoin the fight against Minas. This time he was successful. Turkish firepower was too great for Minas' imperial forces, and they were put to flight at a battle fought in the district of Enderta. Here the Portuguese who had earlier been made captive were set free again. Among them were Oviedo and the other Jesuit missionaries, and they were all moved north into Yeshaq's province and given protection at a place called Mai Gwa Gwa, near Adwa. It was here that Oviedo established the first permanent Jesuit mission station. Mai Gwa Gwa was renamed Fremona, and it became the headquarters of Jesuit activity in the Highlands until the Portuguese were expelled in 1634.

João Nunes Barreto died at Goa in December, 1562, never having taken up his appointment as Roman Catholic prelate in Ethiopia. Oviedo, being his bishop and named successor, thus automatically became prelate in his place. It was a majestic title, but it really only meant that he would continue, as he already was, leader of the Highland Jesuits.

## Rebellion

Emperor Minas died in February, 1563, and was replaced by his young son, Sartsa Dengal. Rebellion had wracked the land during Minas' reign, and this intensified under the new emperor. For the first two years after his succession he was constantly fleeing rivals for his throne, one of whom was fiercely supported by Yeshaq.

Oviedo's position became increasingly more difficult as Sartsa Dengal's power base grew in strength. He had compromised himself by siding with Yeshaq, by condoning Yeshaq's alliance with the Turks, and also by accepting Yeshaq's protection at Fremona. He had placed himself in such a position that he had little choice but to go along with the rebel's confrontation. At the same time he continued pleading with Goa for Portuguese troops. These, he hoped, would side with the Tigray governor against Sartsa Dengal and thus impose the Church of Rome by force.

Once again the troops failed to appear. Dom Sebastião was now on the throne in Portugal, with his great uncle the saintly Dom Henrique acting as regent, and it was well understood by this time that Ethiopia's emperor had no intention of becoming Roman Catholic. At this juncture the Portuguese were loath to commit an army to what had all the appearances of a fruitless cause.

For all his faults, a quick temper and a tactless tongue in his dealings with the Ethiopian clergy, nobles and emperor, Oviedo had about him a quiet personal pride and a sense of human worth. Behind an austere facade he was an essentially decent man, and possessed those aesthetic qualities that forbade him, even in the face of hardship, to abandon what he had poured his heart and life into building. Forgiven his follies by a generous Sartsa Dengal, the old man had the chance to take up a useful mission post in China. He elected instead to remain at Fremona, a courtly bishop who quietly tended his own vegetable garden on his hands and knees. As the years passed he became known and respected for the many simple and kindly Christian acts he performed for the poor people living in the district so that, before his time was up, he had succeeded in making numerous converts to his faith. His grander plan to conquer the souls of all Ethiopians had failed lamentably, but as an unornamented Christian he left his mark. He died at Fremona in 1577.

Yeshaq made his peace with Sartsa Dengal and retained his governorship in Tigray. Later, and foolishly, he renewed his pact with the Turks, and he rebelled yet again in 1579. This time his luck ran out. He was killed in a final battle against his emperor the following year, and the Turks who had fought with him were driven out of the Highlands of Tigray, back to the coast at Massawa.

**Heresy: Rome's Rebuttal**

The Inquisition, established in Portugal in 1536, had had a peculiar and indirect effect on Ethiopia. In the 1530's Damião de Gois, the famous Portuguese humanist, had met Saga Zaab, the Ethiopian monk-diplomat, in Portugal. The great thinker was intrigued by his new friend's explanations of the Ethiopian Orthodox Church, and he persuaded him to write out a detailed description of it. Saga Zaab was happy to do so, and forthwith penned a lengthy treatise. Delighted, de Gois translated it into Latin, called it *Fides, Religio, Moresque Aethiopum*, and published it at Louvain in 1540.

It was a scandal. True Christians, whose Holy day is a Saturday? Who refrain from eating pork? Who practice circumcision? This was Jewry, not Christianity! That the Ethiopian Orthodox Church should consider the three heads of the Trinity as the same, and equal, was not only ignorance, but little short of outright heresy. The two churches professed the same god, but there were great differences in the fundamentals of theology and liturgy: differences in concepts of The Creation, the passage of the human soul after death, baptism and confession. While in the north of Europe, the Reform churches had been throwing off the burdens of Rome, the Roman Church itself was busy seeking out heretics, setting them ablaze, persecuting Protestants and Jews with all their inspired Christian fervour. Rome was anything but tolerant towards those who appeared to buck her claim to truth and correctness. Here was a supposedly Christian church in the Highlands of Ethiopia, bulwark of the True Faith in the midst of Islam, ally to Portugal and, by extension, to Rome itself. Suddenly it was abundantly clear that its ministry was not only schismatic, but heretic too.

Oh benighted and misguided Prester John! What he really needed most of all was the faithful guiding hand of a Jesuit mission.

It was at this point, in 1554, that João Nunes Barreto was appointed Roman Catholic prelate and André de Oviedo his bishop. Oviedo was the first Jesuit destined to wear a bishop's awesome robes and headgear, presumably with the notion that such ornate vestment and mitre would suitably impress the new adherents to the congregation of the pope. And it was with all these ideas of ecclesiastical conquest that Padre Gonçalo Rodrigues and his companion, Diogo Dias, entered the Highlands as the first ambassadors of their church to prepare the way for their superiors. The bidding had been concluded satisfactorily, they thought; time, now, to close the deal.

Well, as noted earlier, it did not work out that way. Rome had by no means abandoned hope of claiming such a prize. In the overall scheme of things, and with a mind ever to the great rift that divided the western Roman Catholics from the eastern Orthodox churches, putting its stamp on such a significant block of Christianity would be a righteous Roman finger in the Orthodox eye, a just and pious claim to the ecclesiastical high ground in a bitter and age-old feud.

By this stage there were many Roman Catholics living in the Highlands; Portuguese, Ethiopian, and the descendants of numerous mixed marriages and unions. The Jesuits, even when it was realized that Rome was to be denied the conquest of the entire congregation of the Christian Highlands, considered it an imperative that these Roman Catholics, especially the converts, be prevented from reverting or going over to Orthodoxy. For many years there remained, in all the Highlands, just two priests to administer the sacraments of the Church of Rome. Then one – and then he died in 1597.

Stranger things had happened; perhaps there might arise, in time, yet another chance to claim Ethiopia for Rome. Things were bad, but hope never quite died.

## Pêro Páez

The stage was set for the dramatic entry of Padre Pêro Páez, a quick, intelligent and energetic Jesuit priest from Castile.

However he was not so quick getting there.

He embarked from Goa for Ethiopia as a young man in February, 1588; he arrived at Massawa a good deal more mature in April, 1603, reaching the Fremona mission a few weeks later. In the intervening years he had been captured by Turks off the coast of Oman, taken as a valued prisoner for ransom across the deserts of Yemen from hot and dusty mud-baked towns to villages huddling in high and well-defended crags. He occupied dungeon cells in most of these places. Finally, at a Red Sea port, he was chained to the oar of a slave galley, fortunately for only a brief duration. Word had filtered back to India that he was being held at Mocha, so ransom monies were collected and sent by special envoy. After being in prison for nearly eight years, Pêro Páez arrived back at the Jesuit headquarters in Goa. It was almost another seven years before he was to realize his ambition of setting foot in Ethiopia.

Much controversy surrounds the nineteen-year ministry of Pêro Páez. He was an incredibly dynamic man. He spoke Arabic like an Arab, and learned both Ge'ez and Amharic with exceptional speed. He was a teacher, a translator, an orator, an astute rhetorician, an architect, builder, diplomat, painter and writer. Whatever needed doing he would tackle with gusto, and it seemed he could do almost anything.

After Emperor Sartsa Dengal's death in 1596 the Highlands had entered a protracted period of internecine war. The emperor, without legitimate heir, had not made it clear who should succeed him, so that the fabric of society was rent almost continuously for eleven years. Ya'qob, child of one of Sartsa Dengal's concubines, mounted the throne as a small boy in 1596 under the regency of two of his maternal uncles, Atnatewos, the governor of Gojjam, and Kiflewahd, the governor of Tigray. He was ousted in 1603 and Za Dengal, one of Sartsa Dengal's nephews, took his place for almost one year before he was killed in one of the on-going actions of the war.

The brevity of Za Dengal's reign is directly attributable to Padre Pêro Páez and his consummate skill as a missionary. Invited to the emperor's court in 1604, the priest wasted no time in using his well-honed rhetoric to win the emperor to the side of the Roman Catholic Church. Za Dengal imprudently issued a decree prohibiting the observance of Saturday as a religious holiday; the nobles forthwith rose in rebellion, the emperor was killed, and young Ya'qob regained his throne.

This extraordinary volatility of the Highlanders concerning their religion should have been a warning to the missionary. True, he did attempt to rein in the emperor before he lost his royal head, but the fact remains that with the power of his arguments alone he was able to set in motion certain trains of action over which he lacked sufficient control. If not exactly fanaticism, the priest exhibited an ardour concealed within his rhetoric that was capable of sowing as great doubts and confusions in the minds of his congregation as it was any level of conviction. It might have been understandable, or even forgivable, had he done it only this once. The sad fact is that Pêro Páez was so convinced of the righteousness of his position that he repeated his performance again and again, and with such an incredibly focused power that he became unquestionably involved, by the end of his life, in triggering one of the bloodiest civil wars in Ethiopian history.

Ya'qob managed to reclaim his throne in 1604, but came immediately under threat from Sussenyos, a great grandson of Emperor Lebna Dengal. Sussenyos had been living and nurturing his popularity in Amhara and Shoa, and had created a state of almost constant rebellion since Sartsa Dengal's death. Within a couple of years Pêro Páez was once again in the thick of the political dicing, this time summoning a Christian army from Goa to smite Orthodox Christians. Ya'qob saw himself being out-manoeuvreed by Sussenyos, and in 1606 ordered Pêro Páez to come from Fremona to his court near Lake Tana. He informed the missionary that he would convert to Roman Catholicism immediately upon the arrival of assistance in the form of a Portuguese army. Pêro Páez wrote letters to both Lisbon and Rome on behalf of the emperor. Neither of the letters seem to have arrived at their destinations.

Ya'qob did his best to contain Sussenyos without Portuguese troops, but at the showdown in 1607 it was Sussenyos who won the day. Ya'qob lost not only his crown, but the head on which it had sat so precariously.

Pêro Páez possessed a range of talents and, among them, he turned out to be a builder of considerable energies. He was responsible for a significant number of structures in the Lake Tana region, and thus is of major significance in the context of this work. Coming from Extremadura he would have been exposed to that special stonework most common to the adjacent area of southern Portugal; a technique that had spread, since the earliest times of the Roman (and later Moorish occupation) of Iberia, across the frontier into his own regions. When, at last, he set foot in the Ethiopian Highlands he would have recognized immediately the significance of the Lusitanian talents with which he came in contact – the numbers of Portuguese and descendents of Portuguese whose building knowledge and techniques were so close to his own cultural vocabulary.

**Emperor Sussenyos Converts to the Church of Rome**

The nobles and princes, in what would appear to have been paroxysms of unvarnished selfishness and ambition, each fielded armies of their own. Sussenyos, being only too well aware of the unpredictable notions of so many local warlords, also thought of calling in the Portuguese on his side. Once again Pêro Páez was happy to oblige with his efforts and contacts, and letters were sent off to Lisbon and Rome. Invasions of the Highlands by the southern Galla in 1608, and uprisings in Gojjam and Tigray, kept the emperor's own army in fighting fettle. In this way he was able to re-establish much of the prestige that the previous emperors had frittered away in ineffectual campaigns, and regain control over the provinces previously lost through internecine wrangling. This was the first time since the wars with Ahmad Grag'n that the emperor of Ethiopia had been able to hold his head up and offer genuine protection to all the people of his widespread and varied domains. In 1611 word came from Portugal's King Filipe II that military assistance would indeed be on its way before too long, but now it seemed that it might not be necessary after all.

If the missionaries appreciated what the emperor was doing in terms of knitting together a multi-faceted empire, for they liked order and absolutism as well in politics as in their religious practices, the emperor was equally impressed by the organizational abilities of the missionaries. For this reason, in addition to the emperor's genuine religious curiosity, the missionaries were welcomed at court, and thus began the famous series of debates and sermons that gradually won over Sussenyos.

These debates were held regularly between the missionaries and the senior Orthodox clergy, the emperor and his family very often attending. The sessions soon became a favourite means of entertainment and diversion. One of the strongest debaters on the Orthodox side was the emperor's younger brother, Sela Cristos. Pêro Páez singled him out, deciding this was the man to convert to Roman Catholicism first. The strategy worked. In 1612 Sela Cristos declared himself for the Church of Rome, and became as outspoken and eloquent a speaker championing this new cause as he had previously been against it. Sussenyos, showing decided bias for the missionaries' cause, but as yet not committing himself, gave Sela Cristos the governorship of the provinces of Damot and Gojjam. Within a very short space of time the first Jesuit missions were opened at Gemb Giorghis (Collala) and Yibaba (Sarca) in Gojjam. The interest of the emperor's household and family in the Church of Rome had a decisive effect on many younger people, and the missionaries opened up numerous centres in the vicinity of Lake Tana. To their way of thinking, the Portuguese were making good progress.

Sussenyos sent an ambassador to Lisbon to explain that he was prepared to declare himself for Roman Catholicism, but preferred to have an army of Portuguese on his side prior to doing so. The ambassador failed in his overland attempt to reach Malindi on the Kenya coast. While the Church of Rome was definitely gathering strength in the Highlands, it was by no means a match in numbers for the adherents to the traditional Ethiopian Orthodox Church. Even considering the prestige of the royal court, it was doubtful whether there would be sufficient political strength to hold off the onslaught of an outraged Orthodox clergy and their followers. By now the debates that took place between Orthodoxy and Catholicism were more often used as occasions to belittle and demean the traditional local church. The very finest Ethiopian debaters, knowing little or nothing of the subtleties of rhetoric, were no match for the debating skills of the Jesuits, especially Padre Pêro Páez.

Sussenyos, his brother, their nobles and attendants, had managed to win over a large number to Catholicism, and there was a move afoot to adopt force to introduce the new church, with or without the assistance of the Portuguese military. At this juncture Sussenyos was about to show the same carelessness as Za Dengal, for he proclaimed himself openly in favour of that part of the Roman Catholic dogma in which the Jesuits taught of the dual nature of God, and he opposed the Orthodox concept of God's perfect unity. He ordered the death penalty for any clergy teaching the Orthodox dogma.

Abun Simon, the Orthodox patriarch, heard this news with alarm, and hurried to court to face his emperor. Sussenyos repeated his condemnation of Orthodoxy, whereupon the Abun proclaimed excommunication for all converting to Catholicism. Sussenyos countered with an imperial edict of freedom of religion for everyone.

Discussions raged bitterly throughout 1613 and 1614, neither side giving any ground to the other, and in this latter year yet another revolt broke out in Begemdir. Other rebellions festered in the north, and some of the traditionally conservative nobles of Gorgora hatched a plot against the emperor. Abun Simon was killed in the rebellion of 1617 and was replaced by Abun Zara Wangel. Throughout this time Pêro Páez was acting as spiritual counsellor to Sussenyos, and never hesitated to assure the emperor that his triumphs over Orthodoxy were signs of God's pleasure.

In 1620 a strong proclamation was issued condemning the doctrine of Christ's single nature. The Saturday Sabbath was once more prohibited. More rebellions broke out in Begemdir and, in Gojjam, Sela Cristos put down an uprising with such extreme ferocity that the emperor himself was alarmed at the brutal passion and the huge numbers of Orthodox peasantry who died rather than submit to the Roman Church. Then in March, 1622, Sussenyos declared formally for Roman Catholicism and accepted the blessings of Pêro Páez in the same church at Gorgora over which the missionary himself had acted as supervisor of construction.

In this way Roman Catholicism became the "official" religion of the empire, though it was far from acceptable to the great majority of the population. In May of the same year Pêro Páez died without ever seeing the full extent of the chaos yet to come, but for which he and Sussenyos were, without a shadow of doubt, entirely responsible.

**"Our sun has been eclipsed…"**

Though promised, Portuguese troops never arrived in the Highlands to support the Jesuit cause. The treasury chests of Goa were empty. Mounting a military expedition of any kind to march into the Highlands of Ethiopia was simply out of the question. With a Spanish king on the throne of Portugal the enemies of Spain had become Portugal's enemies. Although there was an agreement between the two countries that Portugal's empire in the east would remain essentially free of Spanish domination, Holland and Britain saw no reason to include themselves within the broad spectrum of this gentlemanly understanding. Both found the pickings were just too tempting not to partake.

There were various attempts to nudge Ethiopia a little closer geographically. At one stage, hoping to avoid the constant attacks and irritations of sailing in the Islamic dominated waters of the Red Sea, or crossing the Islamic controlled coastal territories, a move was made to open a direct road to the Lake Tana region from Malindi and Mombassa. This would have meant crossing even more hostile lands dominated by forbiddingly difficult terrain, deserts and unfriendly tribesmen. The plan was soon abandoned.

The Portuguese continued to use Massawa and Arkiko as entry points and, although a few of them lost their heads to Islamic swords, many got through into the Highlands. The 1620's saw a significant influx into the Highlands of missionaries, lay preachers – and others. They quickly spread themselves among the various mission stations, and they helped in the construction of yet other centres. They were made welcome by Emperor Sussenyos and despite the fact that they were the objects of considerable propagandizing by their own Jesuit order, they were clearly not popular with the masses they had come to convert. All Jesuit residences had to be built as fortifications against possible attack by individuals and groups drawn from the local populace. The number of enemies of Catholicism appeared to grow in direct proportion to the number of mission converts.

Afonso Mendes, the Jesuit prelate, arrived at the end of 1625. He brought other missionaries with him, and soldiers enough to guard their party. Once again Sussenyos pledged his loyalty to the pope, and so did his son, the crown prince Fasiladas. In a famous speech to a congregation of converts, Sussenyos gave historical imperative to his choice of the Church of Rome, and outlined why it was honourable and necessary for all Ethiopia to do the same. Back at the time of Galawdewos, he claimed, an agreement had been made between the emperor and Rome: introduction of Roman Catholicism throughout the Highlands to replace Orthodoxy, plus one third of the entire empire to be signed over to Portugal, in return for assistance against Ahmad Grag'n.

No trace of any such agreement has ever been found, however. The story appears to have originated with Pêro Páez. Whatever its wellspring, Sussenyos was no doubt convinced of its authenticity and hung, like a fly trapped in honey, upon every word and idea Pêro Páez expressed.

After the missionary died, Sussenyos wrote to the Jesuit Provincial at Goa:

> "The virtuous Father Páez was father of our soul, bright sun of faith lighting the darkness of Ethiopia. Since our sun has been eclipsed and set our joy is turned to sadness, our happiness to mourning. If this paper was as wide as the sky and the ink as like to the sea, it would not be sufficient to write his virtues and teachings... "

If it is an indication of the emperor's great love for the missionary, so also may it be seen as a measure of the control that Pêro Páez had over Sussenyos. With Páez gone, Sussenyos for some reason again found it necessary to reaffirm his beliefs in front of the new leader of the Jesuits. There is in this the sad indication of at least one significant factor to aid our understanding of the catastrophe to come, and why. There can be little doubt that Sussenyos was held under some kind of spell by the brilliant Pêro Páez. In the expression of his beliefs to Afonso Mendes the emperor was to give the impression that the groundwork for the general acceptance of Roman Catholicism had a wider base, and had been better prepared than it actually was.

The result of this was a deal of callous obduracy on the part of the Jesuits. Firstly, in their lightning quick spread across the landscape and, secondly, in their dogged assumption of the correctness of their theological arguments and the manner in which this righteousness was expressed to the locals. Major errors were made because of simple misjudgement and lack of feeling. Not only was the Roman Catholic faith introduced with power tactics and a bulldozing absence of sensitivity, it came with such extraordinary rapidity that the common parishioners were offended. Concurrently, there was an insistence on the dismantling of Orthodoxy, and this, too, with unseemly and totally unacceptable haste.

When, ultimately, the Roman Catholic mission collapsed, much of the blame was laid on the back of Afonso Mendes; probably unfairly, in retrospect, even if he was foolishly inflexible. He was ill prepared for the situation he walked into, and ill informed of both the strengths and weaknesses of the Jesuit foothold. Emperor Sussenyos and his immediate entourage were enthusiastic, but they were doubtless under false impressions concerning the countryside as a whole. In 1625 Mendes blithely took over the reins of a situation already out of anyone's control, a runaway that had been whipped into full gallop by the ardour of Pêro Páez. He was still holding those reins when this metaphorical animal, by now wild and bucking frantically, cut loose and bucked him off. Recent studies by Ethiopian historians indicate that Afonso Mendes did in fact attempt to rein in this runaway, that he attempted to avert the catastrophe which he realized too late was about to engulf them all.

By June, 1632, civil war was raging. In the uprising in Begemdir over eight thousand peasants championing the Ethiopian Orthodox Church were killed in a single day. It had become obvious that a clear return to Orthodoxy was the only thing that would ensure peace. A council of state was held, and Sussenyos sought the permission of the prelate to restore the traditional church. Afonso Mendes, of course, could not agree to this and, under extreme pressure, Sussenyos at last turned over all his powers of governance to his son, Fasiladas.

The restoration of the traditional church was proclaimed immediately. Emperor Fasiladas himself had become totally disenchanted by the Roman Catholic insistence on the correctness of their faith, theology and liturgy. He specifically criticized what he considered to be Rome's intolerance, something that ran absolutely counter to the traditions of Orthodoxy and which he saw as the root cause of the current crisis.

Sussenyos died in September of that year. Disillusioned and confused, he renounced Roman Catholicism and on his deathbed refused confession. Fearful of Portuguese intervention, Fasiladas ordered all Roman Catholic missionaries and priests to leave Ethiopia. Some attempted to remain, but they were caught and executed. In time, Roman Catholicism, too, was denied. It had been superimposed over something that was much deeper in terms of local tradition, and many of those who professed it were, above all, simple and honest subjects who had no inclination to run counter to the wishes and orders of their emperor. Once the old emperor was gone and they were free to return to their traditional ways things settled down again.

It was to be several centuries before Ethiopia would again see fit to treat with any European nation. Where Pêro da Covilhã's brand of liberal Renaissance thinking and tolerance had been accepted and honoured by the Highlanders, the later impositions of Portugal and the Roman Catholic Church came to be resented and totally rejected.

Perhaps this particular historical vignette might serve to underscore the danger of people who play what are called, in modern parlance, "mind games" with others who do not possess the same cultural or historical references. Some might consider such games "good business." More accurately, though, it is taking unfair advantage. It is, baldly, one of the most devastating ways in which a so-called "truth" (ironically sometimes actually true) has the ability to be used as a destructive weapon. The knack of using the "rhetorical" or "common sense" process can have devastating consequences on the unsuspecting. Afterwards the rhetorician or imposer may, and usually does, claim total guiltlessness. Politicians do it all the time. It was little different in the XIX and XX centuries when Ethiopia again had to deal with a European power intent on forcing its way, this time Italy. As before, the attentions were accepted to a point. When they also became oppressive Ethiopia seemed quite ready to take a stand based upon its previous unpleasant experience.

It is all history, now. What remains, of course, are the stones.

# Part Two

# The Stones

## Portugal's Cultural and Architectural Influences

History has long underestimated the considerable number of Portuguese who beat a path into Ethiopia's Highland regions. In addition there is a great deal of Portuguese building, even of a minor or residential nature, that has never been specifically pinpointed or identified as such. Today, much of Ethiopia's modern building employs the principle of mimesis, or the quite unconscious adopting of previously learned methods, forms and decorations. It is the building of a house the way one's father built his house because his father before him had built it that way. In any case, that is how a house is built – and it works.

When it comes to the structures in the Highlands this principle has been so closely adhered to that even some buildings of today tend to demonstrate a distinct Portuguese flavour. Many of the existing structures are original, dating from the period of this influx of the Portuguese. They were tough soldiers or sailors when required, but at their root men of the soil who moved and built with great purpose on the fertile lands that surround Lake Tana. They took themselves local wives and settled. Back home they had been farmers, fishermen, artisans or builders – men of considerable skills and abilities. Now they constructed farmhouses and outbuildings for themselves and their new families in much the way they would have done back in the Alentejo or Minho, fished the waters of the lake and tilled the black soil. Their aptitude as builders was particularly useful to the growing number of religious moving into the area, and they were put to work as *pedreiros,* or stonemasons, overseers teaching others to fashion stone walls, buttresses, arches and *cupolas*. Their settlements, in fact, spread further than Lake Tana, north to Gondar and up into Tigray along the Highland route they had originally followed from the coast to the interior.

In several parts of the Highlands today one will find pockets of people who yet claim Portuguese ancestry. This may or may not be the case as there are no traces or names. To date there has been no DNA analysis. After a single generation the offspring of a Portuguese-Ethiopian relationship would likely be much the same skin colouring as any of the indigenous peoples, and in any case not white. Names were quickly lost. The Ethiopian tradition of naming a child is to christen it with but a single name, most often a word with some special significance to the parents, or to the circumstances of the birth. If further identification is required, the father's single name is used in much the same way as a family name is used in Europe. Let us presume, for instance, that a Portuguese soldier named João Ribeiro sires a son; he and the mother call their son by a local name - say, Tadele. Tadele will come to be known as Tadele João. When it is his turn to have an offspring he may call the child Sisay, who will come to be known locally as Sisay Tadele. In this way, within a generation or two, the father's name is lost altogether.

What is noticeable in this area, though, are the remnants of Portuguese architectural endeavour. The castles of Gondar are the most widely known. In many other areas, too, there are churches and monasteries, bridges, palaces and simple houses. Most of this inventory of stone structure is in ruins, but many of the old buildings are still in use. All of them tell of this Portuguese "invasion."

In August, 2008, the Japanese Embassy in Addis Ababa sponsored a weekend conference on historic cities. This conference was held in Queen Mentuabe's palace inside the castle compound at Gondar, and was attended by numerous dignitaries and scholars.

As part of these celebrations, delegates gathered outside the compound in a small near-by park for the dedication of a diminutive Japanese pavilion and a "Gondarine" pavilion. The two structures, side-by-side, were not quite finished.

The Japanese building, delightful replica of a typical XVI century wooden house of that country, seemed incongruous in its particular setting, but sat comfortably enough at the edge of a flower garden; the Gondarine structure was also a typical replica of the same era – a round house, about four metres wall-to-wall in its interior, with an incomplete roof that would, in time, be of thatch.

One of the guests of honour at the conference was the Portuguese ambassador. We stood together in the garden as civic dignitaries and structural experts expounded their various theories concerning the two small buildings juxtaposed before them.

Knowing something of my background, and nodding her head towards the Gondarine pavilion, the ambassador at one point leaned over towards me and whispered:

"Do you see anything familiar here …?"

We both laughed. Indeed we did. The Gondarine structure, in fact, was a virtual knock-off of the type of rural round houses that were built by the farmers of southern Portugal for centuries – shelters (*abrigos*), sometimes houses, that are a beloved feature of the Alentejo landscape. The style goes back to Moorish times, at least, and possibly even pre-dates the period of the Roman occupation.

**Before Setting Out**

Explorations over several years took me into all those corners of Ethiopia's Western Highlands that had been frequented by Portuguese travellers and missionaries some five hundred years earlier. The search was propelled by a purely personal curiosity, and that can be difficult to explain to someone whose sentimental and artistic drives issue from an entirely different educational or cultural launch pad. It delighted me, thrilled me, to see here in these remote places not only forms of architecture that I recognized and knew well, but also examples of the very stonework with which I had become so familiar during my years of residence in southern Portugal.

As explained elsewhere, I am a stonemason and sculptor; three-dimensional stonework has a special resonance for me. For twelve of the many years that I lived in Portugal I worked with local builders in the restoration of traditional Portuguese houses, none of which was newer than three hundred years old – and some a good deal older than that. We did this work in the south of the country, and there I was able to learn from hands-on experience many local secrets and techniques. It is the south of Portugal, particularly the hinterland of the Alentejo, that is the principal geographical area from which were derived by far the greater proportion of the discoverers and adventurers who went overseas in the Portuguese ships as military and naval personnel. As a consequence this has meant that much of the building the Portuguese undertook throughout their old empire (and for purposes of design recognition this would definitely include the Western Highlands of Ethiopia) followed patterns and skills they had recognizably developed in the south of their homeland.

My first contact with any architecture is always, naturally, visual. A Portuguese wall looks mightily Portuguese to me. Although I may be gifted to see this at a glance, and believe in my convictions, such facility would hardly be considered proof positive. Considering matters of scientific proof, therefore, I would hope other scholars continue research in this area to further establish the validity of these findings.

One story that always amused me, and which is worth relating here, concerns some information passed along to me at the time I entered the Highlands: that the Portuguese builders of the XV, XVI and XVII centuries had used eggs for mortar. My Ethiopian hosts would tell me this story with a knowing smile on their faces, their tongues poked firmly into their cheeks fully expecting me to chuckle along with them at such an old wives' tale of ridiculously sentimental and parochial nonsense. A funny story, they would tell me, and of course I would chuckle – but not for the reasons they would suppose. This "story" has a measurable basis in fact. This I know precisely because I laboured with *pedreiros*, or stonemasons, who still use the technique today. Working on site in Portugal, we would sometimes break eggs into a mortar mix, perhaps as many as half-a-dozen of them, in order to slick the slurry, to make it creamier and smoother in those instances in which such consistency was desirable. It was an age-old technique my Portuguese companions assured me, and it was a technique that had been used by local builders for ages, certainly as long ago as the XV century – and much earlier. It was carried overseas to Ethiopia and, with time and doubtless a good deal of exaggeration, the technique became "egg mortar" – and a rollicking good joke.

There are many little stories of this nature, a number of them layered into the descriptions that follow. In all something more than thirty sites are examined, each somehow triggering its individual pattern of ideas and thoughts. It should be noted that at the time of each visit I did not have the necessary tools for anything like scientific examination. Instead, through description and images, an attempt is made to present the scene at each place, and perhaps to convey some of the ambient to be found there.

Now the invitation must be extended to scientists who might be enticed to follow up this presentation. Only in this way will it ever be possible to establish definitively the historical worth and verity of each individual site.

**Ankober – Assessing the Ancient Land**

The escarpment of the Rift Valley near Ankober

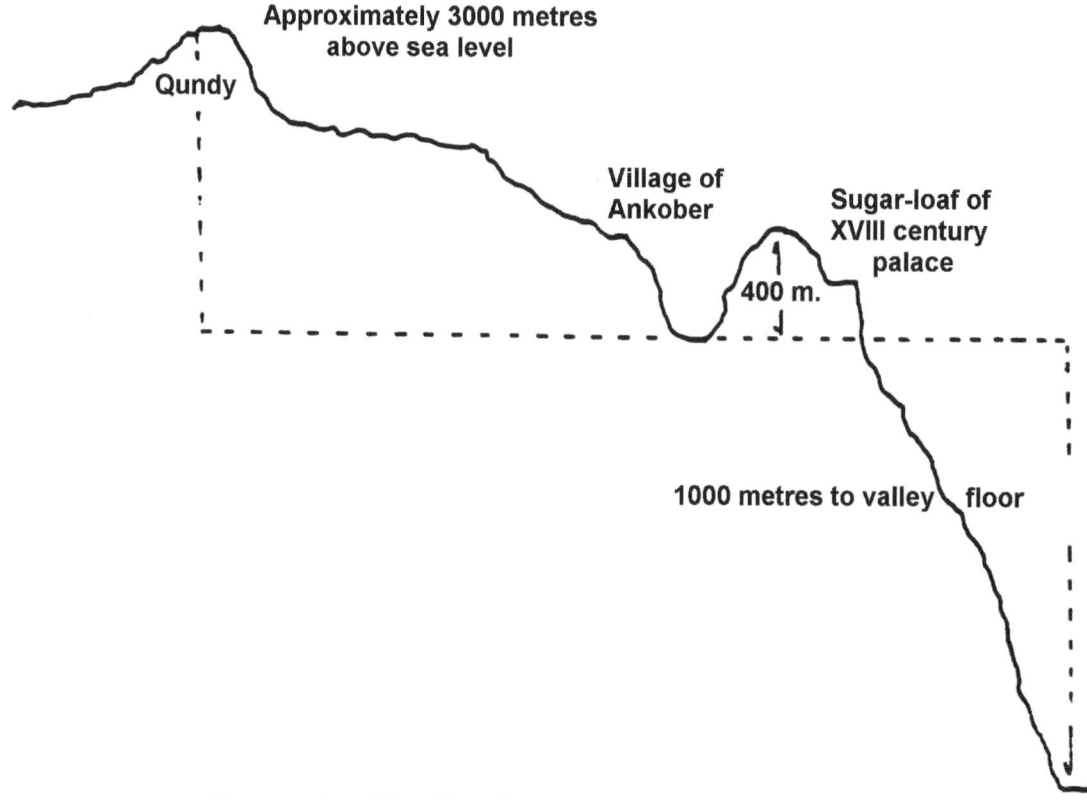

Cross-section of the Rift Valley escarpment at Ankober – not to scale

This ancient town some one-hundred and seventy kilometres to the northeast of Addis Ababa was the capital of the Kingdom of Shoa at various stages throughout the history of the Highlands. Here, or close by, is believed to be the location where the Portuguese envoy, Pêro da Covilhã, first came into contact with "Prester John," Emperor Eskendar, after making his way overland from Zeila in present-day Somaliland, the port town on the Gulf of Aden just south of Djibouti. This would have been late 1492, or early 1493.

One might show an interest in Pêro da Covilhã for any of several reasons: he was a great explorer-diplomat; he was a soldier; he was a highly accomplished linguist and translator; he was a wise counsellor to the court of the emperor. He was also recognized by the Ethiopians as an administrator of considerable ability. It appears he exercised all these pursuits simultaneously. Quite an extraordinary combination.

In addition, in his lifetime da Covilhã became personally acquainted with the monarchs of both Portugal and Ethiopia, and possessed an innate understanding of court etiquette and protocol in each of the two domains. He became a particular friend to the Dowager Empress Eleni, Emperor Eskendar's stepmother, who administered vast lands in the region of Gojjam. Da Covilhã quickly earned the trust and respect of these royals, for he was appointed advisor to the court in military and diplomatic matters and, as a result, became the first contact between Portugal and Ethiopia. He was made steward of the province of Gojjam on behalf of Empress Eleni, and this at a time when Shoa was yet expanding its influence to become the dominant region of an Ethiopian empire. The frontiers of Ethiopia have fluctuated a great deal throughout the broad scope of the country's history, but at this particular moment in time the empire incorporated all of Shoa, Gojjam, parts of Welega, Gondar, Wallo, Tigray and large sections of present-day Eritrea – and it was still expanding. There can be little argument but that any king of Shoa might legitimately present himself as emperor over all these other Highland kingdoms and regions, the more so if he could support his claim with military muscle. There are stories, very probably true even though precise records are not available, that Pêro da Covilhã was a counsellor to Lebna Dengal during the emperor's minority when Empress Eleni acted as regent. There are records to indicate the two adults were working closely together at this time, so it is no great stretch to see the Portuguese assuming the role of advisor to the young monarch even if such advice was administered via the dowager empress. In much the same way one may associate da Covilhã, through legend, with a number of building projects – notably Mertule Maryam in Gojjam and, possibly, the church of Bhary Gemb in Gondar.

One cannot help but be impressed by the extent and difficulty of Pêro da Covilhã's voyages, but particularly his walk from Zeila southwest to Ankober over some of the most difficult terrain in the land. Ankober itself is on the edge of a gigantic escarpment overlooking the Awash Valley. To get there from the coast da Covilhã would have had to traverse more than four hundred and fifty kilometres of formidable desert and dry river bed scrublands, well to the north of the Ahmar Mountains where one might reasonably expect to find water or shelter from lowland heat. He would then have had to cross the Awash River, a haven for crocodiles, into an area teeming with all manner of aggressive wildlife. Then he would have had to climb as much as two thousand metres to the lip of the escarpment that delineates the Highlands proper. No small feat, even today, a cross-country journey from Zeila; more difficult yet in the days of limited hiking gear.

Royal enclosures or palaces in those days of almost constant struggle and warfare were invariably located on the tops of mountains, or at least on high ground, the better to protect them. Ankober is no exception. Although the present small town is located on a stretch of nearly level land on the upper reaches of the escarpment proper, the ancient royal location occupied the crest of a sugarloaf projecting out from the escarpment's edge and rising an additional four hundred metres. There would have been no shortage of womanpower to lug equipment and water buckets to the tops of even the loftiest peaks; it is the sort of thing that women did unless they were born to privilege.

Ankober was last a royal city towards the close of the XIX century, and at that time a palace was built of which there is nothing remaining today except a single low stone wall. A recently-built tourist lodge now occupies the site. In the days when Pêro da Covilhã would have visited these parts, the "capital" was considered to be the site of the royal court, a nomadic encampment of tents and makeshift houses occupying any one of several choice locations widely scattered throughout the empire. The ruling monarch and his retinue would have circulated from one to the other at intervals, so that the capital as such was not a fixed entity.

This type of nomadic imperial capital usually consisted of several hundreds of thousands of people, and would likely have remained in place for a number of years at a time, usually until local lands were exhausted, firewood supplies had been depleted, or water sources had been dried up or fouled. Nowadays there is no trace of any of this at Ankober. Seeing the location, it is a simple matter to understand da Covilhã's ordeal and personal determination in getting there. One can also learn something useful concerning the type of terrain the ancient emperors favoured for their camps.

After turning off the main road at Debre Birhan, and some kilometres prior to arriving at Ankober, one comes to a mountain known locally as Qundy. There is a micro-transmission tower at the top of it, and a dirt road all the way up. It can get cold up there, and can be subject to quick and dramatic changes in temperature. It is a bracing and worthwhile excursion, rewarding to take advantage of this feature to gain a majestic view of the surrounding lands. To the west, when it is clear and sunny, one can see all the way back to Debre Birhan, some thirty kilometres behind and below. To the east the view is often obscured by heavy clouds boiling up from the depths of the Awash Valley. On a clear evening one may quite easily make out the lights of Awash itself some eighty kilometres distant to the southeast as the crow flies.

Qundy is high enough that it has its own brisk semi-Alpine microclimate, and a windy mountain's vegetation, which includes a particularly lovely species of giant lobelia. At the general level of the surface of the Highland plateau, and spilling over the edge of the escarpment towards the valley floor, the vegetation consists largely of a local pine forest. There is also a species of Australian eucalyptus which was imported and planted in great quantities throughout Ethiopia during the second half of the XIX century. Even from the great height at Ankober, and from the "palace sugarloaf," it is possible to see that the floor of the valley close to the escarpment is extremely fertile and heavily cultivated. These two modern visual features, the eucalyptus and the cultivated landscape below, actually preclude one from gleaning a true picture of how the area would have appeared at the close of the XV century.

The valley floor basks in a much warmer climate than one will experience at the level of Ankober. It is quite possible to imagine how, in past centuries, it and the steeply rising ground of the escarpment itself, except for extensive faces of sheer cliff, was more densely covered by forest. Though thinned out considerably now, pines would have been abundant at the higher altitudes in Pêro da Covilhã's day. Lower down the face of the escarpment there would have been a thick tropical vegetation continuing all the way down to the lowest level, where the Awash River flows. Past that, way off towards the town of Awash itself, and beyond, the terrain is transformed into the desert and scrubland that it was in the XV century, and that it yet remains today.

Even so, looking out towards the northeast, one may catch considerably more than just a simple sense of the enormities and difficulties confronting any expedition bound across that countryside. Trying to convert such an overland voyage into a XV century context might tax the imaginative skills of even the most poetic.

I knew I could not stay there for long, so I clicked away with my camera at some of the most outstanding and lovely landscapes in all Africa.

The police arrived.

"What are you taking pictures of?" they demanded sternly.

"You, if you like!" We all laughed and, at the police post, clustered in front of my lens for a memento shot.

For all the breathtaking landscape, it was the people themselves that provided the most memorable contact with Ankober. The police, curious, and conscious all the while of their responsibilities to their laws and superiors were, after all, just a group of guys saddled with a necessary but rather prosaic job. Once they were satisfied our party meant no harm they opened up, rallying with kindnesses and jocular conversation, offers of food and drink, or shelter if we needed it.

At the lip of the escarpment a young peasant family passed by our parked car and stopped to watch while I took photographs. The mother carried her child papoose-style on her back. Her features and colourful attire, the child's wide and curious eyes peeping confidently from the safety of his wrappings, the generous good looks of the husband, all somehow completed perfectly the setting of that lovely place. As they posed for me I caught a glimpse of intricate but faded traditional tattooings on the mother's jaw, and on the front of her throat. I was reminded of a line from Os Lusíadas, in which Luís Vaz de Camões describes the exquisite adornment of the nymphs of Paradise island:

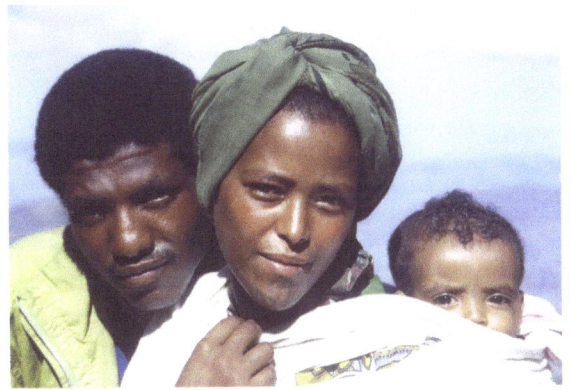

"... such as human beings, themselves beautiful as the rose, will wear to make their beauty rarer still and incite more potently to love."

By his innocent and unaffected attentions one could tell at a glance that this mother and her child filled the young husband with immense joy and pride. Perhaps these good people were poor, but indeed there was no impoverishment here.

**Examples of Typical Portuguese Stonework**

Before proceeding to examine the various Highland sites listed here, it might be helpful to spend a moment reviewing a few typical examples of traditional Portuguese stonework and architectural form.

Historically the Portuguese stonemason has taken enormous pride in his craftsmanship, building not just for effect but for posterity. One may see this in every corner of Portugal, her former empire, and everywhere the Portuguese adventurer has set foot. For hundreds of years the Lusitanian stonemason has directed the love of his craft towards those he knows will follow him. He employs his considerable skill for his family, and for the affection and loyalty he feels towards his *terra,* his land, his village. This in turn speaks to his concept of quality. One will unfailingly find examples of such craftsmanship even in the humblest of structures. It is a quality that has made Portuguese stonework famous throughout the world.

The sceptic might eye the examples illustrated below and declare them obvious or commonplace. Perhaps a more accurate word would be logical – and they are. The forms illustrated are by no means the only ones available to a builder; the selection is far wider. Who is to say the variation of one wall form compared with another has been executed by a Portuguese rather than by a Greek? There is physical and gravitational logic in the piling of one stone atop others. How can it be possible to identify one rock wall from another?

The secret to the identity of any particular wall is contained within a combination of the elements of its structure, and these really only reveal themselves after long hours of examining form, method, expertise and tradition. Even an untrained eye would be able to tell the difference between a brick wall laid up by a novice and one laid up by a master bricklayer – but if the novice's wall is straight and true, what is it that one notices? There is a knack to seeing it all, but not a mystery. In the simplest brick wall there are literally scores of elements that could be noted, the most basic perhaps being its uniformity. In a stone wall one might also seek uniformity, but it would be something infinitely more complex because the stones themselves would not be uniform or symmetrical one with another. The elements of difference would be multiplied many many fold.

Undoubtedly it is a fundamental and elemental tradition that creates an elemental uniformity, and the manner in which a master in that tradition applies his touch or chooses to create his variations adds immeasurably to the mystique. Over centuries the traditions of stonemasonry in Portugal have evolved into techniques that vary enormously from those developed, for instance, next door in Spain – and they in turn vary from those applied in France, which vary from those in Italy, and so on. Sure, it is possible to trick the trained eye now and again, but in the total reckoning of what it sees the differences will be more than just reasonably clear. Without waving a wand, looking into a crystal ball or claiming special powers, suffice it to say that familiarity with the skills of the trade in all its manifestations does indeed furnish one with the extraordinary ability to "read stones." Some people are better at it than others and the sceptic may just have to bite his lip.

In one of the final sections of this edition there is a brief essay entitled "Denial." It draws attention to a vociferous segment of Ethiopia's academic population that argues forcefully to negate what this author considers an Ethiopian historical imperative, namely: that the Portuguese entered the Highlands in significant numbers, remained over one hundred and forty years, mixed and married and created a considerable inter-mingling of bloodlines, attempted to convert the country's Orthodox Christians to the Church of Rome, and carried out a not inconsiderable – though haphazard – building programme. Those opposing this view would prefer to consider the Portuguese presence negligible, that their building programme was Ethiopian rather than Portuguese, that they made little other than a meddlesome nuisance of themselves and wereced out of the country in 1634. I urge the reader to turn to that section of this edition (page 165) in order to consider its statements and opinions within a wider context than we shall examine at this immediate juncture. For the moment we are examining stones.

The kernel of my limited hypothesis at this stage can be summarised very briefly: stonework, like two-dimensional artwork, is identifiable. The art historian will examine many facets of a painting to determine its provenance: the material canvas, board or wall upon which the painting is executed, its pigmentation and colouring, the brush strokes, the subject matter itself. There may be a thousand and one ways to recount the detailed story of that painting. The same basic principals exist for discovery of a piece of sculpture. The art historian will look carefully at the material from which it is made, any markings or tell-tale evidences upon its surfaces, the style, its story, its subject matter, and so on.

Similarly, a building will also have its artistic and sculptural manifestations – things about it that will stamp its story indelibly. To know it intimately one would have to pay close attention to all manner of detail, its material, its design, its use, its geographical and historical location, its environs. The additional minutiae being studied in this case are complex: one would be looking at not only design and structural method, but such things as the size and shape of the stones or bricks used, whether or not they have been dressed or sized, how they are held together by mud or mortar (the quality of that mud or mortar), or whether they are assembled drystone. One would examine dimensions and proportions of walls, niches, doorways and lintels, pinning, framing and woodwork. And intruding on all these details, like a wash over a watercolour, there is the tradition that belies method and intent.

It is the combination of such myriad details that will reveal to the art historian, as the obscure path of a wild animal will be revealed to the tracker, something akin to precision and accuracy.

"Proof!" will scream the neurotic historian who considers himself an objective scientist.

"That can never be!" the art historian will reply, muted by what he knows to be the limitations of his essential subjectivity.

It is, perhaps, the reason why history and art history, close cousins the academic criteria of which frequently overlap, are really two distinct and separate fields of study.

Framed irregular stonework – mortar

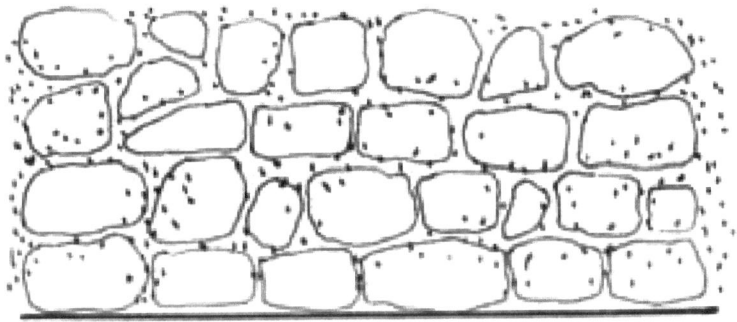

Large "join stone" – interspersed with smaller stones and mud or mortar – perhaps rendered

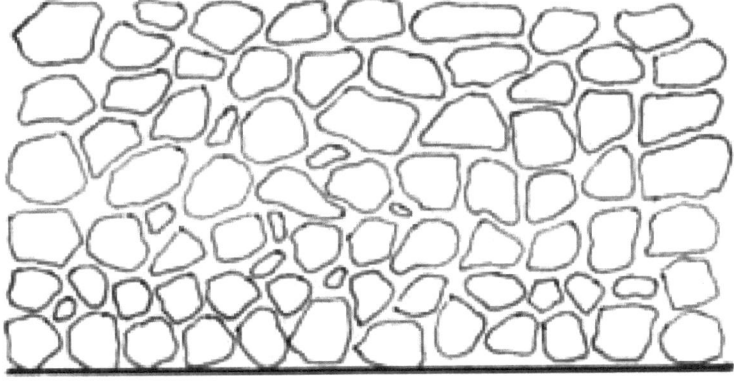

Irregular "found stone" – mud, mortar, drystone

Flat stone files – usually mortared, rendered

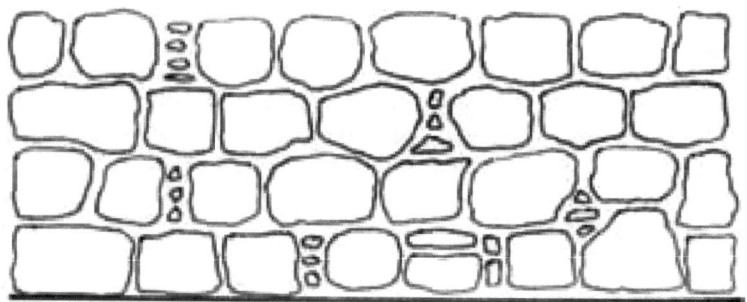

Irregular found rock – with/without mortar, usually unrendered

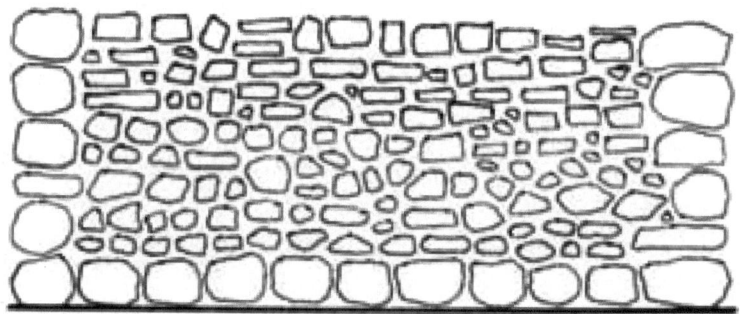

Ordered (corrected) irregular found rock – usually mortared and rendered

Low weight-bearing arch of brick (or stone) in file over lintel

Keystone arch over lintel

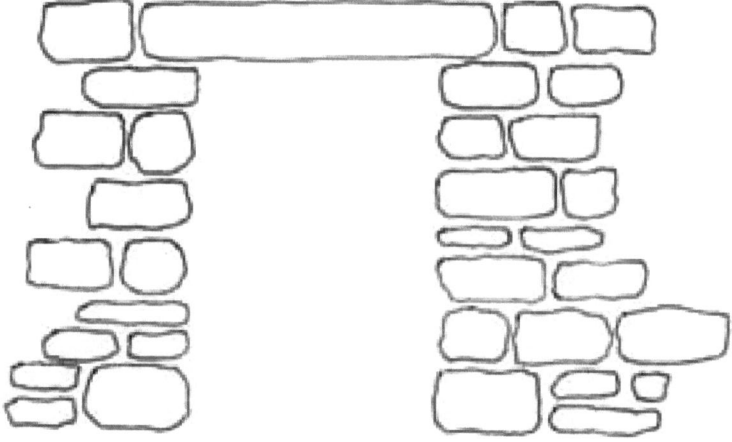

Integrated stone lintel

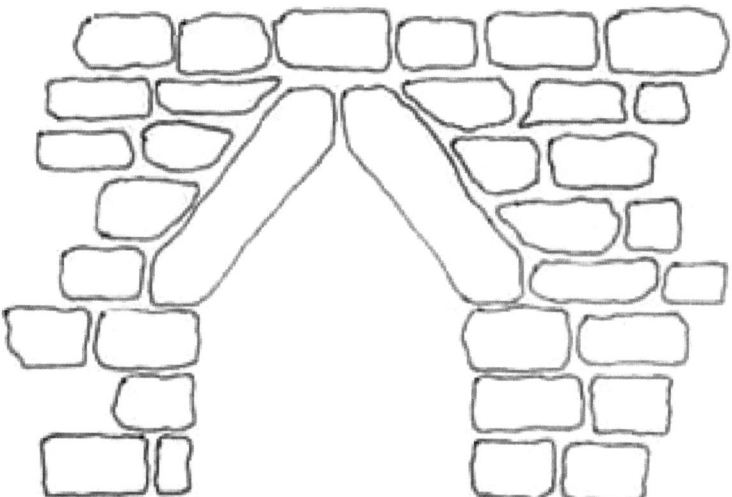

Angled stone lintel

## Goze

Drystone wall at Goze

At Debre Birhan I had the opportunity to meet the commissioner in charge of local archaeological investigations, and was curious to know about recent findings in the vicinity, the district of Manz. He showed me a number of photographs, all of which seemed to be outside the area of my own enquiries – except one captioned simply the mosque at Goze.

"Tell me about this," I prodded him.

"We don't know a great deal at this stage. It is a very old building, perhaps seventeenth century. It is small, as you can see. At present it is used as a mosque, but we don't know if it was always used for that purpose. Perhaps not… "

From the photographs it seemed possible to detect a certain familiar pattern of stonework.

"Where is the place? Can I go see it?"

"Goze is in the valley, north of Shoarobit. You can get to Shoarobit by car. From there you must walk."

On my map Shoarobit was marked as Robi, but my experience with various maps of Ethiopia has taught me not to seek consistency in the spelling of place names. Nor, in fact, should one assume that just because a place exists it is necessarily going to be marked on any or all maps. Such variations as one will find create a measure of charm, to say nothing of adventure, as one moves about the Ethiopian countryside.

Two young colleagues had expressed an interest in going with me, so before first light the following morning we met up with our guide Tsegaye Kebede, and headed north out of Debre Birhan towards what I had come to call the "Mussolini Tunnel." The proper name of this feature is T'armaber Pass. It is the point at which the northbound road burrows its way through a massive red rock and plunges dramatically over the edge of the escarpment into the Great Rift Valley. On the face of the rock at each end of this tunnel the name Mussolini had been chiselled in brutal deep relief by Italian fascists during their years of occupation, 1935-1941. The Italian military had built the road, so no doubt felt quite entitled to sign the name of its beloved Duce; once defeated, though, the signs did not long remain. Ethiopian partisans carved even deeper into the rock in an effort to erase such a hated reminder of their humiliation. Though damaged and the level of Ethiopian disgust clearly registered, the name is still legible at both ends of the tunnel.

At the tunnel's eastern end the road takes a sharp turn to the left, and races downhill all the way to Debre Sina. We stopped there for a scanty breakfast of oily egg sandwiches and then continued on our way north across the valley floor to Shoarobit.

Then we hiked.

Tsegaye estimated the distance at ten kilometres. To me, sadly out of condition and at this juncture easily intimidated, the mountain of Goze rose in the distance like Bali Hai, a full day's dream across a flat ocean. I was alright on the level, but as soon as we started to climb I was done for. I could take no more than a half-dozen paces before having to stop and gasp for air. It had been cool enough when we started to walk, but as the sun rose in the sky it turned blisteringly hot on the open valley floor, and there seemed not a wisp of air as we started on the rise.

In time we came up to the village of Goze nestled on the side of the mountain, but it was still a substantial hike to the mosque at the top. By now I was worried by my condition. My legs had turned to lead. My chest felt like a balloon inflated to bursting. All of us were alarmed. These last several hundred metres were impossible for me.

"I stop here. You guys go on, take my camera. Photograph everything."

It was, I am sure, the wisest course. It was a failure on my part, and I felt it keenly, but still I knew in my gut there was nothing to be done. I sank onto the ground and stretched out. Perhaps I could rest for an hour before the others returned and we faced the long hike back to Shoarobit. It would be downhill all the way to the flats and, as it turned out, I would make it with a gasp. Really, I needed something to eat.

As I rested there at the entrance to Goze, though, I became aware of whisperings all around me. I kept my eyes shut, then someone jabbed a sharp stick into my ribs. I had thrown one arm over my eyes to block the intense sunlight, but now I stirred and sat up blinking.

Twenty or thirty people had gathered about me, and they jumped back en masse at my sudden movement. A young woman cried out in alarm.

The crowd comprised mostly children of all ages and women. There was an old man who carried a stout staff, and it was this that had been used to awaken me. They stared and stared, silently, their brows furrowed suspiciously.

I could not speak to them, but it did not require a university diploma in psychology to comprehend that they were expressing far greater uncertainty and fear than mere curiosity. I spread out my hands and smiled, sat cross-legged and pointed out my friends where they could be seen well above us on the side of the mountain. Making a small clearing in the dirt in front of me, I drew an X and walked my fingers into it. Then I pointed to my chest and made the sign for exhaustion and sleep.

They stared back at me, a comprehensive sullenness. Then one of the younger women coquettishly stepped forward and made the hand sign for "no," at the same time clicking her tongue in mock castigation. She squatted down beside me and rubbed out my X, replacing it with a finger-drawn crescent moon. She pointed to it, and then pointed up the hill. Her message was clear: she had taken the X as some kind of Christian representation and wished to correct me, for this place was Muslim.

I smiled and nodded my head. Indeed, I smiled and nodded my head for most of an hour as we attempted to establish some sort of communion between us. By the time the others returned from the mosque on top of the hill, I was seated on the ground with a substantial portion of the village population gathered about, and the children had started singing me songs. Happily I had discovered a compensation for my lack of sufficient stamina to climb to the top of the mountain.

Tsegaye was able to act as translator when he came back down to the level of the village.

"They were afraid of you when they first saw you sleeping on the ground," he explained. "Your white skin and white hair alarmed them. They say that for them the devil is white…"

My colleague had used my camera to take numerous shots of the old building. Much later, back in the capital, I was able to give careful attention to an examination of the prints. It was a small building, measuring perhaps five metres by nine, tight drystone construction, and with a single door. There were no windows. The place may have looked like a tool shed, but its structure was a stonemason's work of art.

Goze remains something of a mystery to me. The stonework was most carefully wrought in drystone layers, a favourite method employed by Portuguese masons. Corner stones, lintels and extended wall-plates supporting roof beams were all of a typical Portuguese pattern. On one corner, inverted and set high into the wall like all the other stones, was one that had been carefully trenched as though it had initially been cut as part of a trough or gutter. It was incongruous, placed as it was, something of a mystery. An ordinary stone would have served just as well.

In the end, though, I did not succeed in seeing the place myself, and have only this set of very fine photographs to use as any form of guide concerning the place's origin. Had I seen Goze in the Gondar area, rather than down in the Great Rift Valley, I would feel on firmer ground pronouncing it of definite Portuguese style. Its location, however, was many kilometres distant from the area in which I would expect to find Portuguese or Gondarine architecture.

That is not to say there is no connection between the place and the style. Goze, to me, is one of those places that warrants much closer scrutiny by scientific experts. After all, its location is not far removed from the area in which Pêro da Covilhã is reported to have first contacted Emperor Eskendar – and there is every possibility he could have remained in that district for a considerable period of time; long enough, perhaps, to have overseen the construction of the drystone building at Goze.

Trenched "mystery stone" at Goze

### The "Portuguese Bridge" on the Gur River

Almost at the junction of the main Addis Ababa-Gojjam highway and the road that leads into Debre Libanos, but still in the province of Shoa, there is a small river, the Gur, that crosses from south to north and drops over a waterfall to join the Zega River far below. Just shy of the fall, and somewhat hidden from the main road, there is a stone bridge that leaps across the Gur in three arches and has been known for years as the "Portuguese Bridge."

Various studies have been done on the origin of this bridge. A photograph of it was taken in 1907 by a German traveller named Kurt Herzbruch. An exhaustive study of it was made by members of the Ethnological Society of the University College of Addis Ababa under Dr. Stanislaw Chojnacki in 1954. In the late 1990's Ian L. Campbell collected what data on it he could and, further, interviewed individuals living in the area who claimed to recall the bridge being built. The Portuguese were expelled from Ethiopia in 1634 so if these locals are correct, and to be believed, clearly the bridge is not Portuguese.

There is a tantalizing story about it – that a European died in an accidental fall from the bridge while he was working on its construction. One might be tempted to think that perhaps he was Portuguese, except that one of those to whom Campbell spoke said he remembered the man, which puts paid to that notion. There is yet another story that the mortar used to hold the stones together was made of limestone and eggs.

We discussed this recipe earlier – a well-known, even traditional, mortar mix among Portuguese builders of the XV century; one known also to East Indian stonemasons. A reliable mix used until present times (indeed, I have used it myself), it is not at all clear whether the Portuguese taught the method to the Indians, or vice-versa – or where the recipe might have come from in the first place.

However, egg mortar is a preparation known to have been introduced into the Highlands at the time of the Portuguese presence there, and it was used in at least some of the structures they built – they and a seeming host of East Indian builders the Portuguese appear to have brought with them from their headquarters at Goa on the Malabar Coast. If this talk of egg mortar had been fabricated, or was only rumour, how could modern day Ethiopians even have guessed at such a strange notion? (Or for that matter the Portuguese still be employing it from time-to-time?)

From a design point of view there can be little question that the bridge looks Portuguese. Roman Portuguese. So if the bridge is relatively modern, why was it built according to such an ancient pattern? Also, why the choice of such an apparently ancient recipe for the mortar mix?

At several points in this narrative there will appear other not dissimilar mysteries, the sort of occurrences which appear to defy satisfactory explanation and remain shrouded in some whacky indefinite. As one travels this land there is an almost palpable sense of the unknowable, as though the ancients who witnessed its earliest links with human knowledge deliberately withheld detail – to the point of obscuring chronicle – in order to confuse or to control. The axiom that "who masters information masters the minds of the masses" would seem to apply in these Highlands. Myth mixes with history so thoroughly it can be difficult to separate the two. Rumour can so bountifully fog fact that intelligent men mumble inanities.

With this caution, one would best be wary of accepting too readily the claims of those who say they watched, when they were children, the construction of the bridge over the Gur. How old would a person have to be in 1990, the date of Campbell's visit, who could remember the building of a finished bridge that had been photographed in 1907? Precisely how much of what would he or she be able to remember? If the witness had been seven years old at the time the photograph was taken, that would make him ninety at the time of his conversation with Campbell. One might legitimately ask how much of the bridge's construction a seven-year-old would know about or understand, let alone note. Perhaps he was not seven, but a much more mature and impressionable eleven – in which case in 1990 our witness would have been ninety-four ... By now my own doubts should have my tongue fumbling about behind my cheek ...

In addition to mysticism, concocted or otherwise, in the course of investigations throughout the Highlands I came across a considerable quantity of what can only be described as "nationalist denial" – a sort of psychological refusal to accept that others might have come from elsewhere and set about doing things – like constructing buildings and bridges in a manner that, for millennia up to the time of the coming of the Portuguese, manifestly did not occur to the locals. Once, on the campus of Addis Ababa University, an academic had scolded me: "Is there nothing we have been capable of doing for ourselves? Do you believe that because we are Africans we are incapable of inventing technologies ourselves?" It was a vehement moment, and in a sense embarrassing. Again I must refer my reader to the essay on denial, page 165.

Ancient Ethiopian technologies are well known so it would be difficult, even foolish, to hold such totally negative opinion. The man who shouted this was wrong on several counts, and of course one must not make special allowances for his errors just because he happened to have been an African in confrontation with someone of European descent. Western political correctness tends to go too far when it becomes overly permissive of incorrect concepts in order to avoid treading on sensitive nationalistic toes. Whether they be minority or majority toes really should make no difference when examining anything falling within the realm of history. One may legitimately make conjecture about history, I believe; but to re-write history, or even to lean towards one interpretation of it over another, is to invite obfuscation and impede honest scholarship. History presents sufficient contention that it does not require the assistance of false concoctions. Mary Lefkowitz's thought provoking book, *Not Out of Africa*, deals courageously with these very fallacies: the reorganization of African or African-American history in order to promote or appease.

That said, there must be the implicit acknowledgement that stonework did indeed exist in Ethiopia's Highlands prior to the arrival of the Portuguese. This simplistic argument is trundled out time and again as something like a disclaimer. The fact is that just as the tradition of stonework in Portugal differs from the stonework in next door Spain, so the stonework of Axum differs from the stonework of Tigray, which in turn differs from the stonework of Lalibela. To confuse one with the other is to admit an inability to distinguish one from the other, and in this particular case to admit a specific ignorance of Portuguese stonework.

Insofar as the bridge over the Gur is concerned, and in many other instances as well, my own explanation is both simple and straightforward: during the presence of the Portuguese a strong and efficient building method was introduced that worked well, caught on, and has been handed down from generation to generation ever since. Coming to the Highlands from Goa, and recognizing from Metropolitan Portuguese architecture the fact that great quantities and all manner of Indian motif was zealously copied and incorporated into Portuguese structures of the era, it is by no means unlikely that both Indian and Portuguese designers worked together on the Ethiopian structures that remain today. My guess would be something along the line of Portuguese overseers, Indian craftsmanship, Ethiopian labour. Once one has learned how to build a Roman/Portuguese bridge, and knows the formula thoroughly, it is quite possible to construct the next one, and very capably, without a Portuguese or Indian overseer on site.

Mimesis is undoubtedly a factor, the copying of a design motif, and even the detailed method of structure. There can be little question that large numbers of both Portuguese and Indians remained permanently in the Highlands and that they taught the locals (probably beginning with their own descendents born to local wives) how to erect certain structures. Once done, it is a simple matter to pass the knowledge on from father to son.

The evidence in this case may indeed point to the likely construction of the bridge at the end of the XIX century, or even early XX century. It remains something of a mystery – perhaps there was a bridge there earlier that was rebuilt in more modern times. Perhaps the seven-year-old witnessed a renovation or remodelling. Campbell is decidedly doubtful.

"I think the theory (of the bridge being Portuguese) is most unlikely, and I cannot believe that the Jesuits would have built it, in the middle of nowhere, far from any Jesuit mission, at great expense, to serve the congregation of an Orthodox church – and never mention it (in their chronicles)!"

Why is it known as the "Portuguese Bridge?"

Maybe it is no more than a token acknowledgement that it was constructed along the lines of some remembered Portuguese prototype. I prefer to be sceptical. While Campbell suggests that the site may in fact be the best example of mimesis, I am not entirely convinced that the bridge is not a good deal older, and would prefer to await scientific examination of its mortar before making a pronouncement.

As a sidebar issue, this "Portuguese Bridge" provides a useful mini-example of an extensive set of problems that currently plague Africa far beyond the borders of Ethiopia. Africans suffered dreadfully at the hands of Europeans, and all over the continent nationalist sensitivities are acute in ways that bumbling newcomers have often failed adequately to assess. Whether the bridge be ancient or modern, in this as in so many other much more significant areas, Africa's tragedy should not be used as an excuse to bypass clear academic evidence. Nor should it be touted in order to ignore, perhaps overpass, reasonable conjecture.

**Mertule Maryam**

The ruins of Mertule Maryam, located in a remote corner of Gojjam, are contained inside a single walled church compound at the southern end of the town. One of these is of particular interest to this study, and is the oldest standing structure of the three buildings within the enclosure. Locals refer to the ancient structure as a "church," claiming its origin to be from the time of the Queen of Sheba – approximately a millennium before the birth of Christ. It is intriguing to contemplate the origin of colourful legend, but the ruins one sees above ground today manifestly do not date to that period. It is very possible that below the present visible structures there indeed lie other ancient foundations. No satisfactory archaeological work has ever been undertaken at the site, so it is impossible to confirm here whether or not a much older structure rests under what may be seen today. One legend recounted to me in breathless excitement by a local deacon was that Jesus Christ himself preached in Mertule Maryam – within the very walls that remain standing. Another claimed the place had been floated into its present location by God. Yet another explained how a very slim stone mounted within the compound, standing perhaps three metres high and topped by an ancient Jesuit stone cross, actually grows millimetre by millimetre each year. I was much charmed by the overall location, and would have loved to remain there longer; but I did not have a year to set aside to verify such claims, nor a handy tape measure and ladder that would permit me to take precise details and perhaps return at a later date.

The remaining two buildings within the compound area are traditional round structures, more recent Ethiopian Orthodox churches. Locals claim the site itself was first chosen for the building of a church by the twin kings, Abraha and Atsbaha, in the IV century, and that a monastery was established here in the XIV century.

What does exist of the visible ruin is clearly Portuguese in origin, though much of the remaining superficial decoration, ashlar, would appear to be either Indian or Armenian. Several "experts" have pronounced conflicting opinions. If, indeed, it proves to be Indian, then of course there is little call for great surprise. Portugal's means of access to Ethiopia was via Goa on India's west coast, and it is not improbable that artisans could have been brought by the Portuguese from Gujarat into the Highlands specifically for this work. If Armenian, then this, too, has logical explanation. Armenian traders had been filtering into the region for many years prior to the arrival of the Portuguese, and the presence of their culture's skilled decorative stonemasons could be easily explained. In addition, corroborative work on the part of any able stone workers present is well within the bounds of reason, regardless of nationality or cultural background.

It is unlikely the ruin at Mertule Maryam was only a church, although it certainly contained a chapel, and a very handsome one. Early chronicles indicate there were, in fact, three chapels laid out side-by-side and connected by decorated doorways. It is much more likely that the main structure was built as a palace, the chapel or chapels forming a central core to the overall complex. The structure had two floor levels, possibly three.

Much of Mertule Maryam's complex history is concealed by legend, and may be only reasonably guessed at; some of it is more precisely recorded. According to believable tradition, the building extant today was undertaken by Empress Eleni. The empress died in 1523, about ten or twelve years after the structure's completion. According to this time line, then, her Mertule Maryam would have been completed about 1512. At the time of its completion it was considered to be the most outstanding building in Ethiopia. It was said to have contained two altar slabs of solid gold; the roofs of the entire building were covered, it was claimed, with gold sheeting.

There are two likely uses for the place: being the paramount administrator of Gojjam, Empress Eleni might well have used it as a formal residence. Being renowned as a pious Christian lady, it unquestionably contained a church or chapels, though it is impossible to tell prior to detailed archaeological work to what degree these were integrated into the overall complex.

A shell motif in mountains several hundred kilometres from any shoreline speaks more
to the nostalgia of the seafaring Portuguese than it does to Highland farmers

The place was sacked during the Islamic invasion of Ahmad Grag'n, likely during the early 1530's. The gold of the roof, if it existed, would have been removed at this time. Legend has it that the altar slabs were saved, but if that is true, their whereabouts are unknown today. Certain items of local Christian religious treasure pre-dating this sacking appear to have survived more or less intact. It is known that, despite deliberate Muslim destruction, in many areas local residents successfully hid their church treasure. This appears to have been the case at Mertule Maryam.

The structure was at least partially rebuilt by Emperor Lebna Dengal (1508-1540), or his son Emperor Galawdewos (1540-1559), but it was sacked a second time around 1560 during the Oromo

Decorated ashlar arch at Mertule Maryam,
inset drawing reveals detail of ashlar design

invasions of the Highlands. Balthazar Tellez, a Jesuit priest who arrived in the area in 1623, claims his predecessor, Pêro Páez, had begun yet another restoration in 1619 or 1620, but had died in 1622 without completing the work. The new Jesuit prelate, Afonso Mendes, arrived in the Highlands in 1625 and Emperor Sussenyos (1607-1632), reconfirming to him his allegiance to the Church of Rome, then instructed Padre Bruno Bruni to tackle restoration in earnest the following year.

However, Mertule Maryam was abandoned just six years later, prior to the completion of this undertaking. In 1632 Emperor Sussenyos was forced to acknowledge the will of his people and their traditional church. He died within months, and in 1633 the site was altogether abandoned when his successor, Emperor Fasiladas, ordered the Jesuits out of Gojjam. The following year Fasiladas ordered Jesuits and Roman Catholics throughout the country to leave Ethiopia on pain of death, and control of Mertule Maryam reverted to the Ethiopian Orthodox Church.

For a time the place was revered and treated as sacrosanct. As the years passed and the building deteriorated, local Orthodox Christians decided a new church was in order and they built themselves a more traditional round structure within the same walled compound. They used the stones of the original building and thus augmented its further deterioration. The second round church within the compound was built in modern times.

Effectively, then, the building and its restoration involved a span of about one century, possibly a little more. All this was during a period of the Highland's tumultuous history when the Portuguese exercised extraordinary influence at the royal court, and particularly in the Gojjam district.

As is recounted in both stories and legend, Empress Eleni was extremely close to the Portuguese emissary, Pêro da Covilhã. The two of them were known to be friends, and though it cannot be confirmed there are stories that they were lovers. Chronicles of the time record that Eleni sought da Covilhã's advice concerning the installation of the altar at Mertule Maryam. It is also recorded that he was made administrator, or steward, of her lands in Gojjam. Clearly, at the very least, he occupied an important and senior position at her side.

An angel in decorated stonework

Mertule Maryam's ruin is basically a rectangular building of mortared stonework. Ethiopian churches traditionally were, and continue to be, round structures, although there are numerous exceptions to this throughout the country. If, as story relates, the building of the structure was supervised by the trusted foreign advisor to the empress, would it not be a natural thing for him to build on the European lines that he knew and more readily understood? Even if hypothetical, the question is at least relevant.

One should also consider this: Axum had been a permanent capital, and remained so throughout the period of the Axumite Empire, until its reigning prince abdicated in favour of the Christian king of Shoa, Yekuno Amlak, in 1268. Lalibela, in the mountains east of Gondar, was a capital in the XIII century. Although there was a series of extraordinary monolithic churches created there which were carved out of solid rock, nothing remains that might be identified as forming an administrative centre.

Throughout the time of Pêro da Covilhã's presence in Ethiopia, and for several hundreds of years before that, and even afterwards, tradition had dictated a nomadic court, a moveable administrative capital as opposed to one rooted in the permanence of stone. It was considered a surer means of defence.

Is it not a peculiar coincidence that only after the arrival of Pêro da Covilhã, and the later influx of Portuguese who came tumbling into those Highlands following his initial contact with the royal court, that Ethiopians started thinking, perhaps again, in terms of a permanent capital, like Axum? Like Lalibela? Is it not possible, indeed even likely, that the renewed idea of a fixed and defended capital might have been proposed by the one man selected to advise the court on military and defence matters?

Furthermore, is it only coincidence that the buildings designed to convey a necessary sense of awe, whether a regional capital at Mertule Maryam or a national capital at Gondar, should so closely resemble not just European prototypes but Portuguese prototypes?

Decorated beam supports

Permanent capitals and permanent buildings had been considered dangerous, too easy to attack and too hard to defend. Nevertheless during this era monumental architecture was one of the foremost and very strongest art forms being developed in Portugal, as in all Europe. The Portuguese, as discussed, constituted a nation of builders; they were so throughout all that period of time, and they remain so even today. Is it so unreasonable to conceive that a clever Portuguese diplomat/advisor whispered an idea into the trusting ear of his friend, or lover, the dowager empress? Once again, legend informs us that Empress Eleni chose to be buried at Mertule Maryam. If there is anything to the story that she and da Covilhã were lovers, is it not conceivable, indeed entirely natural, that she would want to be buried in the place he had built for her – a place they had built together, and which replicated the imposing architecture of his homeland, the finest building in the Ethiopia of the day?

These are bold conjectures to make out of so little that is known for sure, let alone that which may be surmised through legend, but there are many, many curious circumstances here. Conjecturing at this point is worth the exercise because it helps to open up a not altogether unlikely channel of discussion and consideration. It could even open an avenue of fruitful investigation: to assume, for instance, that Pêro da Covilhã indeed was responsible for the initial construction of the palace/chapel at Mertule Maryam. Make the further assumption that it was a palace, a capital complex, intended as the residence of Gojjam's senior citizen, and as a district administrative seat for herself and her governor; and, further, that it also contained a chapel, or chapels, built in the style of Portuguese structures of that era.

The hypothesis is interesting even if the science is currently none too precise.

Assuming that Mertule Maryam served as some kind of district capital, there are yet further coincidences. For instance later, when Guzara was built and served as a royal residence it, too, appears to have been assembled along recognizable Portuguese lines. Again, at Denqaz, another royal residence-cum-capital, and the seat of a Roman Catholic bishopric, was definitively of Portuguese origin. (We have on ample record that Father Pêro Páez designed and built it.) When Emperor Fasiladas established Gondar as his permanent capital city it, too, followed a Portuguese pattern almost as though the Portuguese format had initiated the Lego of the day. Who or what established this form? Surely the later buildings would indicate an earlier model or pattern, an earlier archetype?

The renovations, too, when they were undertaken in the century that followed the original construction of Mertule Maryam, were completed in quite typical Portuguese style, although the stone facing decoration, the ashlar, itself is not typically Portuguese. As mentioned, the most obvious explanation of this is that the stonemasons themselves were brought in from Goa and Portuguese India by the Portuguese *mestres*, who would have been working for the Jesuits and overseeing the project. In more than one well-recorded instance, as noted, the Jesuit missionary Pêro Páez was himself a stonemason. Portugal's centre of operations in that era was precisely Goa; Portugal's route to Ethiopia was via Goa. The west coast of the Indian sub-continent was very much dominated by the Portuguese in those years, so it can hardly be seen as surprising that Indians and Indo-Portuguese, perhaps in large numbers, negotiated the *caminho* into the Ethiopian Highlands. If, as some hold, the ashlar at Mertule Maryam is actually of Armenian design, it would not necessarily detract from the overall concept of Portuguese input; rather it might simply indicate that Portuguese overseers had hired Armenian stonemasons locally.

The architectural and decorative indications of Mertule Maryam's Portuguese origin and/or restoration are too numerous to ignore. Nonetheless, the stonework itself provides sufficient information for some definitive conclusions.

The very first indication is simply the aspect of the building, its proportions, and the manner in which it sits into its landscape – its exterior design or silhouette. Portuguese architecture of the time has a unique and unmistakable appearance to the designer's eye, having a rather solid, squat appearance, "low" in terms of overall horizontal extension, well-balanced even when in fact rising to a height of two or perhaps three storeys. This very quality of appearance is a giveaway, a primary indicator not just for Mertule Maryam but for all the Portuguese-style sites in the Highlands. There is an unmistakable architectural demeanour that simply cannot fool the practiced eye or even, with a modicum of exposure, the unpractised eye, and which talks loud and clear about the folk attitude of the Portuguese builder, his awareness of physical landscape coupled with an uncanny optimum use of local scales, materials and colourings. It was, and remains, an exceptional skill the Portuguese succeeded in transporting to every corner of the globe in which they built.

Refer to stick-figure drawing above: the angled door lintel gives a false horizon, permitting anyone passing through to know instinctively to duck and avoid cracking his head; through time it became a design feature

Other indicators: the manner in which the stones are selected and placed in their individual positions; the rutting of door and window lintels and posts to form flanges for the acceptance of a final *reboco*, or rendering, of both indoor and outdoor "plaster." At Mertule Maryam, and many other locations as well, some of this rendering is still visible. Still other indicators include: the angles of the side walls within window and door frames – embrasures or splays – to allow for light or easy passage; the weight-bearing stone arch built over horizontal lintels, usually covered by the *reboco*, but which is very often worn away to reveal this feature; the angles of these lintels, particularly door lintels in instances when the door must pierce an unusually thick wall, and also the use of wood in constructing them. Initially these angled lintels were intended for low doorways, allowing for a tall person to "bob" his head as he went through rather than hunch over or squat and maintain that uncomfortable position for several paces to avoid cracking his head. Later it became a design feature, and may be found even in high doorways where head room is not a consideration. The relative thickness of the walls themselves, and the manner in which they are tapered; door-lock niches and hinge-stones; through-wall niches permitting the interior of a wall to "breathe" and so on – all of these are also tell-tale signs.

The question of mortar is an intriguing one. If one is to believe the words of Pêro Páez, all stone structures erected by the Jesuits and their helpers used mud or clay as a binder. Páez died in 1622, the same year the Portuguese builder Manuel Magro entered the Highlands. It is he who is credited with the introduction of lime mortar, which appears not to have been in common use in the area until after 1624.

Still, in my visits to the numerous sites examined in these pages lime mortar was in common use everywhere. Indeed, I paid special attention to it. This would seem to indicate that none of the walls of the buildings I surveyed were erected prior to 1624 – which information most certainly did not gel with other of my findings.

One possible explanation is the knowledge that lime mortar was in general use in all areas of Europe centuries prior to 1624, so its use most definitely would have been known to Portuguese builders entering the Highlands earlier than that date. It is possible – I think probable – that a form of lime mortar was, indeed, in use prior to the days of Pêro Páez, even if he was not using it himself. He was not the builder of all local structures within the genre. It would also seem very likely that lime mortar would have been used in the repair of walls in the decades and centuries that followed the epoch of the Portuguese presence. The seasonal torrential rains in the Highlands would tend, rather rapidly, to wash out mud or clay used to bind wall stones together; repairs effected with a more permanent mortar mix would thus be a matter of common sense, once it became generally available.

Mortar can be dated fairly accurately, and no doubt this will be done once detailed scientific study of these sites is seriously undertaken.

None of this yet addresses the subject of decorative stone carving. Some of it is decidedly Portuguese, for instance the shell, rose and angel motifs. Other carvings, the geometric and interwoven flower patterns in and over many of the arches, as has been referred to above, has been "positively" identified – by one expert source as Gujarati, by another as Armenian.

I would like to refer the reader to certain illustrations that appear in these pages: the photograph of the angel's winged head in stone relief that appears high on the far wall somewhat below the decorated arch depicted on page 83, and it's close-up repeated at the bottom of page 84; and then the angel's winged head in stone relief below the lancet window at the bottom of page 88.

Apart from the fact that the Portuguese were past masters at detailed relief sculpture, the shell motif, the bowl of roses, the angel's winged head are all typical Portuguese themes, and they fit very comfortably into the interior décor at Mertule Maryam. Such items, particularly the winged head, help to identify the Portuguese provenance of the site. Not always great innovators, but certainly great copyists when inspired to produce something "new," Ethiopian religious painters of only a slightly later period have been quick to "borrow" these same themes – and particularly the winged angel head – squeezing it through a sort of Ethiopian-style metamorphosis into something of a conga line of heads and wings, repeating it over and over. It is mesmerizing, a form of hypnosis; the angels' heads are depicted with typical Afro-style hair and enormously outsized eyes. They may be identified in at least two religious venues in the Highlands – the most famous being the ceiling at Gondar's Debre Birhan Selassie, the other at Narga Selassie. I have no reason to suppose the motif is not lovingly reproduced in many other churches and monasteries as well. It is, I feel, a startling example of how the Portuguese presence surreptitiously, possibly quite unintentionally, worked its way into the consciousness of Ethiopian religious decorators of the era. This theme is discussed in greater detail in the commentary on page 165.

Both Charles Beke (1846) and Paul Henze (1997) have written scholarly and informative detail concerning the history of Mertule Maryam. One may in no way criticize the historical perspectives that each has presented, nor the hypotheses that each has been obliged to put forward in the absence of detailed scientific and archaeological investigation. On the contrary, both scholars have done their utmost to open up discussion on this site, and in this way to promote more arduous criticism and research; but both scholars, though acknowledging Portugal's historical presence in the Highlands, have omitted two very important points in their respective examinations of Mertule Maryam.

The first is the whole matter of architectural design and structural method, the "Portugueseness" of the place. The second is the glaring historical fact that the structure was initially built and then restored twice during a period of time when Portugal's migration, contact and influence in Ethiopia was at its height.

In both of these oversights I believe that each scholar, while certainly aware of a measure of Portuguese input, was not particularly conversant with a much more extensive history involving Portugal, nor the medium, in a general way, of Portuguese architecture, the use of bas relief, for example, or such religious depiction such as the winged angel heads.

In truth this would have to be offered as a more general comment on the whole area under review. The reference is to most academic study of the entire field and is not intended as a critique of just these two particular and very competent scholars. Gondarine architecture is widely discussed; the Portuguese architecture that was its genesis historically seems to get short shrift. Portugal's presence in the Highlands, where it is acknowledged, appears to be measured chiefly from the time the

Vase of roses, typical
Portuguese decorative theme

diplomatic embassy arrived in 1520. The fact that Pêro da Covilhã by that time had been a dominant influence in the country for nearly thirty years appears to be almost entirely overlooked.

The accumulation of these points provides the best of all reasons why this present work is being undertaken.

Specific figures do not exist, but it is believed that within a short period of time after the defeat of Ahmad Grag'n there were some six thousand "Portuguese" migrants in the Lake Tana region alone. It is unlikely they were all Portuguese nationals. To the Ethiopians the Portuguese presence had become so unquestionably prominent in the area that any foreigner in the Highlands was taken for Portuguese. Apart from European-looking merchants from such places as Greece or Armenia, whose transient trading activities had filtered them into the region for many centuries, it is very likely indeed that most non-Portuguese foreigners had in some way or another been in Portuguese service, many of them as mariners or soldiers. Beke himself, at the conclusion of his paper, talks of lands being set aside in the neighbourhood of Sabara Dildiy, quite close to Mertule Maryam, specifically for "Portuguese" settlers.

**The Church Museum**

Mertule Maryam's so-called church "museum" is worthy of elaboration, if only for the crisis it indicates.

"Museum" is a word used by the locals, but it clearly paints an incorrect picture of the manner in which church and religious treasure is being handled and stored. At Mertule Maryam the museum is a concrete blockhouse. The whole is a showcase of lamentable disgrace. Doors are inadequate. Windows are two or three holes let through the block walls that contain no glass, and the shutters of which do not necessarily prevent the entry of chickens, pigeons, rats, dust and filth – and humidity.

It is of no use to be overly critical, but in this place and many others like it throughout the Highlands there is a treasure trove of wondrous and precious items, some of which are described by Henze in his paper referring to the time when he and other scholars attempted to make an inventory. Sometimes in such cases it is necessary to cry alarm; this is in no way to assign blame. Nevertheless, conditions in this and other "museums" are so bad that one naturally feels a sense of responsibility to cast one's vote for improvement. Clearly something must be done to preserve the rare treasures that are tossed into these places.

Inventories barely exist, but would be essential to the initiation of any clean-up program. That would take more time than is available to a mere visitor. In a place like Mertule Maryam there is simply too much material to be listed by anyone short of a professional anthropologist or museum curator. It could take weeks, or months, to do proper justice to the job.

At the time of my visit, ancient books were strewn all over the floor of Mertule Maryam's museum. Many were written in Ge'ez, and it was impossible to pinpoint their respective ages. All of them, at any rate, were hand scripted on velum. Many had been elaborately illuminated. One volume, bound as were many of them between decoratively carved wooden covers, was described by the local priest as being from the VI century. Doubtful. Maybe it was XVI, or XVII, or XVIII. It would require scientific expertise to confirm. Whatever the date, it was a beautiful work of art, and it should not have been on the floor in a heap with others like it.

Bundled into every corner, stacked or leaning against cement block walls, were religious vestments in many richly coloured fabrics, some of them embroidered in gold and silver. Numerous crosses carved in wood, or cast, or hammered in bronze, gold or silver, roosted in the dust and feathers in these dismal corners, some of them mounted on the ends of long wooden shafts. There were prayer sticks and tall embroidered processional umbrellas; dozens of them. Draped across a dressmaker's mannequin, collecting dust like everything else, was a lovely deep royal blue velvet cape decorated on its buttons, edges and around the collar with intricate silver filigree. When asked what it was and to whom it had belonged, the answer came that it was a cape of rank, and that it had probably belonged to Empress Eleni herself. She died in 1523; the garment was in extraordinarily well preserved condition if it was, indeed, that age. My tongue had located a comfortable niche inside my cheek as I listened to guides at Mertule Maryam proclaim without hesitation the dates of the site's indisputable wonders.

Perhaps most extraordinary of all the "exhibits" on this occasion was a simple rough and heavy cotton shirt hung on nails against one wall, its long sleeves stretched straight out at its sides, crucifix-like. It was enormous. Pacing across the front of it from cuff-to-cuff, I stepped out three long strides. When I enquired as to which giant had once pulled the garment over his enormous chest, the answer came back, matter-of-factly: Ahmad Ibn Ibrahim el Ghazi of Adel, Ahmad Grag'n himself.

How much truth or fiction is contained in all this one simply cannot tell without recourse to many more sophisticated technical facilities. It does not take a very highly trained eye to see that there are many, many items of exceptional value stored in this dreadful manner in this miserable little "museum."

**Alata Bridge at Tis'isat**

The "dog's leg" bend in the bridge's deck is a defence feature: it is impossible to shoot an arrow the length of the bridge between its parapets. For architectural style, compare the Alata Bridge with the Pipa Bridge at Barrancos, southern Portugal, next page

This eight-arch structure, approximately seventy metres in length, crosses a narrows of the Blue Nile River a few hundred metres below the Tis'isat waterfall, which is about thirty kilometres southeast of Bahir Dar. It links the two provinces of Gojjam and Gondar. Some sources claim it is one of many structures erected at the behest of Emperor Fasiladas (1632-1667); others that it was built much earlier by Portuguese missionaries, settlers or soldiers. It is an acknowledged work of Portuguese origin, in any event, and is also frequently dubbed the "Portuguese Bridge."

Emperor Fasiladas forbade the Roman Catholic liturgy in 1632, confining Jesuits, Roman Catholic missionaries and their sympathizers; the simultaneous return of the people's religious affiliation to Orthodoxy triggered many years of persecution of Roman Catholics. Two years later the emperor ordered all Roman Catholics to leave the Highlands, and anyone caught practicing the outlawed form was put to death. Even so, by no means all the "Portuguese" left.

By this time Portugal's association with Ethiopia was about one hundred and forty years old. Settlers – missionaries, mission staff, soldiers, guards, runaways – had been coming into the Highlands for practically this entire period, all of them male, and the greatest majority of them taking local wives or companions. There is a spread of perhaps five or even six generations over the entire period under review. It is much more than probable, indeed a foregone conclusion, that the descendents of these original Portuguese settlers were, by the mid-XVII century, dark-skinned in their colouring, not white-skinned like their forefathers of a few generations before. In other words, visually they would have blended in very closely with the local indigenous population. They would have looked "Ethiopian" rather than "Portuguese." It is also entirely likely that they would have adopted most, if not all the cultural traits of the people that surrounded their everyday lives, including religious affiliation. Portuguese as a minority language survived many years, and it was considered elite to speak it. Eventually it was swamped by the language of the majority of indigenous Highlanders. Further, after Fasiladas came to power and issued his edict expelling followers of the foreign religion, to speak Portuguese would have been a negative indicator likely to bring about persecution; those who spoke it would lay themselves open to being considered Roman Catholic sympathizers.

Consequently by the early 1600's far and away the greater majority of the "Portuguese" had been assimilated as "Ethiopians." Only two cultural areas were likely to set these people apart from the overall population: one was the possibility of their Roman Catholic faith, the other was the acquisition of imported "Portuguese" skills. Had they professed their faith openly, they would have found themselves in the gravest danger. But the ability to build, being the predominant local "Portuguese" skill, would have proved a valued meal ticket for anybody regardless of religion or skin colour. The religion was rooted out forcibly. The building skills remained but were now possessed by dark-skinned men – Ethiopian men. The method, initially Portuguese, had been transferred. Certainly there were Portuguese who worked on the Alata Bridge that crosses the Blue Nile River below Tis'isat. They were soldiers. Records of proof exist in the royal chronicles. As with many of the other structures claimed to be "Portuguese," it is not entirely improbable that many, maybe most, of the workmen looked like Ethiopians and shuffled off to say their prayers in an Orthodox church.

In this way, and by a fairly logical extension, it is not an exaggeration to say that what is called Gondarine architecture and what is recognized as Portuguese architecture criss-cross tightly in the region of the Ethiopian Highlands. In the majority of cases they have blended into one and the same thing. "Portugal" is stamped all over the Gondarine architectural creations one examines, and this can be seen very clearly in the building methods used in all major and many minor structures erected at the behest of Emperor Fasiladas, as well as by the leaders who came after him.

As a postscript to discussion of the Alata Bridge, it could be usefully and accurately claimed that anyone who has travelled in Portugal will recognize this structure in an instant. *Ponte Romano* is a method used throughout the country and introduced into Iberia, as its name indicates, by early Roman colonizers. It is immediately recognizable by its tell-tale rounded arches, its heavy buttresses with angled *talha-mars* or cutwaters jutting upstream, its typical decking with water runoff apertures let through the stone parapets on either side. The most obvious feature is the "dog-leg" angle of the deck, built as a defensive measure; one cannot shoot an arrow the full length of a bridge between its parapets if the bridge has such a pronounced kink in it. These bridges have proved so useful, so sturdy and so practical, that they are found in all parts of Iberia, and many of them are still in use. Indeed, the style continued long after the Romans had left. In the case of the Alata Bridge, the stonework is unmistakably Portuguese.

A curious anecdote here concerns the similar bridge about four kilometres north of Barrancos, in Portugal's Alentejo province, where it crosses the Murtiga River carrying the roadway to Noudar Castle. Presented with a photograph of this bridge alongside one taken from a similar angle of the bridge at Tis'isat, the mayor of Barrancos at first was unable to tell the difference. Even the landscapes are similar. (Note also the photos of the stonework at Mai Gwa Gwa, page 158.)

The Blue Nile River flows under Alata Bridge

**Páez house in the Compound of St. Giorghis Church at Bahir Dar**

Right in the centre of town, this tiny building at the back of the St. Giorghis church compound remains something of a mystery concerning its original purpose, but it can most certainly be identified as "Portuguese," or at least "Jesuit" if, as story has it, Pêro Páez was its builder.

Whether he was or not, the building does have a very Portuguese flavour to it and might be regarded as entirely consistent with structures found in the Saloio or Sintra area of Portugal. It is very tall, perhaps eight or nine metres in height, stone built but with an outer rendering, *reboco*, in very good condition. It has a single room slightly below ground level entered by a small door at its western end, an outdoor stairway, the steps and parapet of which are of heavy masonry, and then an upstairs portion which must remain a mystery until the whole can be more thoroughly examined. From the appearance of the masonry roof it looks as though the upper level might have an *abobadilha*, or barrel vaulted ceiling, but it is impossible to be certain without entering, permission for which was denied when it was requested.

An intriguing feature is the arrangement of windows, or window apertures, which could indicate a third level. This is also suggested by a short stair surmounted by a rough ladder that is within the single lower room, at the rear, and leads to a trap door in the ceiling above. One is left to assume that this trap door leads to a level between the ground floor room and the upper story reached by the outdoor stair on the building's north side.

In all of Bahir Dar this building is undoubtedly the most intact example of its period, and so is worthy of much closer scientific examination. It stands on church property, so that a diplomatic approach to the religious authorities would be necessary. Securing this sort of permission is not always as easy as it might seem. Religious authorities in Ethiopia tend to take what they understand to be areas of their responsibility very seriously. They defend their turf. Closed for many years, and fiercely proud, Ethiopian society as a whole tends to keep one foot back in its dealings with outsiders. By and large Ethiopians are a conservative people, very much respectful of the senior status and authority of church and clergy. On the other side of the coin, the clergy is not noted for its liberal and progressive views on any matter, particularly in instances in which the matter concerned is perceived as encroaching upon church rights or church property. There are many and noted senior clergymen within the Ethiopian Orthodox Church who are highly educated and wise to the ways of the world. By far the greater majority of churchmen, however, have an education circumscribed by a knowledge of their scriptures and other holy writings, and the suspicions and even superstitions that accrue through years of essentially inward thinking.

Time and again as I worked my way across these Christian Highlands I was forced to deal with these sorts of attitudes. One cannot force an issue of this kind. If sweet reason does not work, it is better by far to back away graciously rather than to be so offensive as to stand firm and argue. It was also my experience, in numerous cases, that a reasoned plea accompanied by a reasoned acceptance of "the way things are" was of itself sufficient to turn the key in many a door.

Not, unfortunately, on the occasion of my visit to the Páez house.

To whomever that privilege is ultimately granted, I would urge particular attention be paid to obtaining a small sample of the building's exterior rendering, or *reboco*, so that it might be dated accurately. If the rendering is of an age approaching what is thought to be the original date of the building, approximately 1620, in other words if the *reboco* itself is likely original, it would be interesting to analyze the mortar securing the stones under the rendering. It is unusual to find among these Highland sites a building with its *reboco* in such good condition; it could mean, of course, that the rendering in this case was renewed at some stage following the building's initial construction.

### Kebran Gabriel, Entos Eyesu, Zege and Liblibo

Kebran Gabriel museum

Entos Eyesu "prison"

Kebran Gabriel is an Orthodox monastery occupying one of two small and adjacent islands on Lake Tana about forty minutes from Bahir Dar by outboard motorboat, in the direction of the Zege peninsula. There are churches on both islands. One, Entos Eyesu, is reserved for women; the larger is Kebran Gabriel, reserved for men. On Entos Eyesu there is also a small building of similar structure to the Páez house in the St. Giorghis church compound in Bahir Dar.

It is a squat, rectangular building, a slight rounding to what is essentially a flat roof, and with a tiny entrance on the west side of its northern end. At its southern end is a covered niche with an arch concealing a second small entry, also arched, leading to a basement space below ground that runs the full length of the building. This is at or below the level of the water of the lake. The entry is blocked with stones, so a detailed inspection is impossible without the co-operation of the local monks, which they denied me when I asked. These same monks claim the building had once been used as a prison.

One of the museum's prized artefacts is this large painted cross. At its base (detail) are rendered a *kwer'ata re'esu* image of Christ's head, and a winged angel's head – both images, as explained in the text, of likely Portuguese provenance (see commentary, The *Kwer'ata Re'esu*, page 177).

If that was indeed its former use, one can only imagine a scant number of prisoners at any one time. The place is small, its exterior dimensions about eleven metres in length, three metres wide and no more than three metres high. It is constructed of mortared stone, all of it rather crude except for the care taken with the arches at the southern end.

Portuguese or not? It is almost impossible to tell without scientific analysis of the structure's mortar. Nothing about the overall design of the little place gives one much of a clue, except for those two arches at the southern end. They could, indeed, be of early Portuguese origin. The island's proximity to Bahir Dar, and the presence there of the Páez house and the old Jesuit walls of Shimbet Mikael, would tend to lend some sort of context to the assumption. The matter needs to be verified more thoroughly; there is not enough visual data to be able to offer much more than a fairly educated guess – other than the obvious fact that islands are generally good places to build prisons.

Above: Fasiladas' bronze church bell at Kebran Gabriel, XVII century

The larger of the two islands, Kebran Gabriel, is the more interesting from the perspective of this study, for the church museum, located just to the north of the church itself, is certainly of Portuguese origin, and is acknowledged by the local monks as having been ordered built by Emperor Fasiladas. It is a small building, the ground floor being the only part of it that serves as a museum housing various church artefacts such as crosses, crowns, religious paraphernalia, and numerous ancient sacred texts. The building itself is of architectural note because of its tell-tale stonework. The overall effect, unfortunately, has been severely crimped by the installation of a tin roof shelter held aloft by unsightly steel pillars that destroy a measure of the aesthetic charm the place would otherwise have.

The peninsula of Zege, northwest of Bahir Dar, is popularly called Portuguese even today. It is said that many Portuguese settled there during the XVI and XVII centuries and, indeed, many of the people still living there claim to be descendents of these early settlers. Many, too, are pleased to flash the same tell-tale grey-green eyes for which the Portuguese are so well known. The peninsula's forest covering is delightfully lush, and the village itself, perched in a lakeshore cove, spreads itself into the surrounding greenery. There are several charming Orthodox churches, but none of the residential structures that smack of Portuguese contact in the manner found, for instance, in Debre Tabor, Gorgora, or Gondar. The stone walls of some of the outbuildings at the church of Ure Kidane Mehret date to the period of Emperor Fasiladas, but the church itself is of the typical round Orthodox type. It houses some of the finest art treasures in the country – mostly on fabric attached to the walls as murals, and many of them in desperate need of repair and restoration.

The stonework of one of the buildings on the grounds of the very small church of Liblibo, located by the shore of the bay just southwest of Zege, caught my interest. It was a small storage shed, Portuguese in style, its stones secured by mud rather than mortar. Whether ancient or modern was of little import; what leaped out was a form that could only have been put together by someone imbued with a deep sense of a locally acquired tradition – examples of which are to be found in many corners of these Highlands.

This stone outbuilding at Liblibo shows distinctive Portuguese style; note mud instead of mortar

The doors to the church itself were of metal and painted the most bilious shade of green, so hideous they drew immediate attention to the beautifully carved wooden bases of the doorposts of the two main doors. Clearly of great age, these carvings were of a totally foreign intricacy – and my guess would be Portuguese. At some point when Liblibo makes it onto the attention list of some restorer's interest, these footings should be carefully examined by experts.

Carved wooden base of Liblibo church doorpost

### The Lake's Grandest Monasteries

Bahir Dar is the point from which one will likely set out to visit any of the more important Lake Tana monasteries and churches. There are some forty of them on the various islands and around the shores of the lake.

Of them all the most significant, and accessible from Bahir Dar, would be the islands of Kebran Gabriel and Entos Eyesu, both a short distance in front of the city; Ure Kidane Mehret, on the peninsula of Zege, which can be reached by road, although the most convenient way to get there would be by boat; and the island monastery of Debre Maryam, very close to the outlet of the lake and only a short distance from where its waters filter over the weir into the Blue Nile. But for Debre Maryam, these sites have all been mentioned in the section above.

More distant from Bahir Dar, at least two hours by motorboat, are the monasteries of Narga Selassie, occupying its own little island on the west side of Dek (the largest of the Lake Tana islands) and Daga Estefanos, at the summit of its own small island just off the eastern shore of Dek. Straight across the lake, going east, is the ancient monastery of Tana Kirkos, considered the most senior monastery of them all.

All of these sites are especially popular as tourist destinations, and would be worth visiting for the displays of historical artefact each houses. The murals and paintings at Kebran Gabriel and Narga Selassie are spectacular, as they are also at Debre Maryam – and in all three one may examine wonderful manuscripts, paintings and ancient musical instruments. The skeletal remains of four emperors are displayed in glass coffins at Daga Estefanos, an island which prizes itself also for a very fine quality of coffee, and where the monks weave uniquely designed blankets. Tana Kirkos, where legend has it Jesus, Joseph and Mary sojourned during their flight from the Holy Land, and where the Ark of the Covenant is supposed to have been sheltered for eight hundred years after it was removed from Jerusalem (prior to being given its present home at Axum) is noted for the sacrificial altar stones that are said to be of pre-Talmudic Jewish origin, and long pre-date Christianity.

One may be sceptical or not of the stories one will hear. What is undeniable is the exceptional sense of antiquity that permeates each of these magnificent sites and *ipso facto* imbues the visitor with the certain knowledge that nothing much has changed during the centuries since they were first established.

My own principal interest was to take a look at the stones used in the building of these sites and to determine, if I could, what link there might be between them and a Portuguese methodology in their structures. To be truthful, I was not anticipating any at all. These monasteries, I thought, would have far pre-dated the influence of the Jesuits. Stories and legends about the area seemed to go far further back in time than anything concerning the Portuguese effort to convert the Orthodox to the Church of Rome, so I was prepared to by-pass them altogether as being outside the scope of this book's theme.

I was wrong. In all of them I found strong Portuguese influence. On many occasions locals would point out to me how some element of a structure was accomplished "… by Emperor Fasiladas," "… ordered by Fasiladas," or "… during the time of Fasiladas," and this, to me, was simply another way of crediting the Portuguese.

Throughout the entire region it was precisely a Portuguese influence in building that had been instituted during the time of Fasiladas. It was Fasiladas himself, a man who commanded the building of numerous structures, who was responsible for the widest distribution of the Portuguese genre. In my stonemason's mind the name "Fasiladas" is virtually synonymous with "Portuguese."

Let us turn to the other sites mentioned.

Although one could spend pleasant hours at XIII-century Debre Maryam, it was the one site of all of them where nothing caught my eye that might have spoken to me of the Portuguese; and yet I came away with the distinct feeling that, had I dug a little deeper, something would have shown itself. The whole area around the lake – and beyond – is simply too saturated with the Portuguese contributions to the local history of their epoch for this pretty site, so close to Bahir Dar, to have been so conspicuously missed. One day it shall be my pleasure to return there and spend more time – in and around the church, in and around the small community that has grown up on the little island.

Such absence was not the case, however, at Narga Selassie, Daga Estefanos or Tana Kirkos.

Landing jetty and Portuguese-style entry gate to Narga Selassie

The charming Narga Selassie is one of several monastery/churches on Dek Island. As stated above, it is actually situated on its own tiny island, but is connected to the main island by a short stone causeway so that it would be possible to walk, ride a bicycle or a mule to any other point on Dek. Approaching the place by boat, one has to circle quite far around the west side of Dek – a low, volcanic feature that has been an agricultural and fishing area for hundreds of years.

Narga Selassie dates to 1739, one hundred years after the demise of the Roman Catholic presence in the area. Yet its Portuguese provenance is very clear from the moment one approaches the dock by boat on the monastery's western side. One may call the gateway at the head of the dock "Gondarine" if one wishes to by-pass the one word that would most accurately describe its true origin, but its derivation is unquestionable. There are three of these stately gates at the site, all of them in quite excellent condition – and all of them could be replications of a thousand structures just like them in Portugal – and not a few in Ethiopia itself. The stonework of the church is masterful, some of the best I have seen in the land, clean, crisp and in every way disciplined. Although the main building sits within walls guarded by gates of such clear Portuguese design, the church itself is the traditional round thatched structure, the magnificent arches of its portico reminiscent of Defeche Kidane Mehret outside Gondar (see page 149) – yet somehow grander. The stonework here, too, is Portuguese in style – but how can all this be when the Portuguese themselves, as a matter of historical record, were ordered out of the area in 1632?

Interior gateway to Narga Selassie church compound

This conundrum recurs again and again at many sites, and the naysayers are quick to leap in, heatedly denying the influence of the Portuguese and shouting loudly for "proof" that the Portuguese were ever there and accomplished anything besides making a bloody nuisance of themselves and getting kicked out of the country in the middle of the XVII century.

"It's Ethiopian!" insist the frenetic ultra-nationalists.

Well, yes. Maybe. But they were Ethiopians who had learned the skills of their trade from master Portuguese craftsmen. This much is writ in stone – and at Narga Selassie the monks themselves will tell you that many of the stones come from the Portuguese quarry at Selassie Gemb (Washa) on the north shore of the lake, near Maryam Gemb [see Selassie Gemb (Washa), page 161].

The argument is made at several points throughout this work that the Portuguese left their seed in these Highlands, that those of them who came there – and they came in great numbers – mixed with the local population and within a generation had become well-blended in. Indeed, they became Ethiopians. These people were particularly numerous in the Gondar, Lake Tana and Gojjam districts. The strongest cultural element the Portuguese left behind, apart from their bloodline, was their instinctive knowledge of a very identifiable strain of stonework – a strain that exists to this very day. Identifying it, as I said, is the *raison d'être* of this book.

Squinch - method of corner corbelling to allow a round *cupola* to be set on squared walls. This ancient classical system is particularly popular in Portuguese structures.

I found in the magnificent paintings on the walls at Narga Selassie great numbers of winged-head angels of the type found on the famous ceiling at Debre Birhan Selassie in Gondar. I could not help but take note of how they appear to be little more than Ethiopian-ized renderings of the very Portuguese relief carving at Mertule Maryam, a photo of which may be found on page 83. To me this is a clear case of religio-cultural transposition, much as may be found, for instance, in the various depictions of the *kwer'ata re'esu*. Throughout Christian history useful iconic figures and symbols have crossed distances and cultural barriers with exceptional ease and rapidity.

Above, left, are the winged-head angels surrounding the holy figure in the centre of this mural at Narga Selassie. Compare these with the ceiling angels at Debre Birhan Selassie, Gondar, right, and the small winged-head angel of the museum cross at Kebran Gabriel, page 96. See also the Mertule Maryam relief depicted on page 83.

The entire island of Daga Estefanos, unfortunately, is closed to women. Only a stone's throw from the eastern shore of the much larger island of Dek, Daga Estefanos is a high sugarloaf that is hazily visible on the horizon from Bahir Dar far to its south. Famed for its prized variety of coffee as well as the woven blankets made and sold by the monks, the monastery was founded in the XII century, the church substantially rebuilt in the XIX century. From water level to the church at the summit of the island is a steep forty-five minute hike; its museum, a clear example of stonework in the Portuguese style, makes a useful comparison with the museums at Kebran Gabriel and Tana Kirkos. Daga Estefanos is famous for housing the earthly remains of four of the nation's emperors – Fasiladas among them. It was here that the Ark of the Covenant was reportedly hidden during the time of the Muslim invasions of Ahmad Grag'n in the XVI century – the onslaught that triggered the landing of the Portuguese army under Cristóvão da Gama in 1541.

The remains of Emperor Fasiladas

The façade of the museum building, Daga Estefanos

Aba Waldehana was the patient and kindly monk who spent time showing me the various artefacts stored in the museum at Daga Estefanos, and he expressed a genuine interest in what I had to say about the stonework of the building we were in. Stepping outside, we took a closer look at the structure, and then moved across to the monastery gate.

As I talked about the stones and how they were put together, I noticed that he was looking at them from a distance of little more than four or five inches. Clearly he was having difficulty with his sight, and I realized that when he had earlier shown me the face pages of the ancient volumes he had taken down from the museum shelves, he seemed to know each more by its size and texture than by reading from it. It had occurred to me that perhaps he did not know how to read, but I had been puzzled because he seemed to know the content of the texts so well.

As though divining my thoughts, he asked:

"Do you think you could buy me some reading glasses and give them to me next time you come here?"

"I would do that happily," I told him, "but I'm not sure when or whether I will ever be coming back … Besides, I don't know what you would require in the way of a prescription …"

I had a pair of fairly strong pharmacy readers on a string about my neck that had served me well for several years, so I took them off and asked him to try them out.

He put them on carefully and squinted, then he opened the text that he was holding in his hand and glanced down at it.

His head jerked back on his shoulders in surprise, radiant joy on his face as he focused on the printed pages. It was a revelation – manifestly many a year since he had seen the written word in such clarity.

I had an auxiliary pair of peepers back in Bahir Dar, so was happy to leave these with him – expressing the wish that he would now continue to enjoy his reading of the sacred texts as well as the beauty of the stones that would be surrounding him for the rest of his life.

Aba Waldehana

Tana Kirkos church – note the odd-sized larger cut stones of the earlier church building

Tana Kirkos, located on the eastern side of the lake, used to be an island. Owing to a fall in the water level it is now a peninsula connected to the main shoreline by a low lying rock strip of papyrus, reeds and bushes.

High above the waters on a craggy ledge, steeped in mystery and legend, the ancient monastery itself was supposedly a holy place long before the coming of Christianity. It is here that the Ark of the Covenant is reputed to have been housed for some eight hundred years prior to its removal to Axum by King Esana in the IV century. It was brought back to the lake to be sheltered briefly at Daga Estefanos during the invasions of Ahmad Grag'n, XVI century.

A brief digression at this point from my principal mission:

I think one can become a little blasé about antiquity in a land as saturated by the mystique of religiosity as is this northwestern corner of Ethiopia. One writer referred to the "vaudeville sanctity" of guides and churchmen encountered in this general geographical area when they manage to pin back the ears of questing visitors, and hold forth on the great mysteries and historic artefact of Ethiopian churches. Dodging the spiel, too often a well-rehearsed patter accompanied by an outstretched hand that seems to be counting the coins in your pocket before you have had a chance to pull them out, there can be no denying that some of these sites are very old indeed. As far as that goes, Tana Kirkos is certainly the venerable old man of Lake Tana.

In the upper echelons of the Amhara region's tourist interests, controls appear to be very slack – and this may, indeed, be a problem throughout the country. There seems to be a disconnect between those who actually control these sites on the ground – the church, the monks – and the government agencies whose interest it is to harness the tourist industry for the benefit of both the visitors (the supply of plentiful, accurate and consistent information; consistent and well-regulated pricing) and, by extension, the resulting economic benefit that accrues to the country as a whole. In so many instances one encounters a sort of wild west freewheeling logic that has taken control over Ethiopia's historic sites: who can spin the whackiest story? Who can get away with charging the most outrageous price to listen to it?

To be sure, the monks at Tana Kirkos see themselves as being in an ideal position to grab the unsuspecting visitor by his short hair. Their site is located so distant from modern civilization that a visitor has to make a major and costly effort to get there. By the time he arrives, having travelled two and a half or three hours by boat, a tourist is hardly likely to refuse payment for entry to the monastery, choosing instead to return forthwith to Bahir Dar. Yet though the going rate for entry to all churches and monasteries on and around Lake Tana is thirty birr; at Tana Kirkos it was two hundred birr. For that price there was no available literature, no guide, and no particular interest on the part of anyone – monk or lay worker – to accommodate even modest enquiry.

Back to the stonework theme:

On the occasion of my own visit to Tana Kirkos I was less interested in its great antiquity than in seeking out what signs there might have been, if any, demonstrating a link with Portugal's presence in these parts in the XV, XVI and XVII centuries. I had come to look at stones stacked into walls, not the supposedly pre-Talmudic Jewish sacrificial stones the monks had piled in cavalier and higgledy-piggledy fashion within the confines of a most un-ceremonial tin outhouse.

There were indeed several buildings that showed a strong Portuguese influence – particularly the one described as a museum.

Pre-Talmudic Jewish sacrificial stones at Tana Kirkos

By far the most intriguing from my perspective, however, was the church itself. It was a simple rectangular stone structure surrounded by a portico, the corrugated iron roof of which was supported by rough-cut and unadorned wooden pillars. The stonework appeared as patchwork, jarring on the aesthetic senses, but an interesting explanation of its provenance filtered to the surface as the priest-cum-guide outlined a cursory history – of which he himself was anything but certain.

There had been, he admitted, a small stone-built church on the same site since earliest times. It was constructed of reddish-brown sandstone, the dressed facings of which formed a flat exterior surface. Its condition had deteriorated over the years, so it had been replaced in the mid-XVII century ("in the time of Fasiladas") with the present rather larger structure – incorporating the same stones that had been used in the initial church. The masons who had built the place used their essentially Portuguese-style

Typical Portuguese-style corner stonework, Tana Kirkos

Talking with monks outside the Tana Kirkos museum building

know-how, manifested by the use of smaller stones surrounding the larger dressed stones. The result is unique in appearance, not especially pleasing, but showing a combination of drystone and mud mortar technique that is unmistakeable.

I saw nothing held together by cement mortar at Tana Kirkos; all walls were either drystone, or else using a mud mortar mixed with straw. People are inclined to think that a drystone wall is unstable. That is not necessarily so. The truth is that when they are well put together they can last for hundreds of years. Mud mortar, also, can last a tremendously long time. It will tend to wash away if exposed to wind and weather, but the secret here is to be sure the wall is well roofed, well protected. Mixing the mud with straw adds enormously to overall strength.

**Gemb Kidane Mehret and Collala**

This site lies to the south of Bahir Dar on the Mota road, some ten kilometres beyond the village of Debre Mai, thus placing it northwest of Mertule Maryam, and about equidistant between that important site and Bahir Dar.

Time and residents in the locale have virtually completed the destruction of Gemb Kidane Mehret. One wall is left standing atop a hill in the middle of a ploughed field. The rest is rubble. A little way off, across the road, is the traditional Orthodox church of Yewezazert, and near here are the remains of what used to be a Roman Catholic church. Portions of its walls, and what was once a staircase, are all that are left now.

Gemb Kidane Mehret itself is believed to have been erected as a palace by Ras Sela Cristos, the brother of Emperor Sussenyos, who converted and became a fervent Roman Catholic. The palace was taken over as a Jesuit residence in the last years of Sussenyos' reign.

A diligent archaeological investigation would doubtless reveal much more than is currently visible, but one can tell a certain amount just by observation of the site's position. It commands the top of a steep hill on the southwest of the current road and about three hundred metres from it. Though one can see virtually nothing of the one remaining wall from the road, from the top of the hill one obtains spectacular views in all directions. Clearly the position was chosen because of this defensive feature; Sela Cristos' unwavering beliefs would have made him many enemies.

**Yibaba**

"Jesuit residence" in the case of Yibaba, as in others, is a euphemism. Vastly outnumbered in this land by followers of the Ethiopian Orthodox faith, the Jesuits and their converts to Roman Catholicism were largely unpopular among their local and close neighbours, and were obliged to sequester themselves in defensive positions behind high walls. Yibaba, like most other Jesuit sites, is just such a place.

It is located some six or seven kilometres to the north of the village of Debre Mai, and about two kilometres across agricultural lands to the east of the Mota road.

It comprises a more-or-less circular wall some two hundred and fifty to three hundred metres in diameter, and in the areas where it remains intact it is possible to see that this wall stood some three metres tall. An eight metre high lookout tower, or *atalaia*, still stands on the eastern side of the compound, and one can see the ring foundations of at least another three presumably similar towers around the southern rim of the wall. A three-arched gate within this southern wall is also still standing.

At one time the interior of this large space had contained other buildings and structures, though little remains today except quantities of the stones of which these had been made. It is within this section of the compound that an archaeologist would be most richly rewarded. Clear spaces within the area would have served as a fruit and vegetable garden.

The *atalaia* stands like a vertical and hollow conical tube. Towers like it can be seen at numerous other sites, most of them physically connected to standing structures, such as at Guzara to the northeast of Lake Tana. It is possible to see how wooden interior stairs and platforms were fitted. Most of this woodwork, though not all, has long since rotted away. From the top of this *atalaia*, and from the others when they were standing, one would have been able to obtain broad vistas in every direction.

Compare the Yibaba *atalaia*, left, with the similar structure at Moura, southern Portugal, right

## Gemb Giorghis and Gemb Maryam

From the centre of Debre Mai one heads almost due west overland to reach the ruins of Gemb Giorghis some five kilometres distant; on another nearby hilltop are the ruins of Gemb Maryam, a Roman Catholic church built by Portuguese Jesuits in about 1625.

In area, the circle defined by the walls of Gemb Giorghis is considerably greater than at Yibaba, perhaps three hundred and fifty to four hundred metres in diameter. Many of the walls and towers remain standing and at their full height of three metres, in some cases more. A great deal of the original crenellation is still in tact. The keep in the centre of the compound, badly overgrown by brambles when I first visited, had crumbled so extensively that it was barely recognizable. Like other Jesuit "residences," Gemb Giorghis occupies a prime defensive position, and there is enough of it intact that one may see very clearly how these places not only resembled forts, but were just that in fact. Euphemism indeed suits more readily those with something to obscure and the Jesuit missionaries, who would have been the first to beg that their message was truer than that espoused by the Ethiopian Orthodox Church, would almost certainly have preferred to talk of their "residence." At the same time they no doubt felt far more comfortable to lodge themselves behind the sturdy walls of a fort.

Gemb Giorghis *atalaia*

Underground amid the central complex of buildings there is a cistern. In parts its roof has collapsed, but it is possible to see how it was built in three corridors, or chambers, each separated from the others by a series of columns and arches. Vaulted ceilings run the full length of each chamber, perhaps fifteen metres in length. The possible collapse of underground masonry is apt to give one pause, but somehow did not bring about the same level of concern as the possibility that some wild animal might have established its lair in a dark corner of the place.

"No lions hiding in here?" I asked, nervous but attempting humour as I inched into the blackness below.

A group of fifteen or twenty children had followed me, anxious to exhibit their limited English language and thereby maybe gain a coin or two in appreciation. I had asked the question because they seemed somehow anxious that I enter first. The biggest boy, who had assumed the responsibility of guide because he proved to be the ablest at communication, pushed past me bravely. The humour of his response stroked my sense of whimsy.

Bats crowd the ceiling of the Gemb Giorghis cistern, note vaulted structure

"Only little lions," he said. "But they must sing before their dinner."

As it turned out, there were indeed wild animals in the cistern: colonies of bats. As I crept through the place in almost total darkness I could feel their slip streams, the beat of their wings fanning my face and hair as they fluttered nervously about my head. The flash of my camera illuminated hundreds of the critters.

It is extremely difficult to arrive at the location of Gemb Giorghis. A good four-wheel-drive vehicle was essential on my first excursion there, but its abilities were rigorously tested. Deep stream gullies traversed the area between the village and the site, and crossing them means driving several kilometres out of one's way. While the site itself is perhaps five kilometres west of Debre Mai, on my first visit I had covered many kilometres before even coming within sight of it; and even then it was necessary to walk. About two kilometres from the site, at the base of a long convex hill, there was a small river. Not even a four-wheel-drive vehicle was of any use at this point, so from here we had to go on foot. In the wet season this route to the site would be almost unthinkable, whether by foot or by car. With even the slightest rainfall the entire area turns to a thick gumbo not unlike molasses.

I spent well over an hour inspecting these ruins, the children following me about as though I was the Pied Piper of Hamelin. In several areas the ground was heaved up into overgrown hummocks. Some of these were quite high, structures that over the years had been so thoroughly covered by the growth of brambles that any view of them was now completely blocked. Others were evidently no more than piles of rubble from buildings that had collapsed.

In the months before the start of the big rains in 2008 I was fortunate enough to encounter a group of German NGO's who wanted to visit the site, and who asked me to take them there.

We plotted our route there a little more carefully than I had done the first time. Rather than attempt an overland hike from the centre of Debre Mai, we drove south of the village and out a country track leading in a more or less southwesterly direction. From this point we could see the site in the distance. We had to hike about seven and a half kilometres, but there was a track that led to the small village at the foot of Gemb Giorghis and it seemed a great deal easier to walk that way than to struggle with the heavily contoured terrain I had met on my first excursion.

To our great delight, Gemb Giorghis had been tidied up considerably. All the extant ruins were now visible, all of them sufficiently cleared of brambles that we could move in really close and examine structure in detail. We spent several hours there, also visiting the ruins of St. Mary's church – which, unfortunately, had not yet been cleared of brambles and undergrowth. The stonework, especially with reference to the interior red stone arch separating the nave from the apse, was carefully wrought in Romanesque manner, a beautiful example of simple Portuguese under-statement.

Distinctive Jesuit arch separates nave and choir of St. Mary's Roman Catholic church, a few hundred yards outside the walls of Gemb Giorghis. Compare this with the choir/nave dividing arch at Denqaz basilica, page 145.

Gemb Giorghis is an important site. In the area relatively close to Bahir Dar there is no other site of its era that presents as much of itself, and about which a lay visitor would be able to glean so much detail. More than any other site in the immediate vicinity, it is this one that deserves attention and conservation. It would not take a government entity a great deal of money or effort to build a decent road out to the place, perhaps to fence it off, maintain guards and charge a modest entry. Doing this could be made to provide revenue for tourism, plus having the added attraction of providing employment for people in the area.

**Shimbet Mikael**

This site is within the city of Bahir Dar itself. There are several residential buildings in the city that are clearly old Portuguese style farmhouses dating from long before any form of municipal incorporation. The land hereabouts would have been an obvious place for any newcomer to choose to settle. It is level and extremely fertile for all manner of farming, and the proximity of the lake with its fishing and irrigation possibilities would simply have enhanced its prospects. Unfortunately it is also a malarial zone.

The location of the ruins of Shimbet Mikael would seem to bear out the farming and fishing thesis. In addition to the monastery, the church would have served a small local community. There is not much left of the site itself except a few broken walls, but the place is superbly nestled near the lake. Although there is no hill on which to locate a residence for defensive purposes, there is nonetheless the very finest defence. At this particular point on the west side of the town Lake Tana forms itself around

Trees destroy walls, but in this case the roots are holding up the last of Shimbet Mikael's walls; almost all of the original stones went towards the construction of a new church at this site. Someone lives under the blue plastic sheet.

a small low-lying peninsula not to be mistaken for Zege, which is the more prominent peninsula a little further to the north. With their backs to the lake, the residents had built a stone wall right across the neck of the point, locating their centre between the wall and the water.

This is an urban area now and destruction of the ancient walls that once stood there is, lamentably, fairly complete. A road to the Orthodox church of St. Mikael has been punched through, houses have been built, ancient walls torn down to use the stones in newer construction. An adjacent modern hotel complex is virtually complete, and the natural growth of the city has ensured that the old appearance of the locale has been altered beyond recognition. Bahir Dar is fast growing, and lakefront properties close to the city centre are at a premium. An isolated collection of old rocks, even if it does resemble a wall, is not about to withstand the momentum of development.

My guide in this instance was Shimelash Bequele, a longtime resident of Bahir Dar who had always taken great interest in his community over the years, and had attempted to compile its history. He walked and taxied me about the town, talking all the while and offering morsels of information, some trivial, some profound, all of it the sort of detail that seldom finds its way into guidebooks. A visit to the ancient walls of Shimbet Mikael proved an opportunity for Shimelash to call on an old friend, the priest of the nearby modern Orthodox church. This venerable elder proudly escorted the two of us through the outer precincts of the circular structure, pointing out the scores of examples of religious paintings adorning the exterior of the *mak'das*, the Holy of Holies. The closed-off centre portion of the church, which only a priest may enter, held the *tabot*, or sacred stones.

Every Orthodox church has these *tabot*, or *tabotat*, customarily two large flat stones or blocks of wood which are representative of the tablets brought down from Mount Sinai by Moses on which were inscribed the Ten Commandments. Great ceremony surrounds the *tabot*, for the Ethiopian Orthodox Church considers that a church building without it is not consecrated. One of the basic tenets of the

Ethiopian Orthodox Church is the unshakable belief that the actual stones of Moses are contained in the original Ark of the Covenant, and that this is housed in the Holy Church of Saint Mary of Zion at Axum.

At various times during my journeys through the Highlands there had been ample opportunity to examine religious paintings and icons. At the Institute of Ethiopian Studies of Addis Ababa University, I had had the great privilege of meeting Dr. Stanislaw Chojnacki, perhaps the world's most knowledgeable scholar in this field. This current work's thrust hardly permits a detailed study of Ethiopian religious art, but it is worth mentioning that, in the broadest of all possible terms, art forms developed in these Christian Highlands occupy a unique and colourful niche within the spectrum of Orthodox ornament. As has been the case with Dr. Chojnacki, one could spend a lifetime examining the multitude of intricate manifestations of Ethiopian religious art. Confining myself to the study of Portuguese style architectural vestige was, in a way, sadly limiting in a country so richly and bountifully endowed with indigenous artwork, religious or otherwise. I have rarely entered a land where sheer colour dominated so forcefully. On every side there was ample opportunity to compare ancient works with their modern counterparts, and the contemporary church of Shimbet Mikael provided a good example of this. Invariably, the distinct impression left behind was that even though artistic expression had modernized, it had done so as the consequence of a continuum in Ethiopian religious and secular life. It was not hard to imagine how those who had walked these Highlands in the XVI and XVII centuries must have been just as resoundingly bombarded by the outstanding colours of landscape and artefact as I was at the beginning of the XXI century. Considering how much artwork was destroyed during the Muslim invasions shortly after Portugal entered into its association with the empire of Prester John, perhaps those earliest travellers enjoyed even more colour. Certainly the vision of the religious painters of so many centuries past, both their manner of seeing and their record, established a strong visual tradition, for it has been rejuvenated and passed on by every generation of artists that has followed.

It was my great pleasure to visit Bahir Dar many times between January, 1996, and the publication of this second edition of my recollections and commentary. Every time I would drop in on my dear friend Shimelash Bequele and we would laugh, go for a meal, compare notes and news, and discuss his projected book on the history of Bahir Dar. He was a kindly and decent gentleman, knowledgeable and anxious to see his city grow into the regional capital it has in fact become.

His death in June, 2008, at the age of eighty-two was a sad occasion. I had spent the previous Christmas with him and his family, and in the months just before his passing I saw him several times both in his home and at Bahir Dar University where he was trying to gain the interest of the senior academics of the History Department in an effort to see his work into print. The pages of his manuscript were laboriously written out by hand in Amharic, but no one at the university was prepared to offer more than a kindly word. The academics would smile and bow to him solicitously, even tell him how important was his work. But then, with transparent gestures and promises of their attention they would turn him away, the backs of their hands hiding the smiles the arrogant reserve for those they consider their inferiors.

The work needed to be on the computer, and clearly Shimelash was a generation or two handicapped in that department. Commentary as he walked away was unkind – but months later these same people came to the old man's funeral. It was a huge event, and a strong lesson for me as to the love that many, many people felt for this man, and the hypocrisy of those who might better have helped him. Everyone of stature in Bahir Dar was present. To have been absent might have been noticed.

## Residential Structures

In the very centre of the town of Bahir Dar is a stone house that would seem to be the mirror image of a typical farmhouse from Portugal's Trás-os-Montes or Minho provinces; in every way, that is, except for the standard corrugated iron roofing.

"Now if I had to point to a typical Portuguese house, *that* would be it!" I exclaimed.

"Ha! Ha!" Shimelash had laughed. "That's not Portuguese ... I remember that house being built! It couldn't be more than forty or fifty years old."

That sort of comment can be deflating, but it was not the first time I had come across something of the kind. Either the house really was relatively new, but had been built in the Portuguese manner, or else this was a case of the very denial I had come to see as a not uncommon occurrence. There are many who would dearly love to use this twist as a means to negate the very idea of a Portuguese presence, or their construction know-how. Some of the houses in the Bahir Dar area are genuinely very old indeed. It is also quite possible that many of them would come under the same category as had this one. It can be difficult to tell the difference without detailed examination. There were several examples. I saw one, a house made of stone and very typically "Portuguese," that was in a state of terrible disrepair, and this precisely because in place of mortar to bind the stones the builder had used mud – and in many places it had washed away. But then mud was very typical in Portugal, also. All over the country, from ancient times, it was used as a method of locking together the stones of a building when there was no mortar to be had. Many houses might fit into this category in Bahir Dar, Debre Tabor, Gondar and elsewhere. Whether or not these are genuinely old houses one cannot presently be in a position to know for sure.

Portuguese style house in Bahir Dar

But the matter of style is unquestionable.

This does, interestingly enough, lead right back to a subject we examined very briefly earlier: the principle of mimesis. It is a term that indicates copying, or mimicry, and it is clearly this that has occurred in the regions of the Highlands through which the Portuguese travelled and in which they settled. In no other art form is this principle of mimesis so apparent as it is in the field of architecture, particularly residential architecture, though more modern industrial design is rampant with it.

Basically, in considering the residential architectural forms in this survey, one should consider this: a man may not be an expert, but he will build his own house in much the same way as his father built his house. And why? Something has been acquired in his cultural make-up, his sense of proportion and

This sketch of the entrance to a very old peasant house was made in a northern Portuguese village; compare it with the photograph from Bahir Dar on the previous page.

design. He may not recall precisely why things must be so, but they are so because they have always been so – and that is the way it is done. A man who is not an innovator tends to remember as a child remembers, only that "it works." People who just need a roof over their heads tend to build the simplest way possible, and to stick to tried methods and understandable decoration:

"I'm building my house like that... because my father built his house like that... and his father before him built his house like that..."

With this form of almost unconscious thinking, one is apt to forget the "why" when certain features are built the way they are. It gets done that special way simply because it is the method best known and understood. Unconscious rather than conscious design: mimesis. It is a recognized phenomenon throughout the entire field of design: the quite inadvertent imitation of form. As soon as a designer is aware of it he might deliberately choose to avoid it, but mimesis certainly exists within the community of skilled but (possibly) unpolished artisans, and particularly in the realm of residential building.

It is easy to see, and logical to believe, that Highland houses were built by Portuguese builders in the way they knew best. Later they taught their skills to their Ethiopian sons, who in turn taught the same skills to their sons, and so on down the generations. Elsewhere in this survey there are other small, seemingly insignificant examples, but in every case, as the expression goes, they are dead giveaways. This is why it is possible to say that in the context of the building and vestige being considered here, "Gondarine" and "Portuguese," in fundamental detail, are one and the same thing. Pedants may insist on pointing out variations with an Ah-ha! element of epiphany, but what I believe they are detailing are little more than the intricate details of an individual *pedreiro*'s personal skills – and his possible success at teaching some of those skills to the people working with him.

Simple but typical trick of Portuguese *pedreiros* when covering an expanse of wood with *reboco*, a plaster or mortar mix: to use bent nails, "*unhas*" – literally fingernails, on the surface of the wood the better to grip the slurry; this example was photographed in Bahir Dar

**Debre Tabor**

The comments on residential buildings included in the previous sections apply equally to Bahir Dar, Debre Tabor, Gondar, and Gorgora, for basic designs have not altered greatly between one town and another. Debre Tabor itself was an area known to have been settled extensively by Portuguese and others coming into the Highlands. In the town centre, as in Bahir Dar, there are numbers of very typical Portuguese style houses.

The journey up to Debre Tabor is little short of spectacular. At first the road snakes along the old lake floor, wide expanses to the left, rising ground to the right. Then one starts climbing and can look back from the curves onto broad vistas far below where the land disappears into distant heat haze before it tumbles over the shoreline of Lake Tana. In front the view is also possibly obscured, but this by clouds and swirling mountain mists. At lunchtime on the particular day in May when I went there with a number of companions, the sky suddenly darkened as though a curtain had been pulled across it, and a Doomsday thunder cracked and rumbled through the high valleys and crevices of the mountains. Then rain pelted down as people ran for the shelter of their houses. Market vendors who had earlier set up at the sides of the dusty main road were forced to bundle their wares into sacks and wrappings, throw them under parked wagons for protection, or carry them quickly to whatever refuge they could find beyond the doorways of cafés and stores. The dust of the street turned to thick mud in an instant.

Then just as suddenly as Heaven had turned on the taps, now it started hurtling down on our heads hailstones as big as children's marbles. So fast and furious did they come at us that, taking shelter in our jeep, we were unable to see as far as the front of the vehicle, nor to hear one another's comments above the colossal racket of the stones drumming on our metal roof. Our driver, coming from the steam heat zones more usual around Lake Tana, was totally unused to this sort of assault by Mother Nature. He crossed himself several times and mumbled urgent prayers, his hands fluttering nervously between his forehead and his lips, where he bestowed abundant kisses to his fingertips. He was fearful, he said, all the while expecting that the jeep's windshield was about to be smashed to smithereens, and that we would all be encased in a smothering mountain of preservative ice balls. In the meantime the temperature had dropped appreciably, and the sharp chill was little alleviated by our huddling together inside the vehicle.

I am generally only passingly surprised or bothered by the onslaughts of nature's capricious weather patterns, but in this instance the sheer rapidity of it was startling. On the surface this would appear to have little to do with architectural vestige, except that perhaps it does in a way. Stone buildings exposed to such extremes tend to crumble rather faster than their counterparts at lower levels, a fact that appeared to be amply borne out by the state of the Jesuit ruins at nearby Aringo.

## Aringo

As with so many journeys in the Highlands, an outing to Aringo is not to be undertaken lightly. It is a most difficult location to arrive at, and the condition of the road leading into it is appalling. When I went, there was no question of accomplishing the journey in anything but a four-wheel drive vehicle, and then at the pace of a slug. The road had not been surfaced, though the "aggregate" had been laid in place. Some of the rock boulders of this were the size of our car wheels.

The present village is only about ten kilometres from Debre Tabor, but it took us a tortuous hour to get there from the town. It is perched on a wide high shelf, and this lies on the western side and slightly to the north of the same mountain on which Debre Tabor is located. Debre Tabor itself has grown up in a saddle at the top of this very prominent mountain. From here the road to Aringo descends behind and to the west, and eventually comes out onto a slightly lower plateau. There is a sense of height at this point, but the sheer drama of it is concealed at first. The shelf's edge is overgrown by a eucalyptus and cane forest, so one is not aware of height until one has pushed through the bush and looked over the edge. The mountain falls away precipitously and far below, lying between the mountain and Lake Tana, is the flatland of the old lakebed. One would need a very wide-angle lens to do photographic justice to such a landscape.

As it is today, the modern village of Aringo has been built around and among a group of old Jesuit buildings. Unfortunately many of the old walls of the place have been dismantled in order to build the newer houses. It is a typical problem, and a harsh mountain climate has exacerbated the overall destruction of the historic site. Since the two villages intertwine the way they do, it is extremely difficult to determine what was what of the older place. The walls are about three metres high; one of them has an angled ramp, possibly once a stairway; in another location there is the half-buried arch of a doorway and some windows. Gigantic eucalyptus trees grow between and through the ruined walls, further assisting in destruction. Without trained archaeologists working very diligently, it is going to be extremely difficult to determine the precise layout of the older place, even though elements of the typical Jesuit defensive ring structure are clearly visible.

The most complete structure of the entire compound, known locally as Af-Mekurabia, measures in the region of nine and a half by three metres, and is about two metres high. Its original use has always been considered something of a mystery. It is located well apart from any of either the ancient or new structures, and is divided into three roughly equal sections. There is an entrance at the north end of the longer western wall, and interior divisions with cut-aways permit access to each of the three interior divisions. Some people have postulated that it was used as a silo. Knowing how hogs are housed in the southern regions of Portugal, an educated guess would be that the place had once been used as a pigpen. The dimensions and style are almost identical. The consumption of pork

PART TWO: THE STONES

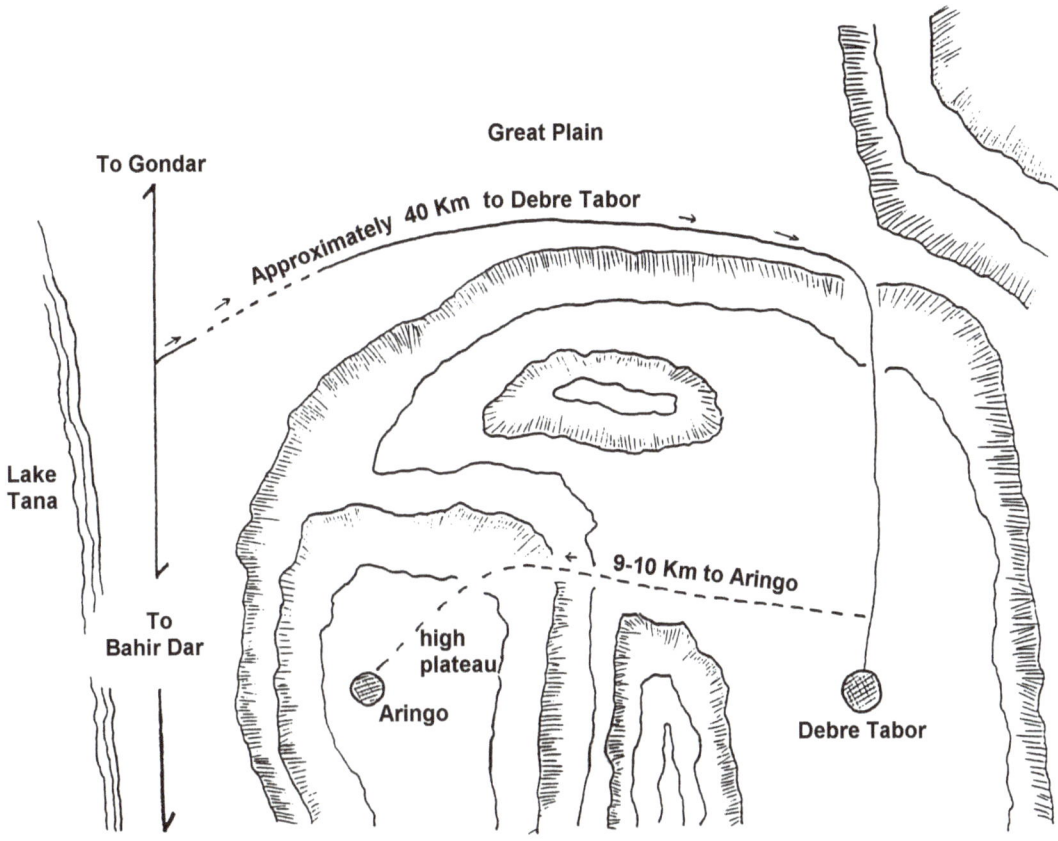

Route to Aringo - not drawn to scale

is forbidden within the Ethiopian Orthodox Church, but it would have been no problem whatsoever to Portuguese Roman Catholics.

An old man and longtime resident of the area produced something he had found some years before buried in a corner of this pigpen. He had no idea what it was but thought it was made of iron and might have some value, so he had kept it. It was a large, twisted and baffling chunk of metal, and had to be turned over several times before it revealed its original shape. There was a slightly green hue to it, so a light scratching of its surface soon revealed not iron, but copper – the remains of a deep round copper bowl which, untwisted, would have measured perhaps thirty-five centimetres across, and with a flat horizontal lip of about two centimetres in width all around its top edge. The bowl's bottom, too, had once been rounded, but much of this had been worn or burnt through. It was heavy, the gauge of the metal being several millimetres thick, and one could tell that it had once been a very fine bowl

The Aringo pigpen

indeed. Now torqued and folded double, a skilled pair of hands probably could have repaired it reasonably well. My guess is that it had once been a table brazier. This is still commonly used today in all areas of Iberia. A bowl of this type is fitted into a special bracket under a communal table. A heavy tablecloth traps heat from the coals in the brazier. In this manner it is possible to keep one's legs warm while seated.

Aringo does not appear by that name in known Jesuit documents. One theory is that it is the actual location of Atqhana – a Jesuit site thought to have existed in the Begemdir district, but which has never been pinpointed. By whatever name, though, there can be little doubt that what is known today as Aringo used to be a Jesuit location of some importance.

**Guzara**

In the bright early morning, the sun rises over the jagged crests of distant mountains revealing the panorama of the lowlands lying at the northeastern edge of Lake Tana, and at the same time burnishing gold the old stones of this lovely castle ruin.

Guzara does not loudly announce itself. It stands silent, immensely proud in its eerie solitude. It can be seen from a long distance away, and the place looks to be some tiny discolouration in a huge panorama, dwarfed by the mass of the mountains that rise on all sides around it. Coming closer along the road it looks more impressive, except that it soon disappears from view as one climbs the convex slope towards it. A pause for a snatch of breath, then on, and suddenly Guzara is there again, now looming a mighty pile at the top of the crest far above the rim of an outer wall.

For a long time I stand there and look on this scene. Some people, I am sure, would see only a pile of rocks heaped into walls that are fast tumbling down. I look on it as a sculpting once finished, once polished, but now battered and aged yet still commanding, with uncounted secrets and immeasurable nobility. The rise on which the castle stands is such that one is forever forced to look up, no doubt a strong psychological impediment to ancient underlings or enemies. The high compound wall surrounding the place is broken down in many sections, but there is enough of it still surviving intact that one can measure out the area, maybe a half-kilometre in diameter.

It is generally acknowledged that Guzara was built at the behest of Emperor Sartsa-Dengal (1563-1597), probably around 1570. For this reason it is also considered the prototype for the palaces and castles that were to follow in Gondar, commencing with the one that bears the name of the emperor who commanded its structure, Fasiladas (1632-1667) after booting the Roman Catholics from the Highlands.

Guzara is a shell. Floors that were made of wood have long since rotted away and the roof, relying on a structure of wooden rafters and joists, has likewise disappeared, fallen into the interior. Even so, if one scrambles inside the base of the towers, at the castle's northeast corner for instance, one may look up and see that stout wooden beams supporting major sections of the upper wall are still solidly in place.

Each tower, tapered to carry its weight more efficiently, was once capped by an *abobada*, a brick *cupola* or dome. A chimney flue rises inside an interior wall to the full height of the structure. It appears that in addition to spacious quarters on the ground and first floors, yet another level may have extended above them. The towers rise considerably higher. There would likely have been a cistern, or some water storage area, but if so it must have collapsed or been filled in. To find it now will require concentrated search.

An eagle owl, over sixty centimetres in height, and with a wingspan of nearly two metres, makes his home inside this empty stone shell. He perches on a ledge of the rock wall in what used to be the main salon. Though the town of Emfraz is only a kilometre or so to the north, Guzara today is a silent and lonely place. The loftiness of its stones and the breathtaking landscape that stretches far below create an atmosphere in which reality and dream, if one wishes it so, are almost inseparable. Birds intuitively recognize such pleasures, which is why mere man warbles so poetically about bird havens as he does his utmost to destroy them. This is one place where many different varieties of birds are to be seen, particularly if one climbs that lovely hill in an early morning.

An impressive study of Guzara was undertaken by Fernanda Durão Ferreira, and published in Lisbon in 2003. Somewhat earlier she had travelled to Goa, and there examined the church of Priorado do Rosário, designed by architect Tomás Fernandes shortly after the turn of the XVI century, and finally erected there in 1544. Born in the Alentejo, and the architect of several churches in that Portuguese province, this was the same man who worked under the command of Afonso de Albuquerque on the defensive forts at Calicut, Goa, Cannanore, Malacca, Ormuz, and others. One of Fernandes' companions and friends during this time, and a man who participated in many of these projects with him, was Captain Francisco Nogueira who, by no small coincidence, landed with Cristóvão da Gama at Massawa in 1541. Two sons he sired while living in the Ethiopian Highlands, António and Jorge Nogueira, learned construction techniques from their father and were collaborators with Emperor Sartsa Dengal in the building of the castle at Guzara.

I am happy to report that in recent years an American group has undertaken conservation work at this delightful site, and locals have been employed to keep an eye on the place.

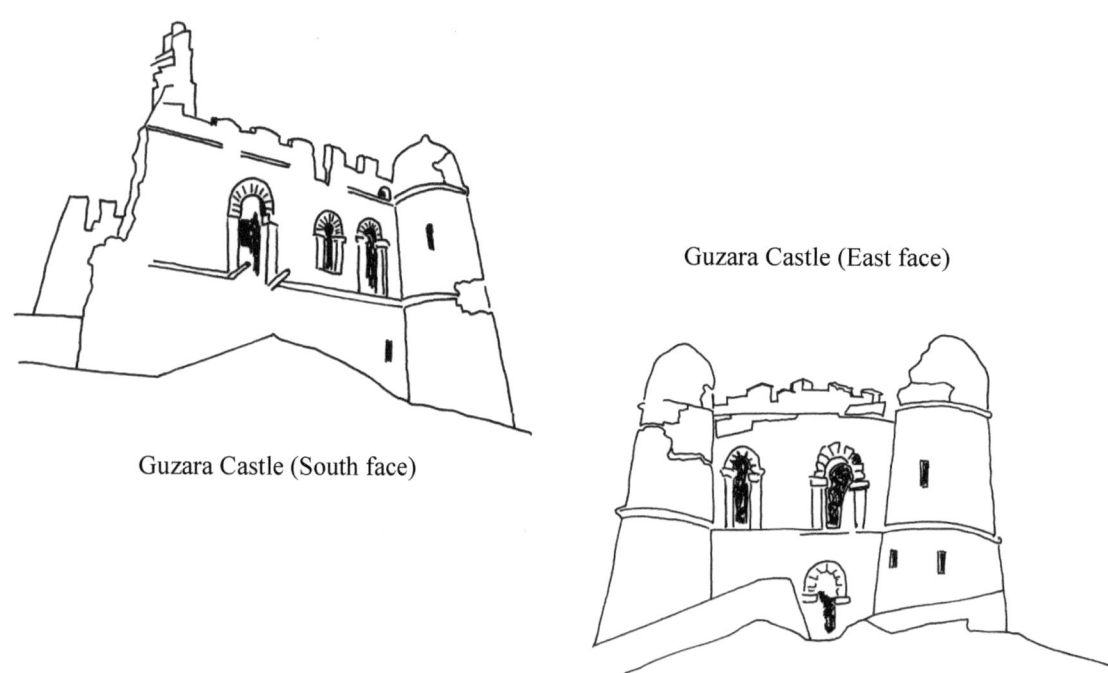

Guzara Castle (East face)

Guzara Castle (South face)

Sketches comparing essential design elements of Priorado do Rosário church in Goa, Fasiladas' Castle, and Guzara Castle. Note particularly: conical towers, domes, shapes and positions of windows and doors, and the frieze "belt" surrounding each structure

Priorado do Rosário

Fasiladas' Castle

## Bhary Gemb

This is a very strange looking cluster of buildings, chiefly because of the exceptional height and form of its two brick *abobadas*, *cupolas* or domes. This, and the fact that the church itself is of the traditionally round Orthodox style, might lead one to expect that the place has little to do with Portuguese design. One could easily walk away from it with the feeling that this is the point at which "Portuguese" and "Gondarine" diverge. I submit it is more likely to be the contrary; that here, at Bhary Gemb, is a prototype of how two ideas were melded together.

It is known that there was a church at this location in the early XVI century, and the names most associated with it are Emperor Lebna Dengal – along with that of his Portuguese advisor, Pêro da Covilhã. There is a strong possibility that it was partially or entirely reconstructed in the XVII or XVIII century. Whatever its story, Bhary Gemb is an architectural oddity.

Close inspection indeed reveals a strong Portuguese connection, chiefly in the manner of its stonework.

The *abobada* of the church itself is old, one might even say original but, like so many features at sites such as this, there is the overpowering impression that a master has taught and someone far less than expert has copied.

An *abobada* is not an easy structure to build, the tradition being one of those fading artisan techniques within southern Portugal that today is having to be consciously revived, and with considerable difficulty, owing to labour shortages and costs. At Serpa, in the Alentejo, there is a school devoted to numerous traditional and cultural construction skills and forms, and which includes in its curriculum the specialized instruction required for the building of *abobadas* and *abobadilhas*. In short, in terms of modern Portuguese construction this is a dying art.

It is likely that the *cupola* atop the church of Bhary Gemb, though, is the fairly successful result of a novice's attempt to copy the idea of a more experienced builder. It in no way follows the traditional Portuguese design or form, but it does sit atop walls that have a distinctive Portuguese technique of construction and stonework. These walls, however, follow the architectural pattern of the traditional round Orthodox church.

One might imagine, in this special instance, that a Portuguese builder of modest abilities, perhaps working with a crew of local artisan apprentices, used a good deal of his artistic license to set about the construction of a church to specifications dictated by an Orthodox patriarch. It is something of a mystery as to why the initial *cupola* should have been built in this manner. Was the constructor carried away with something like Gothic zeal, perhaps finding some spiritual expression in the manner in which the structure seems to force its way heavenwards? In structural terms the design would only be necessary in the event that the one who built it had no clear idea as to how to stop, or to set about capping off his *abobada*.

As is clearly evident, the *abobada* of the small pavilion at the rear of the church is of recent construction; it was set on its concrete lintel at the time of Emperor Haile Selassie (1930-1974). In form it appears to be an attempt to copy the structure atop the main building. Because of this its builder succeeds admirably in conveying the illusion of a conscious design running throughout the entire complex. As designers would say, "It works."

From a builder's standpoint it is not a particularly difficult accomplishment to fashion either of these two *abobadas*. Rising to the height that each does, it is a relatively uncomplicated matter of laying the bricks flat upon the supporting walls in ever-diminishing circles.

However this is not the way in which the seemingly simple, but in fact very difficult and typical low-slung *abobada*, is built in Portugal. Both a high and full-bowed arch, or a catenary arch, would be structurally much easier to build than a low, or shallow, arch; and this is especially the case when a form, or mould, is not employed. The traditional Portuguese *abobada* is built without a mould. Just as with the arch, the same basic principle would apply to the building of a shallow *cupola*.

Of particular interest from the point of view of identification are the broken arches on the outside of the church's core, or *mak'das*, and the barrel vaultings that were built between the columns of these arches. These, surely, were expertly erected by someone very familiar with Portuguese form. Which begs the question: why would the external walls and arches be so competently executed, and the crowning *cupolas* be so clearly the work of someone less capable? It would seem that the *mestre* who began the work was not the one who finished it.

Having said all that, which I consider a reasonable commentary because I am convinced of considerable Portuguese input in the body of the stonework, it should be pointed out that there are, in fact, similar high *cupolas* to be found in Yemen. Is there, therefore, a possibility that it is these that are the prototype for what one sees at Bhary Gemb; that the builder of Bhary Gemb, maybe, was more than passingly familiar with what existed just on the other side of the Red Sea?

## Teklahaimanot Church Complex at Azezo

Complex angles reveal details of outbuilding's interior structure: stone wall, left; wooden door, right, with its hinge post slotted into lintel; above are ceiling rafters and underside of upper storey floorboards

The church itself is of typical Ethiopian Orthodox style, round in its structure and, though a beautiful example of its kind, what is of particular interest in the context of this thesis are the surrounding outbuildings and walls. These demonstrate a strong Portuguese influence.

Though not as high as the *abobadas* at Bhary Gemb, one of the buildings in the Teklahaimanot church complex had an atypical rendered *cupola*.

The arched structures are very much in the Portuguese manner, and an examination of the interior of one of these buildings, a storehouse for all types of construction and gardening paraphernalia, reveals a number of typically Portuguese details - door hinges, locking systems, and support beams for the building's upper floor. Similar accoutrements and details are to be found at numerous other locations, particularly in the Gondar area.

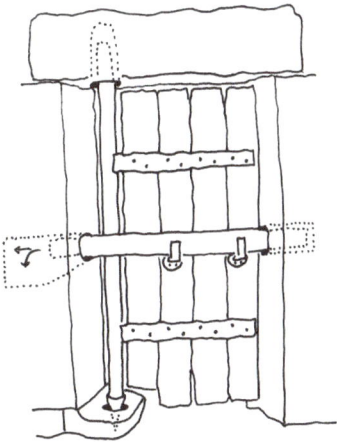

Door lock and hinge system

## The Winter Palace of Geneta Yesus at Azezo

A pile of stones and rubble is all that remains of Emperor Sussenyos' fabled Winter Palace
and its Geneta Yesus, once lovingly tended by Jesuit missionaries

Emperor Sussenyos had built his capital at Denqaz, high in the mountains to the northeast of Lake Tana. Though a beautiful place, it is possibly a little too Spartan for regal comfort during the cold and rainy seasons. For this reason he built himself a winter palace at Azezo, much lower in altitude and just to the north of the lake. Since he had converted to Roman Catholicism, the Jesuits were encouraged to accompany his sojourns there, and the result was to become a Roman Catholic compound known as Geneta Yesus, the Garden of Jesus. The emperor had heard of beautiful gardens created in Europe, and at this site were planted numerous types of vegetables, fruits and flowers.

It was here that Sussenyos was buried, as well as his successor, Emperor Fasiladas, though the remains of the both emperors were subsequently transferred to the monastery of Daga Estefanos on Lake Tana.

Fasiladas took little interest in Geneta Yesus and, following the expulsion of the Jesuits, he turned the lands over to the monks of the great monastery of Debre Libanos.

The site is just down the hill and slightly to the west of Teklahaimanot church. Although it was a popular retreat for royalty in successive reigns throughout the XVII and into the XVIII centuries, there is now, unfortunately, very little left to see. Much of the area was destroyed in the Dervish invasions of the XIX century. A team of Spanish archaeologists are currently conducting investigations on site.

## Gondar's "Chicken House"

The road between Gondar and Azezo has chopped this once fine palace into a small fraction of what it must once have been. A very typical Portuguese structure a kilometre or so south of Gondar, its ruins lying right alongside a well-travelled road, this building has now been reduced to an unplumbed and unofficial public toilet. Needless to say exploring this site was not a pleasant experience.

It is called the "chicken house" because in recent times that was precisely its use, headquarters of a small private business. "Palace," more likely, judging by the luxuriousness of its dimensions, though there is no record of it ever having been a royal residence. In its day it would have been many notches superior to local housing standards. It very much resembles one of the more substantial southern Portuguese *montes*, or farmhouses, so common in the Alentejo province. Although maybe something less than half the building is left standing, it is still possible to ascertain that its rooms were big and airy, its walls well and expensively rendered, arches and stonework of a high quality. If it was a farmhouse, as may well have been the case, then it belonged most assuredly to a group or family of considerable means.

There are finer and more important relics to be studied in the Gondar area, no doubt, but it would still be worthwhile at some point in the future for scholars to search through civic archives to see if it is possible to discover something more about this building. Being so close to town it is likely there is some fairly recent reference to its use before it became the "chicken house."

### Fasil Bridge Over the Angreb River

This site, known also as Defeche, is not far outside Gondar, but neither is it particularly easy to reach. It is in the valley to the northeast of the town, downstream of the reservoir, and is a substantial walk from the last drop-off point for any type of transport.

A first and distant view of Fasil Bridge gives the impression that it is very small indeed, perhaps barely worth the effort of getting there. The ground over which one must walk is irksomely difficult and uneven. Coming up to it one realizes that what at first appears as the bridge itself is actually only a portion of a small defensive tower or gate at one end of a much larger structure. The bridge proper is really a very impressive piece of workmanship. It is still possible to cross it, but it is not in good repair. The main stream of the Angreb has attacked the base of the structure and substantially undercut the two principal support columns. The parapets have completely disappeared, and the guard tower or gate on the north side, a most Iberian item, is now only a shell. The deck is in severely damaged condition, portions of it having been torn away at the south end. Even so, one can easily see its four-arch framework was once a major utilitarian landmark, its southern ramp leading up onto the deck once extending perhaps as much as thirty five metres. The defensive "dog-leg" bend of the bridge is clearly evident. In its entirety the intact structure would have stretched over seventy metres between entry and exit.

## Gondar's Castle Bridges

Two ancient entry bridges cross the road to the northeast of the castle complex, while on the opposite side of the compound, immediately next to the present main entrance, there are the remains of an ancient wall. Abandoned, for years of no particular use and left to deteriorate, these three features nonetheless give a clear concept of the original and excellent quality stonework of the period they survive.

## Old Quarters of Gondar and Gorgora

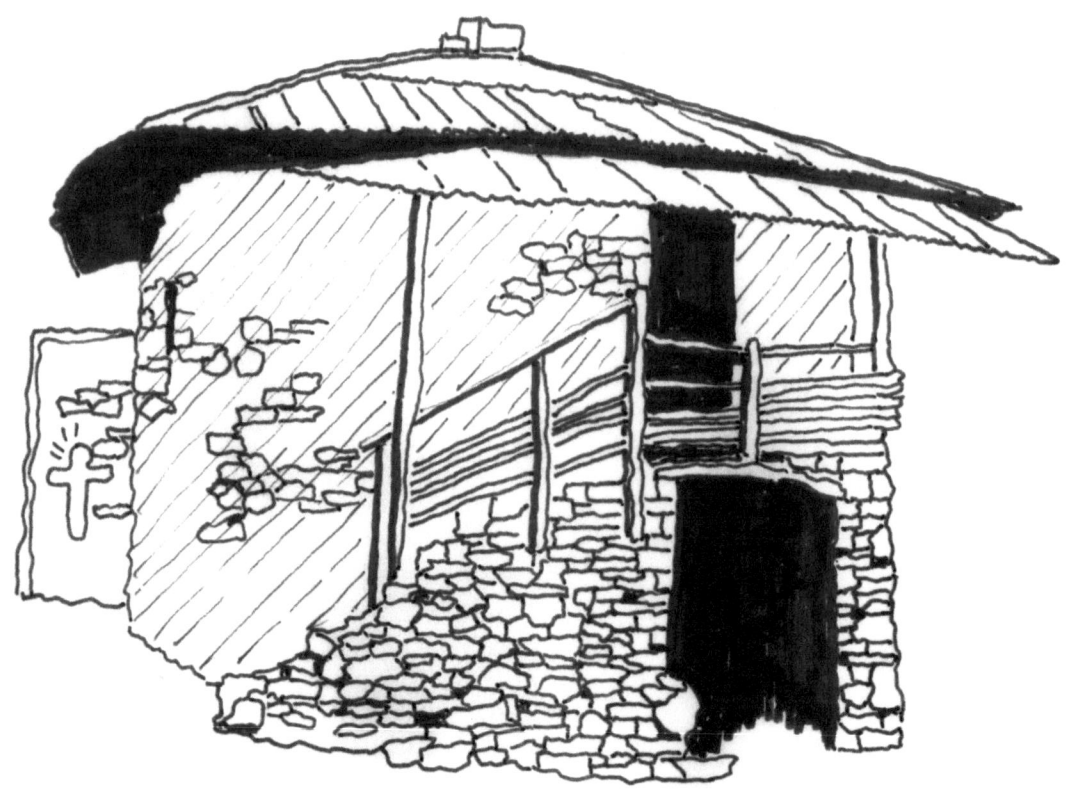

Old Gondar residence

Emperor Fasiladas is credited with building seven churches in the Gondar area, but in fact he built more than that, and not just churches. In a number of these churches, though, it is possible to find many examples of Portuguese building method; sometimes a wall, sometimes an entire building or shed.

At one house in particular, located right at the entrance to one of the churches, the occupant permitted a closer examination. It is about as exact a replica of a Portuguese rural peasant cottage as one is likely ever to see. It could be a living diorama for some sort of museum of Portuguese ethnic heritage, the only significant difference being the tin roof. Floor structure, *lajes* or flagstones, beams, walls, lintels, alcoves and niches, door hinges and locks – everything is in place, everything familiar as though the Portuguese owner had just stepped out for a moment to sample the wine at some local *tasca*.

Inside the various church compounds there is example after example of familiar stonework. What is original is patently obvious; but not all the stonework is original. Repairs have been made in numerous instances and these are particularly interesting because attempt has been made to maintain both style and method of structure. It is possible to see at a glance, however, that if the builder himself was not actually a Portuguese he was certainly influenced by the work of one. This readily calls to mind a remark made by Sir Richard Burton, early British explorer and renowned author, in reference to houses built in another part of the Horn of Africa, the Somali *mos majorum*: " …where father built there son builds, and there shall grandson build." And not just where, but how.

Once again, the principle of mimesis at its most glaringly apparent: the manner in which a man builds, and passes on to successive generations (albeit unconsciously) not only his skills as a builder but his dormant and dominant ideas as a designer. Just as unknowingly each generation learns from the ones before it – method, technique and, seeping through it all, design. The principle of mimesis would seem to be the very foundation of a folk, or ethnic architecture.

Much of Old Gondar appears to be a ramshackle town, many parts of it not unlike wandering about in one of Portugal's old run down *bairros da lata*. How much of the structure is original, and how much is not, is difficult to assess without the detailed investigation that would require one first to seek access to people's private homes and lives. During the hours one might spend walking in these areas many, many houses will be seen that are almost purely Portuguese in style. People familiar with Portuguese rural architecture will recognize these examples in an instant. Those not so familiar with this style would need to examine such things as the proportion of the overall structure, the doorways, windows and balconies, and perhaps particularly the whitewashing, much of it pigmented in a distinctly Portuguese manner. It would be necessary to pay attention to decorative elements around doors and windows, for these also provide clear indications. It is all far too close a similarity to be a coincidence. In fact it is not at all coincidental. These themes were originally transported to this place, and they have since become a localized architectural expression. The origin of a forgotten form can hardly be described as indigenous.

Pigment in whitewash – red, blue and mustard yellow – here seen in Old Gondar, is typical of indigenous decoration in all parts of Portugal particularly in the south

Whitewashing, and blue, red or ochre pigmentation, especially the use of coloured borders around windows and doors – *alizars* – or as decoration around the base of a house, was an Arab form that was imported into Iberia long before the political formation of either Spain or Portugal. This decoration is prevalent in the south of Iberia. I have heard it argued that this is an embellishment that could have come into Ethiopia via some form of contact between Highlanders and an Arab influence that had nothing to do with Portugal's XVI and XVII century contact. If that is the case, the fact that this form of residential decoration should be on such prominent display in areas in which the Portuguese, particularly, had been present and active is inclined to pose more questions than it answers. If we are considering a basic Portuguese form, why should it not also be quite logical to consider the adornment of that form a known Portuguese theme or pattern?

Note whitewash and pigmentation on peasant row housing in Portugal's Alentejo province

Mustard yellow pigmentation around the door and window of a house in Gorgora

I saw many examples of exactly this as I walked about Gorgora, on the north shore of the lake. Perhaps few of the houses were built of stone in the typical Portuguese manner. Where they were constructed of sticks and mud in the African mode they nonetheless remained faithful to typically Portuguese dimensions and exterior decoration.

In Gondar my guide, Bibi Giamberi, drew my attention to a number of old and beautifully constructed round stone houses. There are about twenty of them scattered throughout the old quarter, most of them private residences. A Muslim family lived in one of them, and was kind enough to permit access. It was big and spacious, and magnificently appointed inside with eastern rugs and prayer mats. It would be difficult to comment on the origin of these houses. The stonework had a definite Portuguese influence, and the circular design very probably originated with some southern Portuguese rural prototype; in remote areas of the Alentejo there exist numerous round stone structures – *abrigos* – used as seasonal habitation by shepherds. (On pages 63 and 64 I have described how a modern one was erected in the small garden outside the Gondar castle compound.) It is very possible, of course, that their origin lies more in the influence of the familiar circular form of the Orthodox churches throughout the country. If ever a study is to be made of the residendial structures within the Old Gondar market zone special attention must be paid to these charming round buildings.

Two charming round houses in Old Gondar

## Gondar's Six-Castle Compound

Emperor Fasiladas', or Fasil's, castle

When people talk about Portuguese architectural involvement in Ethiopia, they are usually referring to the six-castle complex at Gondar. The city was the capital for many years, from 1632 until 1855, and in its time became the centre of Ethiopian cultural development. This was at a period of the country's history when there was a conscious effort to fall in alongside, if not actually compete with, other great and developing empires and cultures of the age. This, plus the prior example of Axum's majestic showcase served to spur on a building program in keeping with the emperors' images of themselves and their importance. Gondar has become a centre of attraction because of this architectural heritage, and today is by far the best known and most accessible of the northern Highland tourist targets.

Axum in the far north of the country is also a popular tourist target, and likewise is famed for its stonework. However, it is important to make a differentiation here: the Axumite Empire lasted from approximately II century BC to X century AD; it boasts many fine monuments, no small number of them pre-dating the empire itself by many hundreds of years. The stonework of Axum should in no way be confused with the stonework brought into Ethiopia by the Portuguese. Strong stonework tradition, no doubt; link between one tradition and the other: none at all. I have heard Ethiopian scholars anxious to debunk Portugal's historic influence, but who clearly have no understanding of stonework or stonework design, lump together as "an Ethiopian tradition in stonework" such forms as are to be found in Axum, Tigray, Lalibela and the Lake Tana/Gojjam region. This is manifest nonsense. They are four quite separate and individual traditions – in terms of historical timeline, geographic location, design, and structural method. Some Portuguese forms and methods filtered back up into Tigray but, other than that, one has nothing whatever to do with the others.

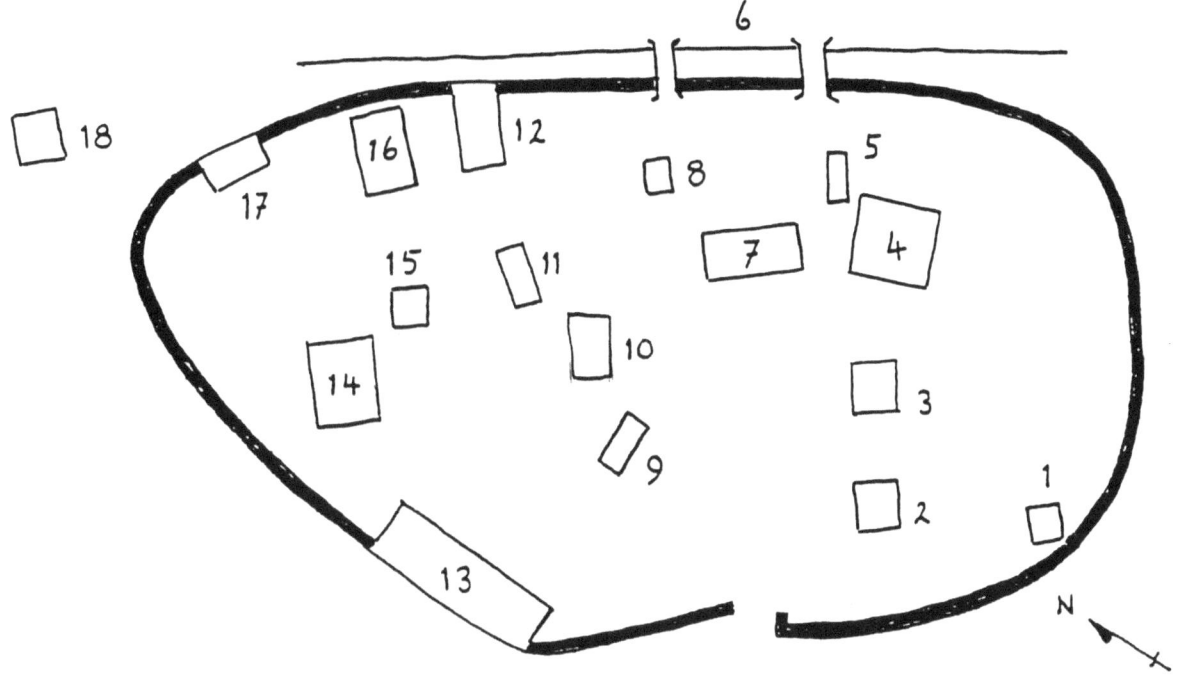

Gondar's castle compound (not to scale)

1 - Bet Maryam church
2 - Yohannes chancellery
3 - Yohannes library
4 - Fasiladas' castle
5 - Fasiladas' pool
6 - Castle bridges
7 - Iyasu I's castle
8 - Fasiladas' Little Palace
9 - Summerhouse
10 - Dawit's choir & music room
11 - Lion house
12 - Wedding house
13 - Bakafa's castle
14 - Mentuabe's & Iyasu II's castle
15 - Turkish baths
16 - Fite Mikael church
17 - Commander of the Cavalry
18 - Ras Mikael Sehul's castle

Perhaps it is too easy to label as "Portuguese" an architectural form that, in terms of its chronology, may be considered an inaccurate term. After all, Gondar's principal Portuguese structures – the ones people travel to the Highlands to see – were built, in the main, following the departure of the Roman Catholic Portuguese. But the thesis of this work is the *origin* of influence, and to try to differentiate between "Portuguese" and "Gondarine" is splitting a fine hair – particularly when the departed Portuguese left such a wide scattering of their seed. No doubt the consideration may be aggravating to someone wishing to champion a purely African form – but origin is the kernel of this discussion, and what developed at Gondar grew out of the momentum of royal prerogative that followed closely on the heels of a concurrent influx of Portuguese settler-builders and their descendents. The settlers had introduced new building ideas, forms and techniques which, for the time, were indicative of a superior imperial growth and development, something to emulate that produced its own force and, with it, a need. "Gondarine" in this context is a confusion – perhaps even an xenophobic means to escape granting due credit to an influence that clearly originated beyond the Highlands.

In essentials, then, "Portuguese" architecture and "Gondarine" architecture are one and the same thing. To throw a sop to those who would still prefer to pinpoint a variance, perhaps it would be possible to claim the first gave birth to the second; the second giving some special (albeit obscure) substance or meaning to forms it might have inherited. Influence in design is a global quantity. Design may be influenced by proximity; it will never be impeded by borders, whether they be cultural or geographical.

One encounters negative qualities on both sides of this architectural coin, so it is important to mention and examine them.

Among Ethiopians one encounters a measure of scoffing and denial:

"Can you accede nothing to our indigenous genius? Do you suppose that we have learned everything from European models? If you think we needed the Portuguese to teach us how to build in stone, what was Axum? What was Lalibela?"

On the Portuguese side, one might well identify a sort of insensitivity rolled up like a fat cigar and puffed in self-contented oblivion, an "us-and-them"-ism which ascribes to the undefined African the status of an amusing little brother. The word "Abyssinia" is bandied about with small regard to the fact that it was really a Portuguese misnomer and a pejorative. To the Portuguese, Prester John is a Portuguese poetic dream figure long before he is an Ethiopian historical reality of another name.

If one knows both cultures, but is adroitly placed as an outsider to the two of them, one might feel a sense of elation at discovering such a precise overlapping of two very different worlds. Perhaps there could even be a feeling of warmth and pride and hope in the recognition of the two, such as a small boy might feel standing between both his grandfathers. Maybe the viewpoint is peculiarly modernistic, even lacking in cultural sensitivity but, standing back as one must, it is possible to smile with a measure of incredulity at the antics of anyone brash enough to champion themselves as superior, more capable, best. Everyone does it. Humans are insistently human. Where, on the surface of this earth, has influence ever ceased? Particularly good influence when it is recognized? The Portuguese themselves took from Morocco and the Moors who inhabited southern Iberia many of the architectural forms that they later imported into Ethiopia. They brought them from India, too.

Moorish style decoration in Fasil's castle

One is cognizant of a delicious academic argument that ascribes to the Maghreb Moors their origin in Ethiopia which, if it possesses even a grain of verity, might justifiably cause one to query just who gave what to whom. The point is, it does not matter. One who emulates the best offered by another should be commended as farsighted, a clever student. Nowadays it is termed "progressive thinking."

Much has been written about the Gondar palaces, and there are numerous excellent descriptions of them. The point of this thesis is to describe a link between them, what is Portuguese and concurrently

Ethiopian. Before examining specific points concerning method and style in relation to historical fact, a useful starting point would be to list the castles according to the dates of the reigns of the monarchs who built them:

| | |
|---|---|
| Fasiladas | 1632-1667 |
| Yohannes I | 1667-1682 |
| Iyasu I | 1682-1706 |
| Dawit III | 1716-1721 |
| Bakafa | 1721-1730 |
| Mentuabe & Iyasu II | 1730-1755 |

Teklahaimanot I ruled for 10 years prior to Dawit III (1706-1716) but did not build his own castle in the Gondar compound.

Ras Mikael Sehul built a castle outside the compound at the time he acted as prime minister/dictator for Iyoas II (reigned 1755-1769).

Emperor Fasiladas expelled the Jesuits from Ethiopia in 1634, and almost immediately began a persecution of Roman Catholics and their sympathizers. He even went so far as to strike a deal with the Muslim leader of Massawa to pay a bounty for the head of every Portuguese caught trying to enter through that port. Such social conditions tend to put paid to the notion of Portuguese nationals functioning as builders. Descendents of Portuguese, perhaps, but not likely first generation nationals – unless there were one or two who had forsaken Roman Catholicism and decided to risk remaining behind. Many families would have wanted to remain intact. We have already examined the matter of just who it was that built such structures as are found in place today and how, if not themselves Portuguese, it cannot be too far fetched to presume they were built by people who benefited from Portuguese training and skills.

Throughout the six compound castles, and even the Ras Mikael castle, are many, many elements of Portuguese building technique and design. During my time in the city, the senior members of the Gondar restoration team, architect Mamo Getahun and chief builder and engineer Endalamaw Sahilu, were anxious to discuss with me all elements of their extraordinarily ambitious work project. In time it is hoped the entire compound will have undergone a complete restoration. In the meanwhile, after years of neglect and the destruction of wars, there are obvious practical and logistical problems in embarking on such a scheme in a country as impoverished as Ethiopia. Only one of these problems is the ability to obtain suitable materials for the job; another is to be able to conduct adequate research to know exactly how particular ancient building techniques were employed. A case in point: how to rebuild or strengthen the many *abobadas* and *abobadilhas* that are incorporated within the complex. Ethiopian crews have had difficulties accomplishing this. They have attempted using moulds, not knowing the Portuguese technique of building or restoring such structures without moulds. This has proved a perplexing and frustrating exercise because in many cases there are existing floors above the *cupolas*, and the use of a mould would require being able to restructure from the upper side of the mould. Clearly, a technique has been lost to Ethiopian builders over the intervening years since Portuguese-trained artisans accomplished the originals.

In Emperor Fasiladas' castle there are many Moorish design motifs, and door-lock and hinge systems that were standard in all Portuguese castles for centuries. In small houses, presumably old

Emperor Iyasu I's castle

workshops, just off the same castle, there are typically Portuguese barrel-vaulted ceilings. *Abobadas* in the castle's towers were built in the Portuguese manner. A brick-ribbed and arched ceiling in a small room atop Fasil's castle, and a similar one above the main hall in Emperor Iyasu I's castle, both completed by laying *lajes*, or flagstones, between the brick ribbing, is an unusual Moorish design. This method of construction had been common when the Moors inhabited Portugal in the VIII to XII centuries. They had used precisely this technique in the water mills they erected throughout the hydrodynamic system of the Guadiana River and its tributaries in southern Portugal (see illustrations pages 138 and 140). Staircases, the stonework around windows and doors, and the stonework in general, *reboco* techniques, towers, wall tapering, wall thickness, design in both specifics and in general – all these legitimately can be said to have had their Ethiopian origins in Portugal notwithstanding the fact that the Portuguese may have robbed these same techniques long before from someone else.

One continually hears, or reads, that the work at Gondar – the castles, and the many other monuments, such as Kusquaum, Fasil's Bath, the Tomb of Zobel, and so on – were undertaken by "Indian" architects and craftsmen, and it cannot be denied that this may, in fact, have been the case. It should not be overlooked, though, that Portugal was dominant in India throughout this period of history, and that it is very likely that any Goan or Gujarati artisans were brought into the Highlands to work under essentially Portuguese direction. In any case, it is also possible that such artisans received earlier training from Portuguese builders in India, or that these same builders before their association with the Portuguese had been strongly influenced by their own subcontinent motifs.

The Portuguese learned many of their designs and techniques in India, but they also took to India from Portugal much of their homeland building know-how. This Portuguese/Indian interchange is something that very likely pertained from the earliest times of Portugal's contact with the Highlands. Both "Indians" and "Egyptians" are reputed to have worked on Mertule Maryam, but this would have been at a time when Egyptian/Gujarati contact and trade was at a peak, and when Portugal was moving onto the subcontinent in force great enough to cause considerable disturbance to that contact. That Egyptians mingled with the Portuguese in India is no more remote a possibility than that the Gujaratis did. Likewise it cannot be a great surprise that numerous of these presumed Egyptian builders, as well as their Gujarati counterparts, filtered into the Ethiopian Highlands along with the mainstream of Portuguese power and influence. Much later these same "Indians" and "Egyptians" survived the persecution of the Jesuits and Roman Catholics by the Ethiopians precisely because they were neither one nor the other. The Orthodox only turned on those whom they saw as having had a negative influence on their own practice of Christianity. They were tolerant of others. Furthermore, these foreign elements offered training in building methods the locals had been assimilating from the Portuguese over a period of years long pre-dating Gondar. There can be no reasonable denying that as a simple matter of acquired habit these foreign craftsmen seasoned their Portuguese-ness with liberal sprinklings of their own powerful cultural backgrounds. Once again, who has influenced? Who has not been influenced?

Although much newer than the compound castles, the palace of Ras Mikael Sehul, just outside the royal compound, might legitimately be considered in the same terms as its nearby companions. The same influences applied many years after the principal buildings of the compound had been completed.

Yohannes' chancellery in the Gondar compound,
a delightful example of Portuguese style stonework and castle design

Typical *abobadilha*, vaulted ceiling, in Portugal's Noudar Castle, left; typical *abobada* at Fasil's castle, Gondar, right

Compare the ceiling in the main hall of Emperor Iyasu I's castle, left, with the structure of the ceiling at Moinho do Gato, right, a 900-year-old water-mill built by the Moors as part of a water use and conservation system on the Guadiana River in southern Portugal. See also repair diagrams page 140.

As a builder and stonemason, I feel I must comment on some disappointing aspects of what is described as "restoration" or "conservation" at the Gondar castle compound. Local authorities have cast themselves aggressively, even enthusiastically, into the role of conservers – and unfortunately some glaring mistakes have been made. The very first thing that one cannot help but notice is that little or no attention whatever has been paid to the historical imperatives of construction. It would have been helpful if instead of charging into reconstruction the civic authorities, the historians, the engineers and builders had been more conversant with – more attentive to – the original XV, XVI and XVII century methods of building. A keener awareness of this historical imperative might have prevented such a widespread use of concrete, for instance, and permitted a rather more authentic all round reconstruction of the site.

For instance, the exterior wall of Bakafa's palace is collapsing, and has to be held up by a hideous frame of girders and supports. The reason? A concrete *plaqua* (ceiling/floor) was poured over the full area contained by the existing stone walls – which, quite simply, were never intended to carry such weight. That a concrete ceiling (floor for the space above it) was attempted at all is tantamount to restoration blasphemy, but that it was set in place without proper footings and anchorage is an example of sheer folly. Now the so-called restorers of the palace have a major and costly problem on their hands – one that could have been avoided in the first place by referral to origin. Possibly less disastrous results were obtained within Fasil's castle itself, where

Bakafa's Palace wall: the disastrous consequence of careless and uninformed "restoration"

liberal quantities of concrete were also poured. The idea of using concrete at all is anathema to the tackling of XVI and XVII century restoration.

Almost as big a blunder has been made in the "restoring" of the ceiling within the great hall of Iyasu's palace. The beautiful line of the original brick arches holding the *lajes* has been corrupted in recent years by the installation of ceiling and roof reinforcement *above* the arches. Its appearance is frankly a ghastly aberration, and is a feature that definitely could have been avoided if, again, more attention had been paid to origin.

Before further damage is done, it would be as well for the Gondar authorities to link with the cultural entities of the Portuguese Embassy in Addis Ababa. As I have written elsewhere in this thesis, there are facilities extant in Portugal that would be well worth consulting prior to charging headlong into further culturally destructive reconstruction in the name of "restoration."

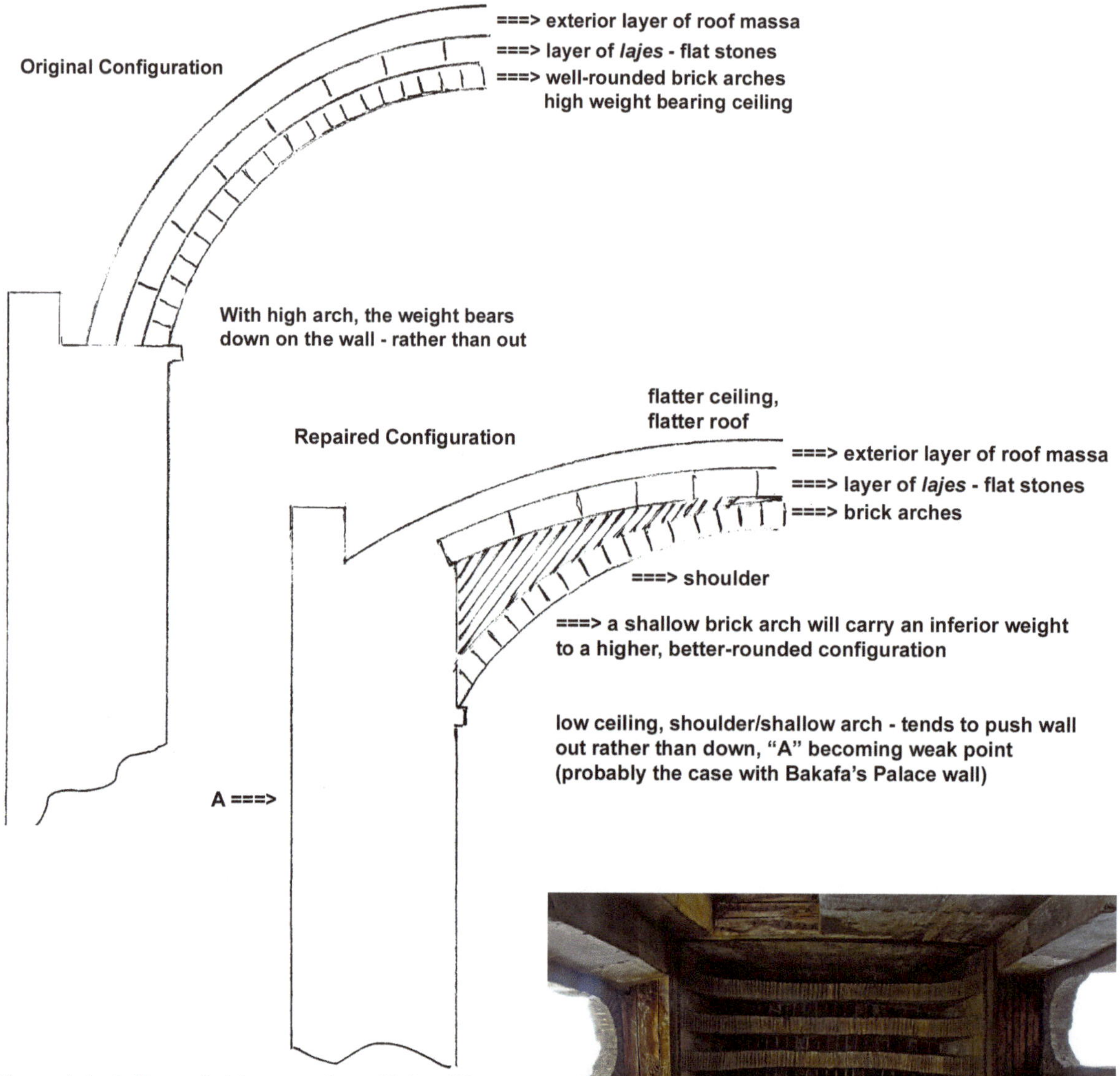

**Original Configuration**

===> exterior layer of roof massa
===> layer of *lajes* - flat stones
===> well-rounded brick arches
high weight bearing ceiling

With high arch, the weight bears down on the wall - rather than out

**Repaired Configuration**

flatter ceiling, flatter roof

===> exterior layer of roof massa
===> layer of *lajes* - flat stones
===> brick arches

===> shoulder

===> a shallow brick arch will carry an inferior weight to a higher, better-rounded configuration

low ceiling, shoulder/shallow arch - tends to push wall out rather than down, "A" becoming weak point (probably the case with Bakafa's Palace wall)

A ===>

The original line of this once beautiful ceiling at Iyasu's castle has been altered through the implementation of improvised repair: the "shoulder" shown clearly in both diagram and photograph. Its installation has flattened out the whole of the ceiling, minimizing the essential role of the *lajes* flat stones, and destroying the roiling harmony and excitement of the once-boisterous brickwork that was simultaneously so intimate. The reasons for doing a repair in this manner are unclear, but are probably due to the availability of easily-worked concrete, and a lack of both historical sensitivity and the background knowledge of how the original was put up in the first place. Money probably had something to do with it, too, although to have done the work properly would likely have incurred little or no greater cost. Fearing the loss of heritage know-how, in recent years a number of specialized schools in Portugal have undertaken to teach the traditional techniques of the country's world-renowned historical structure methods in brick and stone. Before too much more "restoration" is undertaken, it would be wise for a creative link to be formed in this area between Portugal and Ethiopia. Compare the before-and-after photographs of this ceiling at right and on page 138.

## Kusquaum, Fasil's Bath and Tomb of Zobel

The palace at Kusquaum is located three kilometres west of Gondar. Abandoned and crumbling, it was developed and built by Empress Mentuabe and her grandson, Emperor Iyasu II (1730-1755). Much the same commentary made concerning the castle compound in Gondar would also apply to this lovely ruin, Fasil's bath and the remains of the Tomb of Zobel, Emperor Fasiladas' much loved horse. These latter are located just outside the city on the road to Kusquaum.

Each of these monuments is an integral piece of the Gondar story. Zobel's tomb has been long overgrown with bushes and trees poking through cracks in its walls. It is open to question as to whether or not the horse is actually buried there.

Kusquaum itself is a sad reminder of how quickly a loyal people will forget an absent monarch. Here yet again, in the mid-XVIII century and with the Portuguese long gone, one can see that this once noble palace could be a stand-in for any of the great *quintas* of Sintra, Portugal.

Fasil's bath, left, Tomb of Zobel, below

## Denqaz and Waina Dega

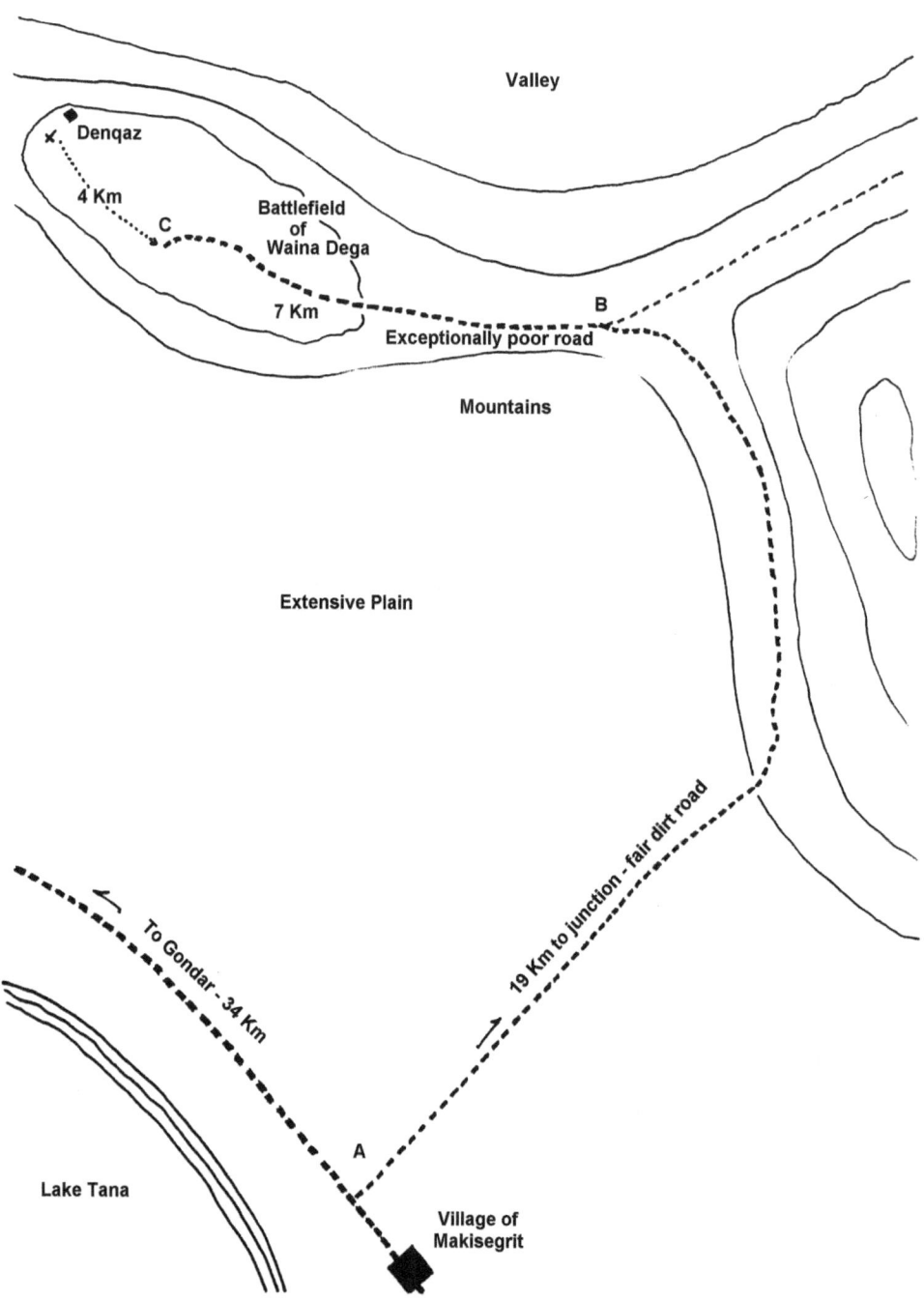

Route to Denqaz and the Waina Dega Battlefield – not to scale

A trip to Denqaz requires patience and organization. One needs transport and guides, and it is advisable to go with an armed escort. Moving unprotected through remote Highland areas can be dangerous. Mountain people very often have dogs as their protectors. These guard dogs are invariably big, strong and extremely aggressive animals. A stout hiking stick might not seem to provide much protection, but it would in all instances be an improvement on nothing.

The distance from Gondar to Denqaz is sixty-four kilometres: A) thirty-four to the turn off to the east just prior to arriving at the village of Makisegrit, B) nineteen up into the mountains to the junction of a left turn in the crest of a saddle, and C) a further seven along this terrible ridge road until the four-wheel-drive vehicle can go no further. A guide is then necessary to show the way for the final four kilometre trudge to the northeast.

It is high up, about three thousand metres. From just beyond point "B" in the diagram one can look back at the road snaking up the side of the mountain, and make out Lake Tana in the hazy distance to the southwest. The seven kilometres of dirt trail to point "C" is the worst imaginable, quite on par but thankfully a little shorter than the road running between Debre Tabor and Aringo. At the point where it is necessary to leave the car and set off on foot, the landscape is a broad savannah opening into an expansive saddle that rises gently to the front, forming an horizon some two kilometres distant. At the cusp of this horizon lies another broad sweep of land, high savannah that runs for perhaps two more kilometres to the edge of an escarpment, and then drops over one thousand metres to the valley floor. It is a dramatic sight. Taking a close look at a map one will see the land is rugged and virtually empty of habitation. It is rough headwater country, with numerous streams tumbling their chaotic courses down to the upper reaches of the Tekeze River near the point where it turns north.

Just before arriving at the ruins there is a typical African village, round mud-and-dung houses with thatch roofs, thorn-fenced yards, and packs of dogs that are mean in daylight, positively lethal after dark. These dogs will start barking when a visitor is still a half-kilometre distant, so that by the outskirts of the village proper a veritable army of curious onlookers will have been notified to gather around. Many of them are children, but many are adults with nothing more to do with themselves than to hang about and try to participate in whatever is happening. The village headman is there, expecting to be thoroughly informed as to why it is so necessary to examine a group of buildings that are not used any more and have, in any case, fallen into ruins. At the conclusion of arduous explanations, and the usual exchange of coin or paper, the whole party by now, allowing for stragglers, numbering some forty souls moves off overland towards the sites.

We come to the basilica first, a magnificent and surprisingly intact ruin of recognizably Portuguese design, a Roman Catholic church in the form of a cross. It is the former seat of Afonso Mendes, Jesuit prelate and mentor to Sussenyos, the emperor who had formally converted to Roman Catholicism in 1622.

As with Gondar, much of the work on the basilica and palace at Denqaz is credited to "Indian" craftsmen and, as noted concerning the Gondar castle complex above, one must keep in mind that "Indians" would most likely have been Goans or Gujaratis working under Portuguese direction. Denqaz, in point of fact, pre-dates the major buildings at Gondar by a substantial margin. Its structure is credited to the Jesuit missionary, Pêro Páez, who arrived in Ethiopia in 1603 and no doubt availed himself of skilled artisans from the subcontinent. The building of such structures would have taken considerable manpower, so it is entirely likely the muscle would have been Ethiopian. This latter cadre might very well have included local *mestres-das-obras* whose knowledge and skill had been drawn from India or Egypt, but who worked not just under the Portuguese but as Portuguese. It is necessary to stress this liberal and very open definition of "Portuguese," and realize that the term in

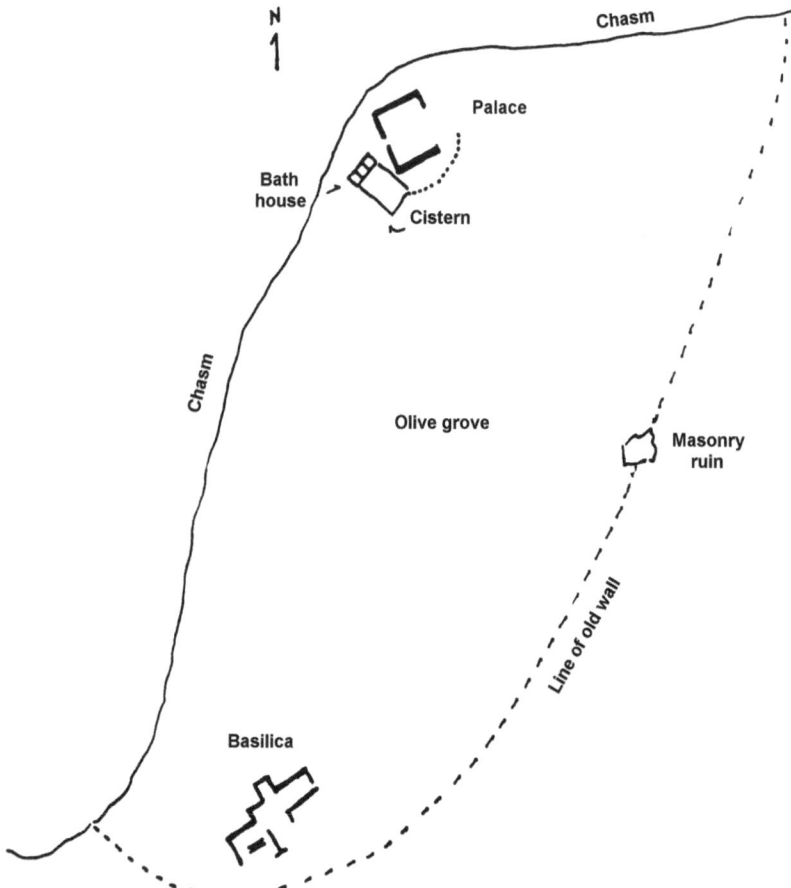

Layout of Denqaz Ruins – not to scale

the XVI or XVII centuries did not carry the same connotation of national boundary as it would today, but rather more the concept of fealty to an overlord, as well as cultural and economic impact.

Here, again, the stonework and decoration of Denqaz followed a Portuguese pattern. It is a delight to discover the similarity in carved stone ashlar between what is to be seen in the Denqaz basilica choir and altar area to that seen in the doorway of Maryam Gemb church at the palace of Emperor Sussenyos on Lake Tana. It is as if the same hand had cut the two, and this may very well have been the case. Arches, stonework, doorways, all are immediately familiar. Of particular note is a window on the north wall of the nave which is so typical that one would not be very surprised to find "Made in Portugal" stamped into the *caixilho*. When one steps into the northern transept, in fact, such a *carimbo*, or seal, is right there! High up and carved in stone, surmounting the crest of what was once a transept altar, the shadow of which yet remains in undressed stone against the north wall, can be seen quite clearly the Portuguese cross, the Cross of Malta, or Cross of the Order of Christ as it is also known. This is the cross immediately recognizable as the one carried on the sails of Portugal's ships of the era, and which is depicted even today on representations of the Portuguese coat of arms.

From here it is perhaps a three hundred metre walk and climb over walls and across rocky ploughed fields to the ancient palace.

The nave of the Roman Catholic basilica, Denqaz

This walk is also a delightful surprise. All about is what looks like an ancient olive grove. It is possible to detect that the trees were once growing in rows. They have seeded themselves over the centuries; many have been cut down for firewood. Though scattered, a pattern is still detectable. Some of them, at least, are very, very old; but then the olive tree is known to live to a great age. In discussion about this phenomenon a local historian remarks:

"I don't know these trees. What are they?"

Perhaps twenty-five villagers stop, and a discussion ensues. Nobody knows these as olive trees. The fruit, they all agree, is bitter

Denqaz basilica choir and altar area; compare upper stonework with similar stonework at Maryam Gemb, page 152 and 154, both attributed to Pêro Páez. Compare this, also, with the choir/nave dividing arch at St. Mary's, Gemb Giorghis (photo page 110).

and quite inedible. The tree is of no use except as firewood. Emperor Sussenyos would have been living here with many Portuguese around him, and they definitely would have known and recognized olive trees. No doubt they would have been the ones who planted them, and they would have known, too, how to prepare the fruit.

Denqaz palace cistern

Several key features are immediately recognizable within the palace: *reboco* on interior walls yet bears fesco decoration in at least a couple of places; channels for water drainage are still detectable; an above ground level cistern has been built over a spring and, outside it, at its northwestern end, are bath chambers; a toilet shaft drains itself to the palace's exterior at the northwest corner at a spot where the waste would have been able to drop over a cliff into a chasm hundreds of feet below.

This chasm itself would have formed part of the defences of the place, located as it is to the northwest, north and east of the area. A walled enclosure to the south of the basilica would have curved from one lip of the chasm to another and would have been sufficient to isolate all of Denqaz from enemy attack. I looked for signs and, sure enough, there they were, though very little of such a wall remains today. Stones have long ago been carted off for building elsewhere. A massive chunk of masonry wall, stones mortared together and too difficult to ever bother separating, stands in the centre of a ploughed area. It was right where a wall logically should have run, and where obviously it once did.

Once adding luxurious decorative luster to one of the palace's many rooms, intricate fresco work, now at the mercy of wind and weather, is yet visible on ancient *reboco* of the walls

Returning to Gondar but still high in the mountains and not far from Denqaz, we passed the old battlefield of Waina Dega where the Portuguese defeated the forces of Islam and Ahmad Grag'n was killed. There is not a great deal to see except for the location of the place, and the wide saddle of the field.

Then Getnet Yigsaw, tourism officer from Gondar, crooked his finger and said: "Come and take a look at this!"

He led the way to a pile of stones in the centre of the field. Once it had had form, but now it was rubble. A lengthy and solid chunk of wood was heaved onto a high section of what passed for a wall.

"See this?" he asked. "Just a few years ago a number of wealthy Muslims got together and decided to erect a monument to Ahmad Grag'n."

"Some monument!" I commented.

"Well, it was a monument. Quite a big structure. The problem was that, when they wanted to build it they had to hire labourers from this district. Costs would have been too high, otherwise. There are people living near here, and they agreed to do it. They needed the wages. But they were Christians, these workers, and they had long memories of what Ahmad Grag'n did to the Christians so many centuries ago. They contracted to build the monument, and actually built it – collecting their wages for the work they did. But they packed the interior of the stonework with dynamite. The day of the inauguration, when the Muslim elders were assembled by the side of the field and about to make the dedication to their hero, the labourers blew up their work. That was the end of it. The Muslims left, and they haven't come back. The people up here on the mountain would never agree to an Islamic monument to such a hated man as Grag'n, so it's not likely ever to be rebuilt."

"Good God!" I exclaimed. "That is a long memory! And what's with that chunk of wood?"

Getnet chuckled.

"Take a look at it!" he said. "It's not just a chunk of wood. It's a commentary. It's the yoke of an ox. These people round here have a clever humour!"

**Gobatit Bridge Over the Angreb River**

This extraordinary little bridge, downstream of the Fasil Bridge on the Angreb River, is quite difficult to reach inasmuch as one must take a three kilometre hike over rough terrain to get to it.

Its main arch is spectacular, high and well over eight metres in width. From the dimensions of the existing deck it is possible to say the bridge was initially designed to carry quite heavy loads ...

But then how, one might ask, would a donkey pulling a cart ever manage to negotiate the hump that has been created over the centre arch ...?

That centre arch, comprising the barest layer of stonework, looks so delicate, so flimsy, that one hesitates to step on it. Gossamer thin, it looks fragile enough that a hefty man might stomp it into ruin simply by walking on it. Perhaps, one might think, it was only ever supposed to be a pedestrian bridge – for very light-footed dancers ...

The fact is, the existing arches are quite sturdy – but a further fact, certainly, is that the bridge was never completed.

For some unknown reason the charming structure we see here was abandoned at this stage of its construction. Happily so, for it permits us to see how, for centuries, this was the way a Roman-style bridge was assembled – a method carried by legions of Roman builders into every far corner of the empire. There are literally hundreds of these bridges to be found everywhere the Romans trod – and probably not a few hundred of those in the Roman colonies of Spain and Portugal.

If one looks carefully at the photograph and its accompanying diagram on the next page, it will be possible to discern quite easily how such bridges were built. Once the lateral footings have been firmly established on either side of the stream, the central arch is built over a mould and secured on

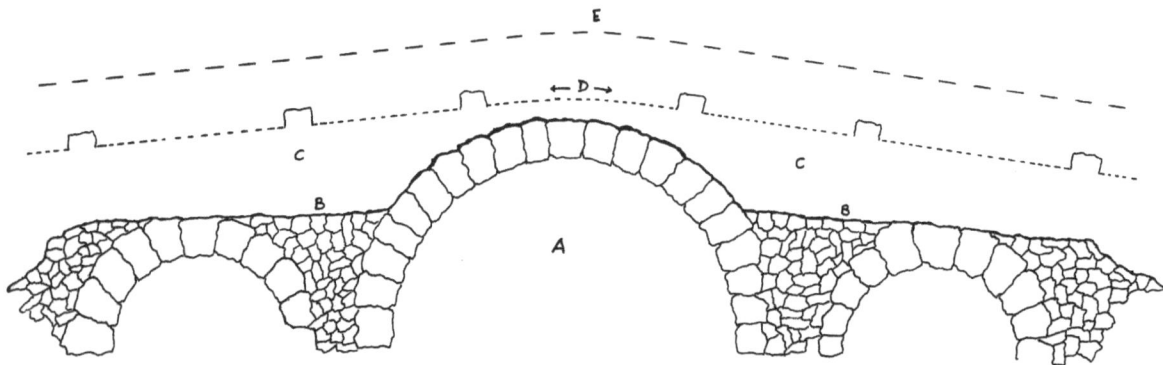

**A** - what one sees at present - initial mortared hoop structure; mortared stones surrounding the hoops structurally and securing them, (B)
**C** - incomplete build-up to ramp level - to be finished and mortared in the same manner as (B)
**D** - level of bridge deck, showing water outlet ports
**E** - level of parapet, a continuation of mortared stones as with (B)

each bank by the massive pillar structures of mortared stone. In this case, secondary arches, formed in like manner, were positioned outside the main pillars. This is the point at which Gobatit was abandoned.

The diagram shows how the bridge would have been completed: the mass of the pillars would have been extended upwards, broadening into what would eventually become the bridge's deck level – the stones mortared in place and giving much more bulk to the overall structure and adding considerable strength to it. The parapet level, though not structural, would have been a visual continuation of the mortared mass of the bridge itself.

Clearly Gobatit Bridge as it stands is a gem, an arrested lesson in Roman-style bridge-building. But it is in urgent need of attention. One might say "restoration," except that what we see is all there ever was. It has stood like that for several hundreds of years, and perhaps it will stand for several hundred more; but it would be a terrible shame if ever that centre arch were to collapse. It would be difficult, and prohibitively expensive, to recover its present charming aspect.

One solution to the problem of conservation might be to complete the bridge; while adding considerably to its strength and its weather and traffic resistance, such a drastic measure would certainly detract from the bridge's delightful contour. Considering its current utility, however, and the distance between the site and any significant population centre, another more practical course of action would be merely to keep a close eye on it, only carrying out restoration as it is needed – but above all to guard this little beauty well and perhaps try to keep people and traffic off it.

Downstream from the Gobatit Bridge, about two kilometres distant, is another structure in a state of advanced ruin, all that now remains of Korata Bridge on the Qaha River where it joins with the Angreb. A single arch in very bad repair, its face parallel to the Angreb, it is impossible to see, now, that there was once a stream that passed under it. It appears to be all that is left of what was once a secondary arch to a larger bridge swept to oblivion long ago.

To say nothing of the aesthetic pleasure one may derive from them, what is left of both bridges gives a very clear idea of the internal structure of stone arches from the period, and for this reason alone they are worth close study and careful preservation.

## Defeche Kidane Mehret

Going to this site entails an expedition not easily or soon forgotten. The place is located on the far side of the Angreb reservoir, at the top of a hill that deserves to be promoted to "mountain." It is a stiff, rather dull climb, no views to speak of. I set off at a reasonable enough pace, guide Bibi Giamberi galloping up in front of me like a gazelle. The going becomes increasingly steep and uneven and, right after rains, it is treacherously slippery to boot. There is no letup. Just up.

The church, when it finally comes into view, is a stunning example of Portuguese stonework. It is in ruins and has no roof now, but the stonework is precise, confident and utterly professional, its formal design in the more common and traditional round configuration of Orthodox churches. Unfortunately the place was largely destroyed in the XIX century during the invasions of the Sudanese Mahdists. The Italians, during their occupation between 1935 and 1941, made a half-hearted attempt to carry out repairs. They did not know what they were doing, using steel reinforced concrete, a minimum of imagination, and a pretty lacklustre effort to complete the destructive effort with which they had begun the "repair." It is a dreadful shame. The unfortunate result is a primary and useful lesson in what NOT to do. In addition, Italian stonework alongside Portuguese stonework stands out like a leaning tower in the Lisbon bullring.

**Desit Giorghis**

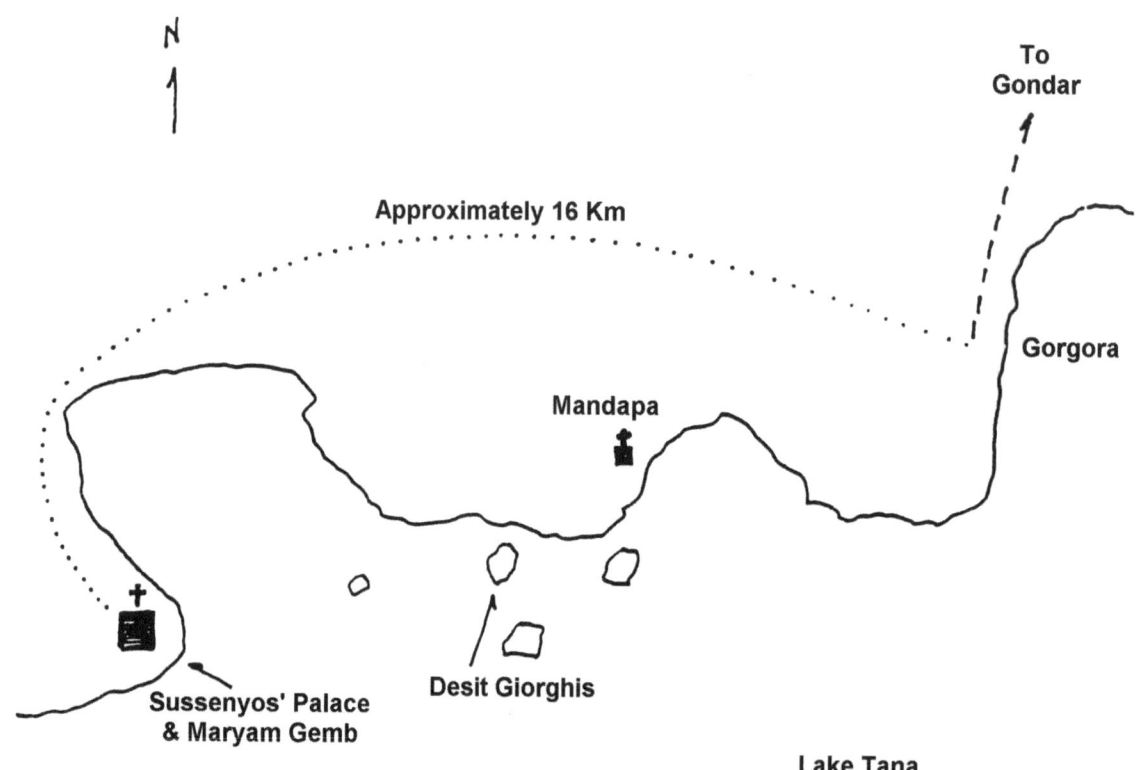

Lake Tana north shore, route to Sussenyos' Palace, Old Gorgora,
and showing Mendapa and Desit Giorghis – not to scale

Just as it might seem that every peak in the Highlands is capped by an isolated Orthodox church, so it might seem just about every sizeable island that peppers the surface of Lake Tana has its monastery. Whether on mountain top or lake, an essential requirement would appear to be remoteness. Desit Giorghis is a site so remote one would have difficulty locating it if one made a deliberate effort to go there, even with the assistance of a map.

It is an island (the meaning of *desit*) no more than a stone's throw from Lake Tana's north shoreline, and tiny. It is located only a short distance from the Orthodox monastery of Mandapa, lying about halfway by boat between Gorgora and the palace of Emperor Sussenyos on the peninsula west of the town.

The place appears to be nowhere on record, and approaching it by boat one might easily miss it. A characteristic Portuguese style stone wall surrounds the island, but has been overgrown in places by verdant bush and trees. There is a natural discolouring caused by lichen and mosses settling on stones that have lain for long centuries at water's edge. Even if unintentional, it is a perfect camouflage and would have mightily pleased the Jesuits who built the place as a fortified residence probably in the first quarter of the 1600's.

Though very small, there is quite enough space to grow essential crops, or have a small vegetable garden. With water all around, the place could be entirely self-sufficient, and would have been

well able to support a community of eight to twelve people. An impressive two-tier gate leads out at the western side onto a rocky shoreline. The gate is well concealed to view from the main shore, and it would have been to this point that supply boats would have pulled up or moored. There is no clear sign of it now, but a small pier or landing built off the lakeside rocks would have been a simple matter to arrange. Brambles and undergrowth covered much of the surface of the island inside the walls, but two buildings stand quite clear, both of them in a state of ruin.

On the north side there is one high wall left standing of what appears to have been a substantial house, perhaps the residence itself. In the very centre of the island, covered with undergrowth to such a thickness that access was impossible when I visited, is the second ruin, a small chapel. For all the growth covering it the island's circumference wall is in remarkably good condition. It was evident that someone had been making fairly regular calls, for a small plot of land inside the wall had been recently cultivated. Later, through an interpreter, I was able to make contact with a hermit who lived under a makeshift shelter on a rock a little further out into the lake. I learned it was he who frequently visited Desit Giorghis and the other several nearby islands where he had planted crops of sweet potatoes and melons. Wild cotton also grows there.

It is the sort of place where I enjoy to linger, taking precious time to soak up the atmosphere. I like to allow my imagination to wander, perhaps, spend a few hours pulling some of the brambles off the central building to see what treasures might lie underneath: a tell-tale stone, a nuance within a wall. Lake boats are expensive when paid for by the hour though. A photograph or two, a quick sketch, and then there is still quite a distance to go before reaching Emperor Sussenyos' palace.

Dock gate, Desit Giorghis

## The Palace of Emperor Sussenyos and Maryam Gemb Church

Sacristy stonework, Maryam Gemb church

A visit to this site is a continuation of the expedition across the northern stretch of Lake Tana.

Crossing the lake on the approach to Sussenyos' palace on the tip of its peninsula is like coming home for me. I had been there before, spent time poring over its contours, crawling on my hands and knees under thickets of brambles in order to get a better idea of how a line of stones turned a corner, or a doorway opened through a wall. Its great pile of masonry is silhouetted on the high ground like an old friend perched on a steamer trunk at the head of a railway station platform.

Locals had conducted an extensive clean-up around the place since the last time I had been there, so that it was now possible to see the full extent of the site. The undergrowth that had been an almost impenetrable cover over the palace in the mid-1990's had been cut away, burned back and raked over so that entering the centre of the complex was now possible. There have been numerous collapses of walls and ceilings over the years, and in many corners there are now stout and well-rooted trees that tend to crack or push walls over. The church fell in, the ceiling pulling down the walls that had supported it, in August of 1995. The full length of the exterior wall of the palace's south wing had collapsed long before that, leaving whatever had been inside exposed to the elements. Despite this, it is possible to walk about at will and unhindered.

The place is gigantic. It was built in the form of a square, with a wide courtyard in the centre of it. In this great space there stands what I call, for want of a clearer description, what seems to be a much more recent structure, a sort of central "keep" that, unlike every other part of the complex, has been built using mud or clay in place of mortar. As a consequence it is in an advanced state of disrepair. Stubby and cramped, it is not a particularly intriguing building, the most interesting of its features being its central location. There is one beautiful stone carved in deep relief that has been fitted into place low down on its south wall. The design of this sculpted stone has nothing whatsoever to do with anything else around it, and was clearly removed from where it had no doubt earlier fallen from its previous situation and had then been stuffed into its present position. One cannot see that it has any special meaning, but it does tend to identify the little building as a later structure altogether than the body of the palace proper. It is really very unlikely that this "keep" was ever designed or

Delicate carving on "keep" stone

intended as a defense for the residence; more probably it was built as some kind of warehouse, possibly an armoury.

Maryam Gemb, the church itself, is such a total destruction it is difficult to read. Once an extraordinary church, it is now an extraordinary heap of rocks; but this pile alone serves to give an idea of the colossal dimensions of the place. Only one piece of wall is left standing at what was once the entranceway, but fortunately it is a glorious piece of the old decorated stone archway. Here it is quite easy to see the vestige of high artwork that must once have graced the entire portico. Indeed, Maryam Gemb was a monumental edifice.

Everything else about the church has fallen into the centre of what used to be the nave. A popular story one hears is that the peeling of the gigantic old church bells could be heard as far away as Bahir Dar, some ninety kilometres south across the lake. Despite the size of this destruction and the sheer tragedy of it, the place is magic. The silence that surrounds Maryam Gemb is far subtler than the whispers that can be detected around the inside rim of a great cathedral dome.

Useful work could be undertaken here to clear the pile of rubble, sort through the stones, putting aside those that have been sculpted and permitting some kind of access to what used to be here. Though in an extremely remote location, and well off the beaten track for tourism, an ideal project for the site would be to construct an inexpensive shelter. A simple building could be erected beside the ruin using the stones that have fallen. Here the more decorative carved stonework may be displayed along with drawings or diagrams of how the site used to appear. It is an important site. A concerted effort should be made, and soon, to preserve what considerable amount of artefact is left and to prevent further deterioration. It would be a terrible shame if what is left of the magnificent portico should go the same way as the rest of the church edifice. Imaginative conservation could save it.

Entry portico, Maryam Gemb church

## Sek'ela and Abba Gish Fasil

By horse to Abba Gish Fasil

The source of a mighty river, if it can be pinpointed, always summons the high priests and soothsayers to their incantations. Great oracles are held to be in such places, and superstitions abound. For these reasons, explorers and adventurers since the beginning of time have risked their lives to be the first to arrive at the top, or the bottom, or at the furthest extremity. Kings and queens, geographical societies and foundations have made great sums of money available in order to encourage and finance such human endeavour. There has been no end of those willing to risk all and head off to God alone knows where "because it is there."

One such adventurer was Sir James Bruce of Kinnaird, an indomitable Scottish giant who travelled to Ethiopia in the last quarter of the XVIII century specifically to search for the source of the Blue Nile River. He published a five volume description of his findings in 1790 – *Travels to Discover the Source of the Nile in the Years 1768, 1769, 1770, 1771, 1772 and 1773* – and few believed him. He was mocked and ridiculed mercilessly, and it was not until the passing of many more years that the general public finally and grudgingly gave him credence. By which time, of course, he was dead.

Although he claimed to have been the first European to find the source of the Blue Nile, in fact he was beaten to the draw by more than one hundred and fifty years by Padre Pêro Páez. That wee fact stuck in Bruce's craw and, while lavishing praise on the Jesuit priest, he nonetheless refused to acknowledge his earlier rival's accomplishment. Instead he writes for us a magnificently detailed description of how, seeing the waters seeping from the ground in the centre of a broad meadow, he gambolled over like a spring lamb and bathed himself in the holy waters, laughing and praising God for having at last guided him to his mission's successful accomplishment.

The people of Sek'ela, the small mountain town not a hundred metres distant from these headwaters, also treat the site with considerable reverence. They call it Gish Abay, and consider the waters of the spring to be holy.

Most people are content to look upon Lake Tana as the source of the Blue Nile, or Abay Wenz as it is known locally. The Little Abay rising at Sek'ela in the mountains east of Dangila and flowing north into the lake west of Bahir Dar creates a slight current across the south end of the lake in the direction of the Blue Nile's exit. Naturally these cheerful mountain people feel they guard the true headwaters of the Blue Nile.

I went to Sek'ela not so much to see the source of the river as to strike out for an old Jesuit centre northeast of there long known as Abba Gish Fasil. Accompanied by my young guide and translator, Tadele Fentahun, we hired horses for the trip.

That was a mistake. I should have insisted on mules, but that was before I knew what we were in for.

We climbed and climbed; first through forests of eucalyptus, and then past fields where farmers paced out behind their weary mules, furrowing their fields with antiquated rustic ploughs. Here and there we came across delicate patches of *tef*, the cereal used in the making of Ethiopia's staple food, the crêpe-like *injera*. Almost without realizing it, we were into the mountains, inching along narrow tracks carved into cliff sides; rock face on one hand, open space and sheer drop on the other.

The horses were not up to it. They were far too small and feeble for the height, the broken surface of the tortuous tracks we were following, the weight they were obliged to carry, and the non-stop pace at which we had to move all day. Twice my nag collapsed under me. I was saddle sore. A patch at the base of my tail bone was worn raw to bleeding by the motion and the furniture upon which I was obliged to perch. At one point my horse stumbled and fell as we were negotiating a narrow trail carved into a cliff face. It was sheer chance that intervened to prevent the two of us toppling off the mountain. Below that particular stretch of the path we would not have so much as bounced for the first three hundred metres. After a full twelve hour span of tension, extreme discomfort, and high alarm, I was barely able to stand upright.

Of all the sites I visited, I was less than enthralled by the route we chose to Abba Gish Fasil. Since that excursion I have talked with a guide who knows the area well and claims there is another and far easier approach to the site. Perhaps. I have this idea in the back of my mind that the next time I visit the place it would be better to leave both horses and mules behind, and instead swoop in aboard a helicopter.

The fortified residence at Abba Gish Fasil was one of the principal Jesuit centres of their operations in that rugged area of north central Gojjam. Now in ruins, having suffered the ignominy of its stones being snitched by locals for other construction, its walls are sprouting trees and shrubs; if there is anything that destroys a wall faster than man it is nature. The location of the site is stunning. As we approached it on horseback, it was as though we had come over the rim of an enormous bowl, ourselves on one side and Abba Gish Fasil in full view on its own rise of ground in the distance, slightly lower and on quite the opposite side from us. There was no going down into the bowl to get to it. It was far too deep and rugged and overgrown. Instead, the place had to be approached by riding around the rim, and gradually descending to the level of the ruins. There were no villages in the immediate vicinity, though there were a number of farm dwellings some distance off. The overall feel of the place was to my mind much like Guzara, lonely on its craggy perch, silent against those vast dark ranges.

The Portuguese stonework was unmistakable, as was the overall design of the main building. Of all the Gojjam sites, this was by far the most difficult to access, but still I have this hope that one day the funding will be secured to send in a team of investigators to reopen the story the place yet conceals.

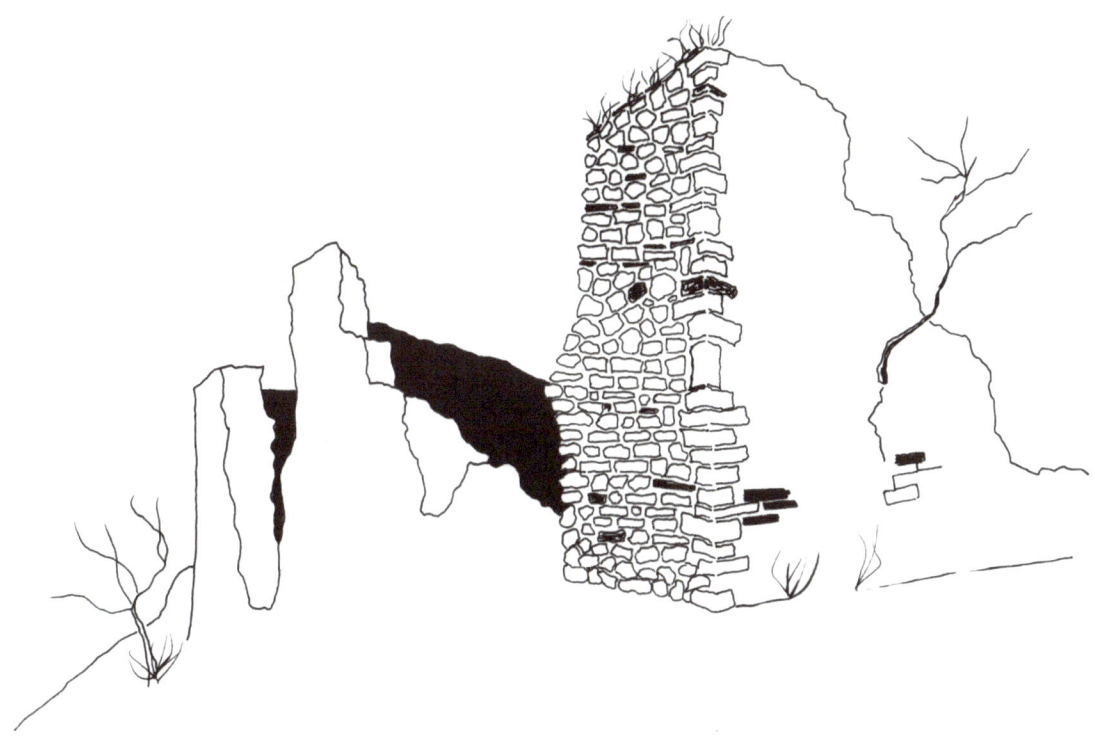

The ruins of Abba Gish Fasil

## Mai Gwa Gwa or Fremona

One of the most impressive and scenic bus rides available in all Africa is aboard the daily transport that plies the road north from Gondar to Tigray. There is a large portion of the route running between Debark and Inda Selassie, or Shire, the drama and beauty of which almost defies description. Nowhere I have ever travelled in Africa has there been a landscape to match it.

Priests and deacons sift the ashes for treasures after fire destroyed the church at Mai Gwa Gwa

It is a tiring drive but the eventual goal at the end of it, at least as far as this thesis is concerned, would be Adwa, locale of the great battle of 1896 when Emperor Menelik's barefoot warriors dealt Italy's considerably better equipped modern army a resounding defeat.

Adwa is a relatively modern town. Near it, on its western extremity, is the site of the old Jesuit headquarters of Mai Gwa Gwa, which the Jesuits chose to rename Fremona.

There is not a great deal left of the ruins at Fremona. There are a few holes in the ground which the local priest claims once constituted here a passageway, there a forge for casting iron. The "passageway" is likely all that is left of a cistern. The forge is a little more difficult to judge, although careful archaeological work would have much to reveal.

Most of the walls of the place have collapsed, and there is a mountain of rubble that is thought to have once been a building of some kind. Not much of anything, one would think, except that when one looks carefully at the structure of what few walls remain standing one should be impressed by the stonework.

The stones themselves are almost identical to a type of stone found in Portugal and known there as *xisto*, or slate. It is not the kind of gray slate associated with roofs and typical of northern Europe. This *xisto* is thicker and heavier, and tends to be brown in colour, with streaks of green or beige, sometimes some rust red. In Portugal, where there are many different kinds of *xisto*, this particular colour and quality is only found and quarried at Barrancos in the province of Alentejo. The town is famous for it. To see something so similar in far-off Ethiopia is an astonishing coincidence. More astonishing yet is to compare the stonework of the walls in both places.

Within a stone's throw of the Eritrean border are a number of ancient walls that are almost a carbon copy of walls that are still built in the same manner as at Barrancos. Walls made of this particular *xisto* need to be assembled in a very special way. The modern method is to use a cement mortar, but the old Barranquenho method is to use mud. When a wall is complete in this way it has an aspect totally unlike any other stone wall in Iberia. There it was, perhaps four-hundred-years-old, but perfect; and several thousand miles away from the one location where its form is commonplace in only that single location in the Alentejo.

Coincidence? Possibly not. It would be a long odds bet, but there are not a few *pedreiros* in Barrancos who would be prepared to state, categorically, that that wall in Fremona was built by one of their ancestors.

The *xisto* or slate wall at Mai Gwa Gwa, left, and a similar wall at Barrancos, Portugal, below

## Cobblestones

Various cities and towns in Ethiopia recently embarked upon the laying of cobblestones on many of their streets. This was certainly true in Bahir Dar, throughout 2009 for instance, when a make-work and urban enhancement program was begun – the whole project, from training and stone cutting through to the finished streets, being paid for and supervised through a German governmental assistance scheme. Hundreds of people have been successfully employed in this most popular of endeavours, and it has made a huge improvement to the appearance of the citiy.

The stonemasonry skills being applied in this work are newly acquired, and in this regard would appear to have no link whatever with anything that might have been passed down from previous generations. It is a European technique being implemented, but it is also interesting to remark that it was the Romans who spread the popularity of cobblestones throughout their old colonial empire. The western extremity of that empire was Portugal – where precisely the same techniques of cobblestoning are employed to this very day.

It is surprising, and delightful, to examine the work being done on the streets of Bahir Dar and make a comparison with what exists in every city of the Portuguese-speaking world. The cobblestoning looks similar, of course; but more than that, the manner in which the work is being undertaken, the cobbles being laid, is identical.

Beautiful cobblestone works, like this in Bahir Dar, are being instituted as make-work projects in many cities throughout Ethiopia, all under the aegis of German supervision and assistance. It is, in fact, the reinstitution of an ancient Roman technique of road-building – still practiced today in Portugal. The decorated sidewalk is particularly common in every town one may happen to visit in the Portuguese-speaking world.

## Amba Wehni

In his thrilling adventure travelogue, *The Mountains of Rasselas*, Thomas Pakenham tells the story of his search for Amba Wehni, the mountain top prison of Ethiopian royalty located in the austere country northeast of Lake Tana.

The idea behind an *amba* was its use as a form of detention camp where excess members of the royal family could be closely watched and guarded. Royal succession was always a problem in Ethiopia. For generations there was never a specific law of succession following a monarch's death. Since any one monarch might take himself numerous wives, there were always any number of children who might legitimately be considered possible successors to the throne. Upstart nobles could, and did, create considerable consternation by throwing their weight and loyalty behind one particular young prince over another. The *amba* system was established over a period of time as an effective means of ensuring that rivalries, jealousies and insurrections could be prevented from ever developing into serious confrontations with a reigning monarch, or creating problems during an interregnum.

Once an emperor had died, it was a relatively simple matter for the political powers of the court to summon a successor from the ranks of those imprisoned in the *amba*.

And the safest place of imprisonment was a mountaintop.

Pakenham had heard stories and legends about the existence of Wehni, and he spent many years trying to find the place. It took him a long time to pinpoint its location on a map; reaching it by travelling overland required a huge effort.

The houses of the prison residence were located on the very pinnacle of a gigantic rock. It rose vertically several hundred metres above its surrounding landscape, the vitrified plug of an ancient volcano. It resembled a giant's thumb, its sides so sheer the summit could only be attained by mounting a dizzying and rickety wooden staircase. This was the only way up or down, servants being forced to trudge its course daily with supplies of food and water; sentry posts were located at various points to make sure that none of the princes descended prior to being summoned by the court.

By the time Packenham arrived at the foot of the mountain the staircase had long since rotted away and he was able to ascend only a short distance before being forced to give up.

He left, but returned much later with a helicopter.

The pilot zoomed in and hovered over the precarious peak, its habitable living space totalling perhaps only two hundred metres in diameter. Stiff cross winds, the uneven ground and the growth of trees and tall shrubbery made landing impossible. Instead the pilot circled his craft a few times while Packenham leaned out and took photographs.

Several of these extraordinary pictures were published in his book, and one of them was of the ruins of a chapel built on the very top. Imagine my surprise when, studying the photograph carefully, I was able to recognize the tell-tale formation of a Portuguese style sanctuary, coupled with the all-too-familiar stonework and *reboco* rendering. As if these were not indication sufficient, the broken walls and caved-in roof gaped in such a way that one could clearly make out the interior form and manner of building. Just like the grand *sala* of Emperor Iyasu I's palace at Gondar, the ceiling and roof structure had once comprised close rows of brick arches, with flagstones, or *lajes*, laid down between them to form a covering and close the roof. Also, as with the numerous water mills up and down the Guadiana River in Portugal, the exterior was rendered with cement in such a way that the whole took on the same unique curved silhouette.

Seeing this photograph in Pakenham's book, and realizing its clear implications, gave me an eerie feeling of déjà vu, but it made complete sense.  Amba Wehni came into use as a detention fortress about the same time that all the other structures were being built in the provinces of Gondar, Begemdir and Gojjam.  The chapel's existence simply reinforces the thesis expressed throughout the pages of this book

This drawing of Thomas Pakenham's aerial photo of Amba Wehni clearly reveals
the brick arch and *lajes* structure of the site's chapel; compare this structure with
the ceiling photographs of Emperor Iyasu I's palace and Moinho do Gato, page 138

### Selassie Gemb (Washa), Sabara Dildiy, Ayba, Galawdewos church

With even the best of intentions, it is nigh on impossible to get to every site one hears about, so this section is necessarily little more than the briefest list of the sites I must leave until another day.

Tim and Kim Otte run a tourist lodge and camp at Gorgora, and have been of immense assistance in gathering local material relevant to this study.  Tim took photographs of Selassie Gemb (Washa), the small church encircled by a broken wall that had been built during the time of Emperor Sussenyos.  He also photographed an adjacent quarry from which masons had cut the stones used in the construction of nearby Maryam Gemb.  The quarry forms a cave, and the manner in which the stones have been neatly separated from the bedrock is clearly visible.

Old Selassie Gemb, on its bluff above Lake Tana, featured an impressive arcade of Portuguese-style stonework

An ornate relief carving in Portuguese style once graced the old circular church

Entrance to the old quarry

Sabara Dildiy is known to be a second Portuguese bridge that crosses the Blue Nile well down from the Alata Bridge at Tis'isat, somewhat east and north of Mota. The bridge's original structure has been broken and locals have erected a precarious substitute to allow passage from one side of the river to the other. As crossing at that point is especially needed, the membership of the Bahir Dar Rotary Club were engaged, in 2010, in the construction of another footbridge at the same site. Members told me that access from the Mota side requires a guide, and entails a four-hour hike over extremely rough terrain. They have been generously assisted by an American cultural heritage organization.

The palace at Ayba is located east of Gondar on an old trail that, in the mid-XVI century, was the main route connecting the Simien Mountains with the settlement at Denqaz. Known to have been built by the Portuguese, it was for several years the seat of Empress Sabla Vanggel, mother of Emperor Galawdewos. If this information is correct, it would indicate a site of about the same antiquity as Guzara. My understanding is that there is little more than a rough track leading there from Gondar.

Two additional sites about which I have heard only the scantiest detail – insufficient detail, in fact, as to keep me in doubt as to their actual existence – include a broken bridge over the Reb River, to the northeast of Lake Tana, and a Galawdewos church some distance to the east of Hamusit.

**Other references**

In *The Indigenous and the Foreign in Christian Ethiopian Art*, Ramos and Boavida, editors, there is a map that indicates several Jesuit structures discussed in this book. Not all of the place names correspond with the names to be found in the pages of this work; also the map, which affixes question marks to several sites, varies in some degree with the present work as to precise location of some of the sites.

Debaroa (Debarwa) and Adegada are marked as located in Eritrea, and are not reviewed in this book.

In Ethiopia itself, Maraba, indicated as being north of Gondar, is unknown to this author. Likewise Ledje Negus, Nafasha and Gabarma are all marked as being located in southwestern Gojjam in the vicinity of Debre Markos, but are not known to me. Depesan, marked as being in southern Gojjam, is also unknown to me – but Debsan is marked in other sources as being located to the northeast of Lake Tana.

Tumha appears to be the name of the place referred to in this work as Abba Gish Fasil; elsewhere the same location is called Nanina. Sarca would appear to be Yibaba, although elsewhere it is also described as being located on the east bank of the Little Abay River. Collala and Maryam Gemb are given as Gemb Giorghis, and Hadasha is the name of the location listed in this work as Gemb Kidane Mehret.

If "Arkana" is to be equated with "Atqhana," and if indeed it is actually Aringo (as suggested in this work), then its place on the Ramos/Boavida map is inaccurately marked, and it should be placed far closer to Debre Tabor.

It would be a mistake to find fault with authors or editors; they are anxious to do their best, but place names may vary a great deal. If discovered I have included alternates whenever possible. In such an ancient terrain many notable landmarks might be given local names, and sometimes several local names, all of which can add to the confusion. Ethiopian maps, particularly where obscure and little-known ruins are concerned, appear to be anything but consistent.

# Sundry Commentary

## Denial

The following essay outlines what I view as a serious problem confronting the intelligent examination of those portions of Ethiopia's past that specifically relate to elements reviewed in this overall study. The "problem" revolves around a denial of Ethiopian history – a factor I had not recognized earlier, or perhaps unconsciously downplayed, and which only presented itself to me once I had burrowed into a most precarious niche within the country's educational milieu at Bahir Dar.

This denial is thankfully espoused by a minority, but it nonetheless exacerbates an extraordinarily limited view of the world beyond Ethiopia's borders. More significantly it seeks to promote, at home, exaggeration to the point of outright dishonesty – a ludicrous attempt on the part of a few nationalistic self-promoters to enhance themselves and what they believe to be the country's status and position. Both the denial and the exaggeration are brute and overt, lacking even the most modest sophistication. One might be tempted to laugh off such blatant drum-beating propaganda, except that the lie encourages neglect of both the true value of Ethiopia's history and the many sites that are residue of that history. Such denial is an unsavoury moral crime.

Unfortunately this naysayer's viewpoint is stubbornly propounded by a lamentably uninformed and xenophobic approach on the part of a few senior university instructors and others – self-professed intellectuals intent, for some obscure and pathological reason (possibly political; certainly self-serving, if not quite capable of re-writing), in re-jigging the events of their country's own past. After learning of my views I was informed how one of these instructors had pronounced my opinions "dangerous." I hasten to turn the table: no, he and his viewpoint are dangerous.

Africa's nations – and here I talk not only about Ethiopia – are destined to remain in a state of tumultuous stasis (minus the equilibrium) until such time as all aspects of their sad histories can be confronted in total honesty and without recourse to corruptive pleadings, blamings, beggings, excusings – or self-serving denials.

I am aware that strong viewpoints can ruffle feathers, but it is almost impossible to discuss this very important matter without running head-on into someone's sensitivities and thus risk causing offence. I have remarked both the Portuguese and the Ethiopians are understandably sensitive towards their respective histories; in the case of either nationality an outsider exploring in this area will very likely find himself picking at the fringes of a most delicate tapestry.

So to start this discussion let us talk about the very basic premise of *A Story in Stones* in which, at numerous points, the terms "Gondarine" and "Portuguese" are freely interchanged.

Quite simply if a person is Portuguese, he or she will have a tendency to look through a Portuguese prism. As a means of abbreviation if not national pride, structural methods that appear familiar would be identified as "Portuguese." Accepted at face value it is really no more than a means to label or categorize. On the other hand, an Ethiopian – especially a naysayer – will see the same data from a totally different perspective, no doubt with a measure of pride as he or she looks upon those same creations appearing against an indigenous backdrop. In an effort to ensure that full credit is not drawn away from such ingenuity, a new name is coined – again, to categorize. After centuries of enslavement, colonization and racist denigration, Africans generally are nothing if not proud of positive achievements which speak directly to their great civilizations.

But the question – and my suspicion – is this: in this specific area of Ethiopia has the term "Gondarine" been coined deliberately in order to refrain from using the word "Portuguese?" I believe there is a valid argument here, and I have attempted to present it in *A Story in Stones*. The simplicity of the argument appears to open up a small can of worms. Such candid publication of the book's thesis appears to have prompted an almost apoplectic spluttering of indignation among the deniers.

In order to outline the issue clearly it is necessary to recount a more contemporary saga.

The English-language edition of *A Story in Stones* was first published in Canada in October, 2006. Based on the contents of that edition, which I was sure exuded impartiality, I was invited to conduct further researches at Bahir Dar University in Ethiopia. What a dream! It seemed at last the interest of Ethiopian scholars had been tweaked, and that there was now a cadre of them who wanted to follow through and examine this aspect of their history.

"Portuguese" or "Gondarine," at last an outside referee was being asked to appear to try to make some form of assessment in the case. It all presented a most exciting prospect, and I eagerly looked forward to returning to a country I had come to love, and to follow through on a theme that by that time had kept me occupied for more than a dozen years.

Well, dream on! The very same scholars who invited me to accompany them in further research were ultimately those responsible for blocking that research – going to considerable lengths to deny me personally, and most forcefully. Their efforts backfired, as malicious negativity tends to. Ultimately I was able to accomplish the bulk of the research on my own, but not without, inevitably, concluding that silencing the viewpoint I expressed – controlling it, squashing it – was the initial motive for inviting me. That could easily read like a pitiful case of paranoia, but in the context of the level of scholarship encountered within the university's History Department the comment actually makes total sense. In the two years of my association with Bahir Dar University, these same scholars failed to conduct any investigation whatever into this area – not a book, not a paper, not a single publication concerning this obvious and important historic theme. Not one. They simply denied, and the basis of their denial was intransigence. Nor have I been able to discover any effort to cover this area in the years since the university's History Department was constituted – some fifteen or twenty years prior to my own arrival.

Why? I put it down to a number of things: xenophobia, laziness, saving face, a twisted form of nationalism, bad teaching habits. The full answer goes to the very heart of the problems that confound Ethiopia's educational system, and requires a greater concentration of investigative research than is the mandate of this study.

**Histories**

When I had initially entered the country years earlier I had travelled south from Athens aboard an Ethiopian Airways flight, and had the opportunity of meeting on board with an Ethiopian historian who exclaimed to me:

"Ah! So you are coming to my country in order to examine an aspect of Ethiopian history …!"

"No," I corrected him, having in mind no more than my search for Pêro da Covilhã. "I am coming to examine an aspect of Portuguese history."

"But it is in Ethiopia that the two histories cross," he commented – by extension claiming Pêro da Covilhã for Ethiopia.

And of course, he was absolutely correct. Indeed, it was in Ethiopia that the two histories melded together and became one and the same thing; and it was in Ethiopia that Pêro da Covilhã spent at least half of his life – possibly more.

The degree of outright antagonism with which these obvious cross-over points were later met came as a complete surprise. I was confronted by Ethiopian historians who categorically refused to accept the evidence that I could see so clearly surrounded them – blindly refuting it, and with extreme force – at the same time brazenly admitting, almost as a mark of pride, that they themselves had done not a scratch of research on their own to prove their denials correct. It was as if it was *their* history, so they did not need to prove anything to some interfering *ferenghi*. This same small cadre of academics proclaimed the Portuguese had accomplished nothing of substance in the Highlands, that there were far too few of them to have built all the edifices I was claiming for them, and that in any case these same buildings were built by Ethiopians, not Portuguese. The few Portuguese that did enter the Highlands simply caused consternation, made a total nuisance of themselves, and were deservedly booted out of the country in 1634. Clinging to this viewpoint, they overlooked entirely the fact that there had been a very strong Portuguese presence in the land extending from 1492 until 1634 – a period of time that would allow for five generations. They did not want to know, or even hear of it.

"Prove it!" the deniers shouted.

It was stunning. I thought I had never heard of such abject idiocy – and out of the mouths of the very academics who had invited my continued research? Why this extraordinary denial in the face of such an accumulation of tangible (stone) evidence?

There are a number of complicated reasons, I believe, all of them trapped deep within the collective psyche of a fiercely proud, essentially traditional and conservative people. Ethiopia is one of only two African nations that has never been colonized. The country was defeated in war and subjugated to Italian tyranny for a period of six years, but it was hardly colonization, and the Italians never had a moment's peace throughout that entire period of time (1935-1941). Even so, Ethiopia's leaders in the modern era, dating back to Tewedros (1855-1868), were keenly aware of what was happening to other lands all around them, and their dealings with the European powers had never been easy. Possibly the one regime, the first and earliest, that had come closest to a form of colonization was precisely the Roman Catholic assault made by the Portuguese Jesuits in the XVI and XVII centuries; and once they had been unceremoniously booted out of the country, Ethiopia went into virtual hibernation for two-hundred years. In the end, the single unit that has always bound together the kaleidoscopic tribal mixture of these mountain peoples was the Ethiopian Orthodox Church. Within the Christian element of the Highlands this is still a major factor. In times past all the lands to the north of Ethiopia – as far as the Nile delta in Egypt – had once been Christian. Islam swept virtually all of it away. The single area that resisted, tenaciously and for two millenniums, has been Highland Ethiopia. This element of resistance to foreign incursion of any sort is yet to be found deeply imbedded within the people's nature.

By no means all Ethiopian academics are died-in-the-wool nationalistic deniers of their past. On the contrary by far the majority of genuine scholars, those who accept the vagaries and whimsies of a complex history, who are not fearful of facing their story with an open mind and an acknowledgement of what is, after all, a matter of most reasonable explanation (even if not immediately obvious), do indeed accept the Portuguese presence. Doubtless they are bemused by the forceful railings of the naysayers, but I believe for the most part they would agree with the general tenets of *A Story in Stones*.

My own contention, of course, is that there is such a bountiful selection of evidence to indicate the verity of the book's theme that the burden of proof now rests with the naysayers; that these same academics have for so long been convinced of their correctness that they by no means wish to consider arguments that might indicate they could be wrong. Not only might such consideration run the risk of being seen as an insidious and disruptive form of zealotry, but it could prove an affront to their well entrenched certainties. ("The inmates of all the world's insane asylums have many, many certainties" – Fernando Pessoa.)

As to the Portuguese sites themselves, it is almost amusing to see how the word "Gondarine" is so readily applied to those elements of architecture that fall within the purview of touristic interest. Further a-field, in remote areas where the Portuguese had been equally active, there is little attempt to identify sites with being of any particular derivation. Sadly, ignorantly, they are left to crumble as though, because of being off the beaten track, they do not exist.

In the meantime, cyclical cause and effect, denial of this kind encourages neglect of the sites themselves.

At times it has seemed to me that someone in a senior position within the educational system must have identified a reason for attempting to re-write, to "correct," the history of Ethiopia – in the same way that Mary Lefkowitz, the American writer, has identified a stream of Afro-American power-seekers in the United States intent on fabricating their history in order to muscle aside truth and shout their way into securing unto themselves a position on the high ground of a sure ignorance.

**Objectivity/Subjectivity**

This book's argument centres almost entirely upon a knowledge of Portuguese stonemasonry dating to the period in question. There is always a danger in confusing the dictates of *objective* history with the *subjective* requirements of art history. Historians consider themselves scientists. They require hard facts in the form of chronology and chronicle – proof, if they can get it. In contrast, the essence of successful art history (and, by extension, architectural history) is the subjective ability of deduction based upon sometimes very obscure secondary elements. Artists and builders do not always sign their work, and even more infrequently do they accompany it with chronology and chronicle.

In order to conduct a competent study of what is being named "Portuguese architecture" in Ethiopia's Highlands, surely it is not unreasonable to suggest that a thorough review be made of buildings of the same epoch within Portugal itself? Apart from certain comparisons made within the pages of *A Story in Stones*, no one I know of has seriously undertaken anything of the kind.

*A Story in Stones* was written by an "outsider," to be sure, but it remains the only work of its kind – identification through stonework – undertaken by anyone since the expulsion of the Portuguese in 1634.

**Stonework**

Bahir Dar is at the geographical fulcrum of a quantity of historic sites dating to the XVI and XVII centuries when the Portuguese, their families and descendants were particularly active in this general area of Highland Ethiopia. *A Story in Stones* attempts to list evidence far greater than mere coincidence that these sites show clear signs of Portuguese workmanship and know-how. Surely Bahir Dar University, therefore, should be the seat of an active centre of study and information on this subject?

But this is not the case. On the contrary, Bahir Dar University's History Department is the one sure place where those who could correct an appalling situation have chosen to hide out, do nothing, and shout their denials when the subject is raised.

Masterful stonework exists in other regions of Ethiopia – in Axum, Tigray, Lalibela, and elsewhere. I have visited and examined much of it. None of it has clear visible link to anything Portuguese. Design and structure clearly show marked differences. The patterns of stonework alluded to in the book, and the structures themselves, most of them in the Gojjam, Lake Tana, Gondar area, are significantly different from the ones found in these other regions. The buildings and walls differ in their concept and design, in the application and finishing of stonework, and in very many instances, in a decorative motif that clearly originates with the presence of the Portuguese.

I have no hesitation whatever in pronouncing Portuguese influence of such magnitude that it has stamped its *carimbo*, its mark, on virtually any buildings that might be sited today as "Gondarine" – and even some that pre-date the accepted "Gondarine" period. This influence is so strong that it may be found in numbers of the structures that have been built in the area – going back to the time of the arrival of Pêro da Covilhã in 1492/3.

Simply put, the building traditions and learned stonemasonry techniques initially introduced by the Portuguese continue – even to the present day, and there are many examples of it. It is subliminal. By now it is Ethiopian, but its origin is clear. Such examples of *mimesis* (the design term that roughly translates "the enforced mimicry brought on by the inability either to escape or forget") may be seen in present stonework, certainly, but also in the designs of doorways and window casings, very often in rendering or decoration.

Anyone who has ever visited a Portuguese or Portuguese colonial city anywhere in the world will recognize in an instant the method and decorative effect of the cobblestones currently being laid down in Bahir Dar and elsewhere in Ethiopia, for it represents a strong Portuguese tradition – even if its current manifestation is being paid for by the Germans. Streets and sidewalks throughout the Portuguese-speaking world have been made this way for centuries, and the tradition continues – a delightful left-over of Roman colonialism.

Had stonework traditions filtered south from northern Ethiopia, as some naysayers claim, one might reasonably expect to see a northern tradition repeated in the south; but this is not the case. Within the text of this book (pages 63 and 64) I recount how, in Gondar, there was an international conference on historic cities sponsored by the Japanese Embassy. To mark the occasion two antique style pavilions were erected in a small park near the castle compound – one Japanese, the other "Gondarine." I was able to study the "Gondarine" pavilion with great care. It follows most precisely in style, measurements and masonry technique, structures that have been built in the south of Portugal for centuries prior to the establishment of a Portuguese state.

**Flux**

It would seem particularly relevant to draw attention to the last paragraph of Professor Richard Pankhurst's very thoughtful Foreword to this book. It is a plea for continued research because this is the best (and only) way to initiate the preservation and restoration of a whole series of magnificent historical monuments. This vital theme is reiterated at several points in the text. The preservation of these old sites is essential to the better comprehension of Ethiopia's true history. By themselves, and just as they are, they constitute a munificent gift of past generations to the present day peoples of Ethiopia. Surely such a gift should be cherished?

The effect of ignoring these sites, or denying them their proper place in the panorama of Ethiopian history, not only constitutes the re-writing of the country's magnificent story – it spites the country itself. Properly tended and administered, these sites could be a source of real income. Due to inattention, one site in Bahir Dar has already all but disappeared – Shimbet Mikael. Instead of preserving what was left of a beautiful Jesuit monastery locals have been permitted to dismantle and carry off the very stones from the walls. Virtually nothing is left.

Even so, and for all time, the Portuguese presence is known. It is Ethiopia's history, and it cannot be denied. To naysayers tempted to warp the true course of events the author commends the excellent and scholarly book by Mary Lefkowitz, *Not Out of Africa – How Afrocentrism Became an*

*Excuse to Teach Myth as History*. This most courageous book details the extraordinary educational and political dangers to be encountered in twisting facts to accommodate short term political goals of narrow cultural expediency – even when the goals of themselves (and the enhancement of the re-writer) might be of noble intent. Ms. Lefkowitz's book deals with an American model, to be sure, but she is talking in most specific terms about the responsibility of all nations in matters of education when she concludes that bending history keeps scholars "… in a state of illusion, both about the true course of history and also the ways in which people have always been able to learn from cultures other than their own."

Ethiopians particularly need to pay attention to this lesson – a timely lesson for scholars who choose to juggle cavalierly with facts and myth and outright propaganda. One way or another the danger of negating essential elements of any history would be the devastating consequences it would have for the sites that tell a country's true story.

**Recap**

a) Portugal's most outstanding cultural expression is in three separate but absolutely inter-linked areas: ***poetry, architecture*** and, perhaps surprisingly to some because it is not widely-known outside Portugal, ***history***. Outsiders examining Portuguese culture would need to know the Portuguese language in order to appreciate the poetry. Architecture, on the other hand, is as universal as it is tangible. One may lack knowledge of the nation's language, or the intricacies of its culture and history, but this most emphatically does *not* indicate an inability to comprehend or appreciate the beauties of architectural form one will encounter in all corners of Portugal. In considering architectural examples in the Highlands of Ethiopia it is necessary, first, to pay close attention to similar examples in Portugal.

And one soon finds that to examine Portugal's history is to tackle something unique and quite extraordinary, unusual in the context of wider European history. The country's borders are the oldest in Europe; it was the first western nation to open up the world we know today. In doing this, Portuguese navigators set fire to the imaginations of all their countrymen. They saw themselves as invincible, god-like, giants among the western peoples who were just setting out on their first tentative steps into the Renaissance. This image of themselves gave rise to great nationalistic flourishes; it was expressed in poetry, and also in the poetry of the stone which was (and had been for centuries) an identifying symbol of the nation's view of its magnificent self. One may agree or disagree with any assessment of Portugal's grandeur, but it would be difficult to disagree with the manner in which Portugal either viewed itself or preferred to portray itself.

b) Portugal is known worldwide as a nation of builders. If a Portuguese is not a *pedreiro* (stonemason) he will in all likelihood, concerning the buildings that surround him, exhibit the self assuredness of the *empreteiro* (contractor). It is a known quantity in those parts of the world that have received large numbers of Portuguese immigrants: if one wants a structure to be built one will seldom do better than to call in a Portuguese craftsman; he and his ancestors have been expressing themselves in stone since before the nation was formed. Portuguese stonework has been transported worldwide and is recognized worldwide.

c) If Portugal's architecture can be judged unique it is because its stonework, also, is unique. Cross the border into Spain and one has immediately entered a totally different milieu in terms of stone. On the Portuguese side of the border scale is unique, design is unique; structure is unique; the lay-up of the stonework is distinct and identifiable. The very thought patterns behind any given construction (of the era and locale under consideration) is uniquely Portuguese, part of a deeply inculcated tradition. For centuries the Portuguese have expressed the poetry of their culture in their architecture and building – as well as in their language. The detail of their structures is essentially sculptural and, as such, is a known quantity. Popular folk forms are spontaneous, never pushing "the limits of admissible stress," as Martins Barata points out in the book he edited, *Architectura Popular Portuguesa*. Monumental and massive, or indigenously folksy and sprung from the rock on which it stands, Portuguese architecture is immediately recognizable to someone intimately, emotionally, connected to it.

d) The architecture in the north of Portugal differs greatly from the architecture in the south. This is due to many factors, not least of which is the ready availability of building materials, but also, and most significantly, to strong cultural influences – Burgundian in the north, Moorish in the south. Climate is also a major consideration.

e) When one is engaged in attempting to identify a painting, one looks for subject, its presentation, its composition and style, the colours and pigmentation, the brush strokes. There could be literally hundreds of considerations. Even without a signature, it is often possible to know who painted the piece. Similarly, when one is examining a sculpture there are tell-tale signs of its authorship, certain qualities that, to an expert, may announce its origin. The exercise differs little in considering architecture and stonework. The scale is grander, possibly, but the same qualities of artistry exist in its creation and, just as forcefully as with a painting or a work of sculpture, these serve to identify its maker(s).

f) Criticism has been offered that *A Story in Stones* did not take sufficiently into account the various early Ethiopian traditions of building in stone. Here my answer must be two-fold: firstly, there is a world of difference (as elaborated above) between the indigenous stonework of Ethiopia and the stonework being discussed in this book; secondly, the sub-title should make it very clear that it is "Portuguese influence" that is the intended theme of the work. While acknowledging that "history" knows no boundaries, the author begs impartiality; no slight or criticism is intended, but "Ethiopian influence," *per se*, would have been outside the book's intended scope – for reasons that should have become abundantly clear through the reading of the text.

g) Doubt has been cast on the numbers of Portuguese that entered the Highlands. As I have said, I believe there were considerably more of them than is generally accepted. Those who have read *A Story in Stones* will understand a wide interpretation of "Portuguese," and that the word in its context does not in any way indicate the colour of any particular man's skin. The Portuguese of the XVI and XVII centuries comprised many nationalities; one owed allegiance to a king or a prince in that era rather than to a chunk of real estate. Columbus was Genoese, lived across the river from Lisbon, sailed for the Spanish; Magellan's family name was Magalhães, a renowned Portuguese family. Likewise he embarked on his famous voyage – and died – for the Spanish. The population of Portugal, as with its navy especially, was drawn from everywhere. The "Portuguese" were present and active in Ethiopia's Highlands for a little more than one hundred and forty years – approximately five generations. It is fair to assume, though it is unlikely we will ever know for sure, that many of them were not Portuguese by blood – but they had sailed under a Portuguese flag, were considered by the Portuguese themselves to be Portuguese, and their service and allegiance was to a Portuguese king. Five generations would allow for the accumulation of a great number of "Portuguese" – of all colours and shades – just as it would also prove sufficient to introduce shifts, key elements of a differing culture. There can be no question that those "Portuguese" who remained in the Highlands were very rapidly "Ethiopianized," but the dominant culture of their paternal linkage, through allegiance if not actually by blood, was clearly much slower in changing. Portugal established, and very early, a vice kingdom – a "capital" – at Goa, on India's western coast. Her control of the entire Arabian Sea coast of India would have ensured that many Indians – Gujaratis, Goans – would have journeyed to Ethiopia as "Portuguese." In the early chapters of his book of travels, Fernão Mendes Pinto makes it clear there were many, many Portuguese to be found at the Red Sea coast, all of them anxious to travel to the lush lands of the interior. In time they became mercenaries, traders, farmers – and virtually all of them husbands.

h) Colleagues have been encouraged to consider the presented thesis not because of any craving for approval, but because to deny it outright would signal "end of argument," "end of discussion." That might conveniently suit the naysayers, but would also crimp effective and much-needed research and discussion into what is in every respect a fascinating hypothesis if not as yet an acceptably "proven" aspect of Ethiopia's history that both pushes outwards and pulls inwards, working in every conceivable direction.

## The Wars with Ahmad Grag'n

After 1526 some personnel from the Portuguese Embassy remained behind, and by now there were considerable numbers of Portuguese and other foreigners who had trekked into the Highlands. None that we know of kept any record that would inform us further on the life of Pêro da Covilhã. The year 1526, then, the date he bade the embassy farewell from Massawa, is the last we hear of him. He would have been sixty-six-years-old. He may have died shortly after that or, for all we know, he may have lived another twenty years.

We do know that just four years later, in 1530, the Muslim prince of Adal, Ahmad ibn Ibrahim el-Gazi, known as Ahmad Grag'n the Left-Handed, launched a massive all-out attack against the Christian Highlands. For eleven years he caused such havoc that even today some Christian Highlanders possess an almost fearful suspicion of Muslim lowlanders. This major attack had been preceded by smaller skirmishes over a considerable period of time, but they had increased in both number and cruelty over the last three years. In most Christian quarters there was a general premonition of the turmoil to come.

A giant whose personal rise to prominence first required the usurpation of a coastal lowland throne, Grag'n had made alliances with seaborne Turks who, since 1513, had been resisting the incursions of the Portuguese into the Red Sea. When he finally turned on the Highlands, it was with such a ferocity that Christianity came very close to being eradicated.

Dowager Empress Eleni who, in 1508, had become regent to the new child emperor, Lebna Dengal, and had contrived to bring Pêro da Covilhã close within court circles, had foreseen serious trouble with coastal Islam. It was for this reason that she had agitated for an alliance with the Portuguese, culminating in the arrival of the embassy led by Rodrigo de Lima in 1520. It is ironic that the Portuguese, who had initially been hoping to ally themselves with a mighty Prester John, and so defeat Islam once and for all, were now being pressed into supplying some sort of assistance to keep the Highland Christian empire intact.

At first the Portuguese appear to have demurred. Their forces were, after all, well occupied in securing the Indian Ocean and beyond. Also, as he grew older and assumed his rightful position on his throne, it was the young Emperor Lebna Dengal himself who demurred. He was wilful and proud, and insisted that the Ethiopians did not require the assistance of any foreigners. Eleni died in 1523, and without her counsel the headstrong young emperor was free to run his affairs as he saw fit. Even Pêro da Covilhã's position appears to have been reduced to something rather lower key than it had been before. From the time of his assuming full responsibility for his empire until the end of his reign in 1540, by which time he had been forced into requesting Portuguese assistance, Lebna Dengal was chased from one mountain top to another fighting rear guard actions or, more often than not, fleeing from battle situations because his own forces were too inadequate.

Grag'n showed the Christians no mercy. His hordes swarmed over the Highlands, destroying churches and burning the precious ecclesiastical heritage of one of the oldest Christian entities in the world. The brutality of his campaign resulted in a catastrophic loss of texts and iconography, precious records going back to the very beginnings of the church in the IV century. Whole congregations of Christians were forced at sword point to convert to Islam; thousands resisted and thousands died.

The Portuguese took their time coming to the rescue. In December, 1541, an expeditionary force consisting of four hundred well-trained and diehard soldiers landed at Massawa under the command of Vasco da Gama's youngest son, Cristóvão. Lebna Dengal had died the year before, and the throne was now occupied by his young son, Emperor Galawdewos.

The new emperor was busy fighting for his life in the interior of the country, and it was the emperor's mother, Queen Sabla Vanggel, with whom the Portuguese had first contact. She accompanied the foreign army into the first of their successful battles at Amba Sanayt, and from then on the combined forces of Ethiopians and Portuguese were able to push the Muslims back. It was in the third confrontation Cristóvão da Gama was caught and killed.

The survivors of the Portuguese army remained with Galawdewos and, in February, 1543, at a fourth encounter, they faced Ahmad Grag'n and his forces at the Battle of Waina Dega, high in the mountains to the northeast of Lake Tana. Grag'n was killed, and his dispirited army was chased back to the coastal lowlands.

This was not the conclusion of all the troubles between the Christians and coastal Islam, but Waina Dega did mark a turning point. In a very real sense this small band of dedicated and well-armed Portuguese was the group that made the essential difference, and was thus able to ensure Christianity survived in the Highlands.

**Legacy**

Pêro da Covilhã and Vasco da Gama, vastly different men in temperament and action, were two of the great Portuguese explorer/discoverers operating in the area of East Africa and the Indian Ocean at approximately the same time. Da Covilhã was actually the first; he was sent out on his famous reconnaissance mission in 1487. Da Gama, who did not embark until 1497, was following up on da Covilhã's findings of the decade before. Nevertheless, it is the heroic actions of da Gama that are celebrated in Portugal's history, and especially literature; recognition of da Covilhã's actions, which were no less heroic and arguably more so, fades into obscurity when stood against those of his contemporary.

Written record of Pêro da Covilhã is meagre, and one must necessarily deduce much concerning the man's character. One thing seems very clear: he entered the Highland world of Ethiopia with an open mind, and it was this that ensured his survival. He accepted what he found. In return he was befriended and loved, made an honoured member of the emperor's court. He was given a position of trust. One would like to think it was da Covilhã's values that were instrumental in bringing Portugal and Ethiopia together as equals, the one accepting of the other. It is a most reasonable assumption that it was due to the influence of Pêro da Covilhã – especially with Empress Eleni – that Portugal established amicable ambassadorial relations with Ethiopia in 1520.

However it was da Gama's set of values, implemented over a far wider region than merely the Highlands of Ethiopia, that won the approval of Portugal's monarch and set the standard of the day.

His actions were those of an intolerant and brutal conqueror. He was an elitist who, while securing great profits for the coffers of the king he served, as well as a chestful of glories for himself, inaugurated for the indigenous communities he subdued an abusive and murderous period of corruption and instability. The world has hardly rid itself of these influences even by the passing of a further five centuries. In Portugal the man is venerated, to be sure, but by no means all conscientious Portuguese feel this way.

Just argument can be made that Vasco da Gama's tumultuous entry into the Indian Ocean constituted the initiation of a rapidly expanding colonial era, setting a dreadful example that was quickly picked up and emulated around the globe. How would the course of subsequent world history have changed if Portugal had instead placed a greater emphasis on the Christian paradigm of tolerance and acceptance exemplified by Pêro da Covilhã? As true today as it was then, personal ambition and greed appear to win every time over altruism.

Luís Vaz de Camões, of even greater cultural import to Portugal than Shakespeare is to Britain, truly the very font of the country's self image, was himself caught up in the great adventure of the day, and wrote his magnificent epic poem about Vasco da Gama, not about Pêro da Covilhã. In very short order, *Os Lusíadas* (1572) became the supreme work that defined Portuguese heroism and the manner in which this plucky maritime nation viewed itself. Prior to Camões one might say the Portuguese constituted an amorphous nation that, while flexing its muscles, was yet not quite big enough, or ready, to know itself. At the height of her power Portugal's population had not attained one and a half million souls. *Os Lusíadas*, however, stamped them and left no doubt whatsoever as to who they were. Even today one may point to this poem as the worthiest definition of the nation, the people and their resilient culture.

Pêro da Covilhã had such an adventurous life, his findings were so significant, it is hard to see how he could have failed to be the subject of heroic historical interest. Yet somehow has he failed to make the grade. One must suppose this was largely due to the fact that he never returned home to collect whatever laurels might have been his due. There was never a great bibliography of his exploits extant in Portugal; perhaps there would be greater evidence of him in the land where he spent the major part of his life, rather than in the homeland he left as a relatively young man. With this in mind I decided to try picking up his trail in Ethiopia, and flew out there for the first time at the beginning of 1996.

In the process of trying to track Pêro da Covilhã, and garnering from locals various fascinating morsels of legend about him and the geography that would have been familiar to him in Ethiopia's Highlands, I unwittingly unearthed something quite different. The initial search was in no way intended to seek out or reveal any specific architectural vestige, and yet the discovery of such a treasure seems to have dovetailed quite fortuitously with Pêro da Covilhã's personal (and local) history – his unique position as advisor to the imperial court, and his possible association with at least a couple of the sites examined in this book.

My own background as sculptor and, more especially, as a stonemason trained in Portugal, was in precisely the same building techniques employed by the Portuguese at the time they arrived in the Highlands. By no means do I consider myself a *mestre pedreiro* the equal of the phenomenal craftsmen with whom I worked in Portugal, but the skill I learned over a period of twelve years has certainly enabled me to identify structures that till now have remained a Highland mystery. Furthermore, in addition to the examples of monumental architecture – castles, churches, bridges, and so on – these years of on-the-job training have permitted me to zero in on a mass of humbler structures such as cottages, residences, utilitarian buildings - and simple walls. This, in turn, has served to demonstrate demographic movement and, in some way, numbers, and is thus a most useful means to assist in indicating the spread of the Portuguese into and over the African hinterland. It is not foolproof, but buildings indicate people; lots of buildings tend to suggest lots of people to use and inhabit them.

The Portuguese remained in the Highlands for approximately one hundred and forty years. After Pêro da Covilhã himself, and the few who followed him in the immediate succeeding years, the first Portuguese of any note to arrive in the Highlands came with Rodrigo de Lima's embassy in 1520. In subsequent years many more followed as missionaries, mainly Jesuits, and soldiers. Many more individuals came as deserters from the hellish life aboard the Portuguese ships plying the Indian Ocean, not a few of whom signed on with Highland warlords as soldiers of fortune.

In light of what we tend to think of Ethiopia today, it is perhaps strange to realize that the popular image of the land of Prester John in the XVI and XVII centuries was that it constituted an Eden, a Paradise. Even as late as 1759, Samuel Johnson's famous fantasy, *The History of Rasselas, Prince of Abissinia*, depicts Ethiopia as an earthly Eden. It is estimated that at one time there were no fewer than six thousand Portuguese living within the great bend of the Blue Nile River as it encompasses the eastern regions of the province of Gojjam.

It is not difficult to believe that a goodly number of them were seeking Paradise as they wound their respective paths into these Highlands.

All these Portuguese were men, though not all were true Portuguese. Some were foreigners who had been press-ganged into serving in the Portuguese navy. They were considered Portuguese by the local Highlanders though, and invariably referred to that way. A great number, particularly those who actually hailed from Portugal, were builders – as the Portuguese remain to this day.

This is an important point: as one might say that the Welsh are singers, the Scots thrifty, or the French most knowledgeable of their kitchens, so one may claim that the Portuguese have always known about building. Architecture is one of their prime cultural expressions. Throughout the land, and no matter the level of education or culture, the Portuguese have a deep sense of structure and their unique form of national architecture. Perhaps it is natural in a people whose land is so well endowed with suitable building materials: granites, some of the finest qualities of marble in the world, and an abundance of different clays which have for centuries nurtured a supportive ceramic industry. This gigantic interest in ceramics, from earliest times, was chiefly utilitarian. Ceramic bricks and roof tiles have been manufactured throughout the country for centuries. Plain and glazed terra cotta forms were developed for both decorative and building purposes. That highly decorative tile work was brought north from the Maghreb into Iberia is well known. It is a toss-up as to whether the Dutch taught the Portuguese the secrets of their *azuleijos* wall tile decoration, or the Portuguese taught the Dutch what later became universally recognized as delftware.

So it was with this intense background in the building trades that these men entered the Highlands. They married local girls, built their homes, raised families and farmed the land. Their offspring commenced a racial blending which, over the full one hundred and forty years, produced a people quite indistinguishable from the indigenous population. It was a total mix – a feature prevalent and well documented in all areas of the Portuguese-speaking world. Not even the Spanish, and certainly not the English or French, promoted the mixing of races to so flamboyant a degree.

By the time the Roman Catholics and Portuguese were expelled from the Highlands in 1634, the strongest cultural trait left behind, apart from the mix of people themselves, was the utility of Portuguese prototypes in stone construction. Stone building was not introduced into Ethiopia by the Portuguese, but the particular form of Portuguese structure where it exists is unmistakable. It is so very utilitarian that the stamp of it has been strong enough to ensure elements of these techniques continue to be seen in Ethiopian building to this present day.

Much of this history had been lost or forgotten, and at both the Portuguese and Ethiopian ends.

For centuries, Portuguese records have been maintained in fearful disarray. The catastrophe of the 1755 Lisbon earthquake and fire destroyed, among other things, the country's principal archive. Duplicates of many lost originals did survive, and more are being discovered every year. Many documents and letters over the years found their way to alternate archives, but were often forgotten and left there to rot. Some were lodged in academic centres or the private libraries of aristocratic homes and they, too, disappeared.

Many captains who sailed the Portuguese ships were favoured sons of noble families; many were courtiers, the sons of privilege and wealth. Their families maintained large houses, *quintas, montes* and *solars*, each having a chapel, a library or perhaps both. Many personal documents and accounts of their voyages were stored by these men in their homes and personal archives; in many cases these homes remained with the same families up into the XX century. Few systematic searches were ever conducted of these private properties. It would have been costly and most families, even if they had the interest, were not sufficiently educated in archaeological method to maintain their documents in good order, or to undertake detailed examination of them. It was only in the two decades following the Portuguese revolution of 1974 that there began a concerted effort within Portugal, along with sufficient funding through the European Union, to find, gather, collate and catalogue what yet remains. Colleges and universities now had the money to train historians, archivists and museum specialists, and throughout the country there has developed a renewed interest and pride in the accomplishments of the past.

Despite what has been lost, what is left still constitutes an immense documentation of Portugal's history. These are exciting years to be an historian or archaeologist in Portugal, for a great deal is coming to light that heretofore has been hidden away on dusty shelving, or packed into boxes in obscure attics. Overseas, too, in long forgotten corners of Lusitanian penetration, records are coming to light, new sense is being made of ancient artefact.

Historically, details of Portugal's ignominious expulsion from Ethiopia, from a national and patriotic point of view, were easily and conveniently forgotten. The simple facts made it into the history books, but the greater story was really one of national failure; even something of a national disgrace. It turned out to be an embarrassment easily shucked into the background by the dazzle of sudden new riches to be gained in Far Eastern trade – in spices, precious metals and fabrics. This wealth exceeded by far the cash value of anything to be gained from the Ethiopian Highlands.

On the Ethiopian side long years of war, poverty and the necessities of daily survival served to act as a blanket obscuring the distant and painful memories of the period of agitation and humiliation brought on by the purveyors of a Roman brand of Christianity.

The true origin of the architectural skills and vestige left behind over so many generations very soon faded into a collective obscurity and amnesia.

Apart from one or two Portuguese words that appear to have entered the Amharic language, the stone ruins to be found today in certain areas of Ethiopia's Western Highlands provide the principal indication that Portugal ever passed that way.

## The Kwer'ata Re'esu

*Kwer'ata re'esu*, "the striking of His head," is the name given to both an attitude and a specific image of Jesus Christ, an icon most often found painted on wood, and venerated throughout Ethiopia's Christian Highlands. Such icons were, and continue to be, usually small and easily transportable. According to research conducted by Prof. Richard Pankhurst, the first icon bearing this motif was brought to Ethiopia from either Egypt or Jerusalem, and presented to Emperor Dawit I (1382-1413). This original was said to have been painted by St. Luke, and was thus held in exceptionally high regard. Subsequently it was lost, no trace of it ever having been found. The original to which the chronicles refer appears to have become a template for hundreds of very similar icons, same image content, which over centuries have become popular depictions of Christ. The words k*wer'ata re'esu*, then, have come to represent both a specific, historic, icon given to the emperor as a gift, and the attitude of the figure – the head of Christ, his crown of thorns, his torso, and his hands presented palms forward as though showing them to his doubting disciples.

Photograph of the *kwer'ata re'esu* stolen by the British at Maqdala in 1868

In his detailed study, Pankhurst referred to many recorded instances when the *kwer'ata re'esu* was used by the reigning emperor as a symbol of his power and majesty. Whether or not it was the original is not stated, neither is the precise point at which the original might have been lost and replaced by another. In the centuries after Dawit there are many references to the icon being used as a focal point of courtly and military ceremony. It appears that knights and senior servants of the emperors were obliged to swear their allegiance before it, particularly during court and religious ceremonies, or prior to entering into battle. Legend grew that the *kwer'ata re'esu* which replaced the lost original was a gift to the emperor of Ethiopia from the king of Portugal, and that it was presented by a Portuguese Jesuit missionary. Emperors Yohannes I, Iyasu I, Iyasu II, Bakafa, Iyoas, Teklahaimanot, Tekla Giorghis, Tewedros II – all are mentioned in numerous chronicles and letters linking their authority to the icon, and venerating it as one of the holiest of relics, capable of extending divine protection during times of tumult.

Over the years the *kwer'ata re'esu* has become a major theme in Ethiopian ecclesiastical art, and the one possessed by the emperor, considered especially holy, gathered about itself an understandable mystique though references to it spasmodically disappeared and reappeared in the years following the city of Gondar's decline in the early XIX century. By 1855, the year of Emperor Tewedros II's coronation, the icon is specifically mentioned as being a part of the imperial regalia as he set off to war in Wallo and Shoa. It was hanging over the head of his bed at his Maqdala redoubt when the British military expedition under General Robert Napier entered the Highlands in April, 1868.

Two examples of the popular *kwer'ata re'esu* motif in Ethiopian iconography

The story of Tewedros' depressions and madness, his ultimate suicide in the face of Napier's brutal punitive expedition, is a matter of well-documented historical record. What is not so well known is that Napier entered the Highlands accompanied by a man named Richard Rivington Holmes, one of the acquisitions curators of the British Museum, and the expedition's appointed archaeologist. The British conducted a massive looting at Maqdala, no small amount of it at the hands of Holmes himself. He wrote about it in letters, making no attempt whatsoever to disguise actions which at that time and place, although undoubtedly theft, were nonetheless considered perfectly normal and above board – spoils of war.

Holmes returned to Britain with a mass of artefact. He carried with him bundles of stolen papers, documents and precious artwork. Amongst it all he had filched an ancient and sacred copy of the *Kebra Nagast*, one of the holiest and most intensely venerated books in the Ethiopian Orthodox Church; moreover, he took the *kwer'ata re'esu* found hanging over the emperor's bed.

Emperor Tewedros was succeeded by Yohannes IV. In 1872 the new emperor wrote to Queen Victoria and the British Foreign Secretary complaining that the two holy items were necessary symbols of his regal authority and he – indeed, the nation – wanted them back. Their absence adversely impacted his governance. The *Kebra Nagast* ultimately found its way home, but the icon had disappeared. Although he had turned over to the British Museum most of the artefacts stolen from Maqdala, Holmes had decided to hang onto the icon. In 1870 he was appointed chief librarian at Windsor Castle, and it was there in 1890, that it was discovered to be hanging on a wall with the simple inscription "Maqdala – 13 April 1868."

Art historians pored over the painting, and there grew to be considerable controversy as to whether it was Flemmish in origin, or Venetian, or Portuguese. Portuguese art historians claim it was painted by the XV century Portuguese artist Jorge Afonso, and that it arrived in Ethiopia in the first quarter of the XVI century. Rendered in tempera, it covered an oak panel measuring just over thirty-one centimetres high and twenty-six centimetres wide.

Holmes died in 1911. It seems that the icon was a part of his estate, and had only been "on loan" to the royal collection at Windsor. In 1917 Holmes' brother auctioned the work at Christie's in

London. It was purchased for the sum of £420 by a Mr. Martin Reid of Wimbledon, and would once more have vanished from the scene except that an art historian from the University of Coimbra in Portugal argued forcefully in one of London's prestigious art magazines that the work was Portuguese, neither Flemmish nor Venetian. He insisted the composition was very typically Portuguese. The "gesture of the hands, the attitude of the head, the drawing of the robe and of the aureole, the treatment of the crown of thorns, modelling of the face and hands," all spoke most convincingly as similar to, and in some aspects the same as, work already well identified as having originated in a XVI century Portuguese school of religious painting.

In 1950 the *kwer'ata re'esu* was once more put up for auction. The Ethiopian government desperately wanted the icon to be returned to Addis Ababa, but its ambassador in London appeared too late at the auction house to place a bid on the work. It had already been sold, and finally fetched all of £315.

The buyer turned out to be none other than the Portuguese art historian who had argued so strenuously that the painting was Portuguese in origin, Professor Luís Reis Santos. The *kwer'ata re'esu* was duly returned to Portugal.

In 1998 I interviewed Senhora Dona Isabel Reis Santos, widow of the famous art historian, at her home in Coimbra. I knew that the painting languished in the vault of a Coimbra bank, and I wanted to see it, possibly take a better photograph, and in colour, than the black and white image of it that had appeared heretofore in newspaper articles. We talked of Ethiopia, and the yearning of the Ethiopians to have their precious icon returned to them.

Senhora Isabel appeared to know nothing of the work's special and mystical meaning. She agonized over her dwindling family fortunes, and saw the work as a means of setting them to rights. Before he died her husband had told her the icon was of "great value." Did I have any idea how much she might be able to get for it?

It was priceless, I told her. To anyone in Portugal, herself included, it was worth money; to the Ethiopians it was – and remains – a portion of their national soul.

She thanked me for coming to see her and telling her about her painting. No, she said, it would not be possible to see it. It was lodged in the bank, and there it must remain – out of sight. In any event, she commented, it would probably be near impossible to sell it. The Portuguese government would consider it *património*, and would surely intervene to prevent it leaving the country.

This generous gift from a Portuguese monarch was held in such high esteem by its recipient that he chose to enter it into his muster of royal treasure. It is ironic that after becoming stolen property, the same treasure should be withheld from its rightful and legal inheritors by those who gave the gift in the first place.

Christ's blessing, *Mestres do Sardoal*, Portugal; Portuguese school, early XVI century: could this have been the prototype for Ethiopia's *kwer'ata re'esu*?

## Select Bibliography

Álvares, Pedro Francisco - *Narrative of the Portuguese Embassy to Abyssinia during the years 1520-1527* - translated into English by Lord Stanley of Alderley - Burt Franklin, New York: The Hakluyt Society, 1970. Originally published in Portuguese as *Verdadera Informação das Terras do Preste João das Índias*, Lisbon, 1540

Arab Faqih (Sihab ad-Din Ahmad bin Abd al-Qader bin Salem bin Utman) - *Futuh al-Habasa* - The Conquest of Abyssinia (16th Century), translated by Paul Lester Stenhouse with annotations by Richard Pankhurst - Tsehai Publishers, Hollywood, 2003

Barata, Martins - editor, *Architectura Popular Portuguesa. Casas Portuguesas*, Resopal Edition, Lisbon, 1989

Barbosa Teixeira, Gabriela de, and Cunha Belém, Margarida da - *Diálogos de Edificação - estudo de técnicas tradicionais de construção restauro* - Associação Arquitectos Portugueses - Lisbon, 1998

Beckford, William - *European Travels* - (letters) - London, 1834

Beckingham, C.F., and Huntingford, G.W.B. - *The Prester John of the Indies* - Cambridge, 1961

Beckwith, Carol, and Fisher, Angela - photographs - text by Graham Hancock - *African Ark - Peoples of the Horn* - Collins Harvill, London, 1990

Beke, Charles T. - A Description of the Ruins of the Church of Martula Mariam in Abessinia - paper submitted to the Society of Antiquaries, May, 1846

Bishop, George - *A Lion to Judah – The Travels and Adventures of Pedro Paez, S.J* - X. Diaz del Rio, S.J., Gujarat Sahitya Prakash, Anand, Gujarat, India, 1998

Boxer, C.R. - *The Portuguese Seaborne Empire, 1415-1825* - Hutchinson & Co., London, 1969

Brooks, Miguel F. - translation and editing - *The Kebra Nagast* (The Glory of Kings) - The Red Sea Press, Lawrenceville, NJ, 1996

Bruce, James of Kinnaird - *Travels to Discover the Source of the Nile in the Years 1768, 1769, 1770, 1771, 1772 and 1773* - Edinburgh, 1790

Budge, E.A. Wallis - *History of Ethiopia - Nubia and Abyssinia* - London, 1928

Burton, R.F. - *First Footsteps in East Africa* - Tylston and Edwards, London, 1894

Camões, Luís Vaz de - *Os Lusíadas* - Lisbon, 1572

Caraman, P. - *The Lost Empire - The Story of the Jesuits in Ethiopia* - London, 1985

Castanhoso, Miguel de - *História das cousas que o muy esforçado capitão Dom Cristóvão da Gama fez nos reynos do Preste João, com quatrocentos Portugueses que consigo levou* - Lisbon, 1558

Cheesman, R.E. - *Lake Tana and the Blue Nile* - London, 1936

Delumeau, Jean - *Une Histoire du Paradis - Le jardin des délices* - Fayard, Paris, 1992

Durão Ferreira, Fernanda - *O Estilo Gondar* - Contra Ponto, Lisbon, 2003

*Encyclopaedia Aethiopica* - Harrassowitz Verlag, Wiesbaden, 2003

Esteves Pereira, F.M. - *Cronica de Sussenyos, Rei de Etiópia* - Lisbon, 1900

Ficalho, Conde de - *Viagens de Pêro da Covilhã* - Lisbon, 1898

Fonseca, Luís Adão da - *Vasco da Gama – o homem, a viagem, a época* - Expo '98, Lisbon, 1998

Girma Beshah and Merid Wolde Aregay - *The Question of the Union of the Churches in Luso-Ethiopian Relations (1500-1632)* - Lisbon, 1964

Gomes de Brito, Bernardo - *The Tragic History of the Sea*, edited by C.R. Boxer, Cambridge University Press for the Hakluyt Society, No. CXII, 1957; No. CXXXII, 1968. Originally published as *História Trágico-Marítima* - Lisbon, 1729-36

Hancock, Graham - *The Sign and the Seal* - William Heinemann, London, 1992

Hastings, Adrian - *The Church in Africa, 1450-1950* - Oxford University Press, 1996

Heldman, Marilyn, with Munro-Hay, Stuart C. - *African Zion - the Sacred Art of Ethiopia* - essays by Donald E. Crummey, Roderick Grierson, Getatchew Haile, Richard Pankhurst, Taddesse Tamrat, Siegbert Uhlig and Carla Zanotti-Eman - Yale University Press, 1993, in association with InterCultura, Fort Worth; The Walters Art Gallery, Baltimore; The Institute of Ethiopian Studies, Addis Ababa

Henze, Paul B. - *Layers of Time – a history of Ethiopia* - Hurst & Co., London, 2000

Huntingford, G.W.B. - *The Historical Geography of Ethiopia, from the First Century AD to 1704* - London, 1989

Isichei, Elizabeth Allo - *A History of Christianity in Africa: from antiquity to the present* - Society for Promoting Christian Knowledge, London, 1995

Johnson, Samuel - *The History of Rasselas, Prince of Abissinia* - London, 1759

Lefkowitz, Mary - *Not Out of Africa - how Afrocentrism became an excuse to teach myth as history* - Basic Books, Perseus Books Group, New York, 1996

Levine, D. - *Wax and Gold - Tradition and Innovation in Ethiopian Culture* - University of Chicago, 1965

Livermore, H.V., editor - *Portugal and Brazil - an introduction* - Oxford University Press, 1953

Macaulay, Rose - *They Went to Portugal* - Jonathan Cape, London, 1946

Marques, Alfred Pinheiro - *Guia de História dos Descobrimentos e Expansão Portuguesa* - Biblioteca Nacional, Lisbon, 1988

McIntyre, Kenneth Gordon - *The Secret Discovery of Australia - Portuguese ventures 200 years before Captain Cook* - Souvenir Press, London, Medindie and Toronto, 1977

Merid Wolde Aregay - A Reappraisal of the Impact of Firearms in the History of Warfare in Ethiopia (c.1500-1800) - *Journal of Ethiopian Studies, XIV* - Addis Ababa, 1980

Moorehead, Alan - *The Blue Nile* - Hamish Hamilton, 1962; revised, 1972; Penguin Books, London, 1983

Murphy, Dervla - *In Ethiopia with a Mule* - John Murray Ltd., London, 1968

Norberto, José (co-ordinator) - *Arquitectura Popular em Portugal* (3 vols.) - Associação Arquitectos Portugueses - Lisbon, 1988

Nowell, Charles - *The Great Discoveries and the First Colonial Empires* - Cornell University Press, 1954

Page, Martin - *The First Global Village - How Portugal Changed the World* - Editorial Noticias, Lisbon, 2002

Pakenham, Thomas - *The Mountains of Rasselas* - Weidenfeld & Nicolson, London, 1998

Pankhurst, Richard - *A Social History of Ethiopia* - Institute of Ethiopian Studies, 1990; The Red Sea Press, Trenton, NJ, 1992

Pennec, Hervé - *Des jésuites au royaume du Prêtre Jean (Ethiopie): stratégies, recontres et tentatives d'implantation 1495-1635* - Paris, 2003

Pinto, Fernão Mendes - *Peregrinação* - Lisbon, 1614. Published as *The Travels of Mendes Pinto* - edited and translated into English by Rebecca D. Catz - The University of Chicago Press, 1989

Ramos, Manuel João, and Boavida, Isabel (editors) - *The Indigenous and the Foreign in Christian Ethiopian Art: On Portuguese-Ethiopian Contacts in the 16th-17th Centuries* - Burlington, 2004

Rey, C.F. - *The Romance of the Portuguese in Abyssinia* - London, 1929

Salt, H. - *A Voyage to Abyssinia* - London, 1814

Sanceau, Elaine - *Portugal in Quest of Prester John* - Hutchinson & Co., London, 1941

Santos, Mª Emília Madeira - *Viagens de Exploração Terrestre dos Portugueses em África* - Lisbon, 1978

Shabot, Leonard Cohen - *The Jesuits in Ethiopia: Missionary Methods and Local Responses to Catholicism (1555-1632)* - University of Haifa, 2005

Sundkler, Bengt and Steed, Christopher - *A History of the Church in Africa* - Cambridge University Press, 2000

Ure, John - *Prince Henry the Navigator* - Constable, London, 1977

Waugh, Evelyn - *Remote People* - Gerald Duckworth & Co., London, 1931

Waugh, Evelyn - *Waugh in Abyssinia* - Longmans, London, 1936

## Chronology

This chronology will provide a useful comparison between the parallel histories of Portugal and Ethiopia during the period of their contact - 1492/3-1634. It opens with events that signalled the beginning of Portugal's era of world exploration. Certain other seemingly unconnected dates are included in order to provide a wider general perspective, and to assist encompassing distant events which nonetheless had, or logically might have had, some impact on the overall scope of the Portuguese/Ethiopian picture - i.e., the Battle of Lepanto, 1571.

| | |
|---|---|
| 1385 | - The Battle of Aljubarrota definitively establishes Portugal's independence |
| 1385-1433 | - Dom João I, King of Portugal |
| 1394 | - Birth of Prince Henry the Navigator |
| 1415 | - Portugal's first overseas venture, the capture of Ceuta in North Africa<br>- Battle of Agincourt |
| 1418 | - Discovery of Madeira and Porto Santo; colonization started 1425 |
| 1424 | - Portuguese voyage to Canary Islands |
| 1427 | - Portuguese discover the Azores Islands |
| 1428 | - Prince Pedro brings from Venice *The Book of Marco Polo* |
| 1433-1438 | - Dom Duarte, King of Portugal |
| 1434 | - Gil Eanes overcomes deep-seated superstitions of treacherous currents off Africa's west coast, and rounds the Cape of Bojador |
| 1434-1468 | - Zara Ya'qob, Emperor of Ethiopia |
| 1438-1481 | - Dom Afonso V, King of Portugal |
| 1444 | - Prince Henry the Navigator presides over Europe's first African slave market at Lagos, Algarve |
| 1453 | - Byzantium falls to Islam<br>- Last battle of the Hundred Years' War fought at Castillon, Aquitaine |
| 1453-1454 | - Movable type introduced by Johannes Gutenberg at Mainz |
| 1456 | - The Vulgate Bible, the first printed book |
| 1460 | - Death of Prince Henry the Navigator<br>- Birth of Vasco da Gama<br>- Birth of Pêro da Covilhã (?) |
| 1462 | - Portuguese colonize Cape Verde Islands |
| 1466 | - Pêro da Covilhã enters service as page of Duke of Medina-Sidonia, Seville<br>- Murderous clashes between Old and New Christians in Toledo |
| 1468 | - Death of Zara Ya'qob, Emperor of Ethiopia |
| 1468-1478 | - Baeda Maryam, Emperor of Ethiopia |
| 1469 | - Plague in Lisbon<br>- Birth of Manuel, Duke of Beja and future Dom Manuel I of Portugal |
| 1470 | - Moors capitulate to Portuguese at Tangiers |

| | |
|---|---|
| 1470 (cont'd) | - Dom Afonso V of Portugal and King Christian I of Denmark finance expedition to Greenland under command of Germans Didrik Pining and Hans Pothorst, taking with them Portuguese navigators João Vaz Corte Real and Álvaro Martins Homem. Pilot of this expedition, Icelander Jon Skulason, himself accustomed to making annual voyages to Baffin Island and Labrador |
| 1471 | - Skulason takes Corte Real and Homem with him to Canadian Arctic, returning to Norway following year. Corte Real returns to home in Portugal 1474 - and stories of this venture are thought to have been inspiration for subsequent voyages of his sons, Vasco, Miguel and Gaspar |
| 1472 | - Portuguese off the mouth of Congo River<br>- Wheat famine in Portugal |
| 1473 | - Clashes between Old and New Christians in Córdoba |
| 1474 | - João Vaz Corte Real reaches Portugal after North American venture (see above 1471)<br>- Death of Gomes Eanes de Zurara (b. 1410) - chronicler of early Portuguese voyages and conquests, biographer of Henry the Navigator |
| 1475 | - Pêro da Covilhã returns to Lisbon, becomes squire to Dom Afonso V |
| 1476 | - Battle of Toro and Dom Afonso V's claim to throne of Castile<br>- Pêro da Covilhã escorts Dom Afonso V to court of Louis XI of France |
| 1477 | - Pêro da Covilhã returns to Portugal, is promoted to King's Squire of Horse & Arms |
| 1478 | - Death of Baeda Maryam, Emperor of Ethiopia<br>- November, establishment of Spanish Inquisition by papal bull of Sixtus IV |
| 1478-1495 | - Eskendar, Emperor of Ethiopia |
| 1479 | - Treaty of Alcáçovas and Dom Afonso V relinquishes his claim to Castile<br>- King Ferdinand V and Queen Isabella I become joint rulers of Castile |
| 1480 | - Portugal abandons Canary Islands<br>- September, King Ferdinand V and Queen Isabella I appoint Inquisitor of Seville |
| 1481 | - Death of Dom Afonso V, King of Portugal |
| 1481-1495 | - Dom João II, King of Portugal |
| 1482 | - Diogo Cão enters mouth of Congo River<br>- Pêro da Covilhã becomes Squire of Royal Guard; undertakes missions to Tlemcen and Fez - the first to convey messages of peace to the Moors and negotiate a trading treaty; the second to buy horses for Prince Manuel and arrange for the return of the bones of martyred Infante Dom Fernando<br>- Venetian monk Francesco Suriano reports meeting 12 foreigners from the court of Prester John, four of whom are Venetian treasure seekers/merchants |
| 1483 | - Diogo Cão lands at various Congo River settlements, returns with Africans to be educated in Lisbon<br>- Tomás de Torquemada appointed Inquisitor-General of Spanish Inquisition<br>- Dom João II executes Duke of Bragança<br>- Birth of Martin Luther in Germany |
| 1484-1486 | - Diogo Cão explores Benin, discovers there a story concerning a Christian king "far to the east" – "Ogané," Prester John (?) |
| 1485 | - Assassination of Inquisitor of Aragón, Pedro de Arbués, at Zaragoza cathedral |
| 1486 | - Christopher Columbus decides to serve Castile rather than Portugal<br>- Casa dos Escravos founded in Lisbon |

| | |
|---|---|
| 1486 (cont'd) | - Bartolomeu Dias sets sail for southern Africa, seeking route around into Indian Ocean<br>- "Overland" expedition of António de Lisboa and Pedro de Montaroyo leaves to seek Prester John; fails, returns to Lisbon |
| 1487 | - May - "overland" expedition of Pêro da Covilhã and Afonso de Paiva leaves for "India" and to seek Prester John in lands east of Cairo, Ethiopia; Gonçalo Eanes and Pêro da Évora leave later for west Africa in search of Prester John, but end up in Tucurol and Timbuktu<br>- Bartolomeu Dias rounds the Cape of Good Hope |
| 1488 | - Pêro da Covilhã and Afonso de Paiva reach Aden and separate - Pêro da Covilhã ultimately to India, Ormuz, East African coast, etc; Afonso de Paiva to Ethiopia and his death |
| c. 1490 | - After his extensive travels – India, Persia, East Africa, Arabia – Pêro da Covilhã returns to Cairo, meets two Jews from Portugal, learns of Afonso de Paiva's death; he writes detailed letter to Dom João II describing his findings, then travels once more to Ormuz with one of the Jews, Rabbi Abraham of Beja; he returns to Red Sea, enters Mecca and Medina – all this travel taking approximately two years |
| 1491 | - Dom João II's son and heir, Afonso, killed in fall from horse |
| 1492 | - Christopher Columbus' first voyage to New World<br>- João Fernandes and Pedro de Barcelos sail to coast of Labrador<br>- Pêro da Covilhã reaches Zeila, end 1492 or early 1493 |
| 1493 | - Columbus' second voyage |
| 1494 | - Treaty of Tordesillas - Spain and Portugal divide the world between them |
| 1495 | - Death of Eskendar, Emperor of Ethiopia<br>- Death of Dom João II, King of Portugal |
| 1495-1508 | - Naod, Emperor of Ethiopia |
| 1495-1521 | - Dom Manuel I, King of Portugal |
| 1496 | - Expulsion of Jews from Lisbon |
| 1497 | - May, John Cabot embarks from Bristol<br>- June, Cabot goes ashore in eastern Canada - southern Labrador (?), Newfoundland (?), Cape Breton Island (?)<br>- July, Vasco da Gama leaves for India |
| 1498 | - May, Vasco da Gama arrives at Calicut, India<br>- Columbus' third voyage<br>- Death of Torquemada, Inquisitor-General of Spain |
| 1499 | - August, Vasco da Gama arrives back in Lisbon |
| 1500 | - April, Pedro Álvares Cabral discovers Brazil<br>- May, Bartolomeu Dias killed rounding the Cape of Good Hope<br>- September, Cabral lands at Calicut<br>- December, massacre of Portuguese at Calicut<br>- Slave trade conducted by Portugal to Brazil and Spanish America averages 4,000 per year throughout this century; Lisbon population is 10% black<br>- Birth of Charles V, Holy Roman Emperor 1519-1556 |
| 1501 | - Gaspar Corte Real re-discovers Newfoundland - "Land of Codfish" - though Azorean fishermen were reported in Grand Banks area some 50 years earlier; voyage of João Vaz Corte Real, 1470, see above |
| 1502-1503 | - Vasco da Gama's second, punitive, voyage to India |

| | |
|---|---|
| 1503 | - Afonso de Albuquerque sent to India<br>- Vincente Sodré goes to Socotra<br>- Spaniard António Lopez appointed ambassador to Ethiopia, but he was lost at sea en route to India |
| 1505 | - Francisco de Almeida appointed Viceroy of India<br>- Portuguese construct fort at Sofala in Mozambique |
| 1506 | - Massacre of New Christians in Lisbon<br>- Birth of Padre Francis Xavier in Spain<br>- Departure of João Gomes, João Sanches, Sid Mohammed for "lands of Prester John" |
| 1507 | - Conquest of Ormuz by Afonso de Albuquerque<br>- Portuguese construct fort on Mozambique Island<br>- March, Gomes, Sanches, Mohammed arrive in Malindi, attempt to travel overland to Ethiopia, but fail and return to coast |
| 1508 | - Death of Naod, Emperor of Ethiopia<br>- Dom Manuel I decrees "Policy of Secrecy" – on pain of death, all maps, logs and notes of all crew members involved in all voyages beyond the Cape of Good Hope to be turned over to Casa da Índia<br>- [James Bruce of Kinnaird contends in his Travels to Discover the Source of the Nile, published 1790, that 1508 is the year of the start of the Turk uprising in the Red Sea area]<br>- First Portuguese missionaries enter Congo<br>- Gomes, Sanches, Mohammed picked up by Afonso de Albuquerque, captain of Socotra, and taken to Filuk, near Cape Guardafui, and succeed in getting through to the Ethiopian court in Shoa<br>- Regency – Dowager Empress Eleni serves as Regent during Lebna Dengal's minority, with guidance of Pêro da Covilhã |
| 1508-1540 | - Lebna Dengal, Emperor of Ethiopia |
| 1509 | - Diogo Lopes de Sequeira explores east coast of Madagascar (São Lourenço)<br>- Matthew the Armenian merchant sent by Empress Eleni as ambassador to Dom Manuel I to draw up military pact against Islam<br>- Portuguese defeat Muslim Egyptian-Gujarati naval forces off Diu |
| 1510 | - Afonso de Albuquerque conquers Goa<br>- Portuguese establish bases at Bombay, Goa, Calicut, and control 3,200 kilometres of East African coast<br>- Portuguese abandon Socotra |
| 1511 | - Portuguese establish base at Malacca |
| 1512 | - Portuguese land at Ternate |
| 1513 | - January, Javanese fleet destroyed off Malacca coast<br>- Afonso de Albuquerque attempts conquest of Aden, enters Red Sea and commences operations against Egyptian-Gujarati fleet along Ethiopian coast; the fleet is replaced by Turkish Muslims, who take issue with allies of Portuguese, the Christian Ethiopians under Emperor Lebna Dengal<br>- António Fernandes explores East African coast |
| 1514 | - February, Matthew the Armenian, upon arrival in Lisbon to represent Ethiopians has difficulty being accepted as genuine ambassador |
| 1515 | - Portuguese finish building fort at Ormuz<br>- Empress Eleni's Regency comes to a close as Lebna Dengal assumes full powers as emperor |

| | |
|---|---|
| 1515 (cont'd) | - April, Matthew the Armenian leaves Lisbon with Duarte Galvão's embassy, arriving in Goa in September |
| 1516 | - Portuguese reach Canton |
| 1517 | - Fernão de Magalhães offers his services to Spain<br>- Turks conquer Egypt and Syria<br>- February, Matthew the Armenian leaves Goa with Lopo Soares, Governor of Goa, bound for Red Sea<br>- Lopo Soares blunders, fails to attack Turkish fleet at Aden and Jeddah<br>- June, death of Duarte Galvão on Camarão Island; party returns to Goa, September<br>- Martin Luther launches the Protestant Reformation - the Ninety-Five Theses |
| 1518 | - September, Diogo Lopes de Sequeira becomes governor at Goa |
| 1519 | - Magalhães commences voyage to girdle globe |
| 1519-1556 | - Charles V, Holy Roman Emperor |
| 1520 | - January, Diogo Lopes de Sequeira leaves Goa for Massawa, taking Matthew the Armenian and Francisco Álvares with him, arriving 7 April<br>- Rodrigo de Lima named ambassador to Court of Prester John, 25 April; Matthew the Armenian, Padre Francisco Álvares accompany de Lima inland; Matthew dies, May; embassy reaches tent capital of Prester John, October<br>- Gregório de Quadra attempts to reach Ethiopia via Congo River<br>- Turks instigate rebellion in southeast Ethiopia |
| 1521 | - Death of Dom Manuel I, King of Portugal<br>- Famine in Portugal<br>- Emperor Charles V declares war on Protestantism at Worms, Edict of Worms, returning to Spain to assume control over a Spanish army<br>- Chinese defeat Portuguese fleet in South China Sea |
| 1521-1557 | - Dom João III, King of Portugal |
| 1522 | - Return to Spain of Sebastián de El Cano, leader of the remnant of Magalhães' expedition that had circumnavigated the globe<br>- Chinese again push Portuguese out of South China Sea |
| 1523 | - Death of Dowager Empress Eleni of Ethiopia |
| 1523-1544 | - Revolt in southeast Ethiopia owing to breakdown of commerce associated with defeated Egyptian-Gujarati fleet; revolt bolstered by Turks from Arabia; severe Muslim invasions plague remainder of Emperor Lebna Dengal's reign |
| 1524 | - Vasco da Gama appointed Viceroy of India - dies at Cochin, December, 1524<br>- Birth of Luís Vaz de Camões (?) - Portugal's pre-eminent poet<br>- Portuguese Embassy leaves court of Emperor Lebna Dengal<br>- Estimates of only 300 Portuguese sailors available for service in all India; report made to king of the harshness of treatment of seamen aboard Portuguese shipping, particularly the *carreira da Índia* |
| 1526 | - Portuguese Embassy leaves Massawa, April, taking Saga Zaab as first official Ethiopian ambassador to Lisbon, arriving July, 1527<br>- Pêro da Covilhã last seen alive by his countrymen<br>- Emperor Charles V marries Isabel, daughter of Dom Manuel I, King of Portugal |
| 1527 | - Ahmad Grag'n's first invasions of Ethiopia's Highland territories<br>- First census of Portugal<br>- May, Sack of Rome |

| | |
|---|---|
| 1529 | - March, Battle of Shembra Kuré; Ahmad Grag'n defeats Emperor Lebna Dengal's larger army<br>- Diet of Speyer - first use of the term "Protestantism" referring to non-Roman Catholics |
| 1530 | - Ahmad Grag'n begins massive incursions into Christian Highlands of Ethiopia<br>- Charles V is the last Holy Roman Emperor to be crowned by the pope |
| 1531 | - Lisbon earthquake destroys 1,500 houses |
| 1533 | - Ahmad Grag'n lays siege to Amba Geshan |
| 1534 | - August, Ignatius Loyola initiates what is to become the Society of Jesus, the Jesuits, at Paris |
| 1535 | - Famine in Portugal<br>- João Bermudez appointed patriarch of Ethiopian church, and special envoy of Emperor Lebna Dengal, sent to Europe arriving Lisbon via Goa in 1537 |
| 1536 | - Inquisition established in Portugal |
| 1538 | - João Bermudez leaves Lisbon with Saga Zaab<br>- Turks occupy Aden |
| 1539 | - Portuguese destroy Mombassa<br>- Garcia de Noronha appointed Viceroy of India<br>- Minas, brother/successor to Emperor Galawdewos, taken hostage by Muslims |
| 1539-1540 | - Famine ravages Arabia and Ethiopian Highlands |
| 1540 | - September, pope approves Loyola's outline for the organization of the Jesuit order<br>- Throughout 1540's - destruction of Hindu temples in Portuguese India<br>- Publication of Francisco Álvares' work, *A Verdadeira Informação das Terras do Preste João das Índias*<br>- Publication of Damião de Gois' work, *Fides, Religio, Moresque Aethiopum*<br>- Death of Lebna Dengal, Emperor of Ethiopia<br>- Death of Garcia de Noronha<br>- Penal laws enacted in Goa against public profession of Islam, Hinduism, Buddhism |
| 1540-1559 | - Galawdewos, Emperor of Ethiopia |
| 1541 | - Estevão da Gama appointed governor of India - sails for Red Sea same year; February, Suez raid; May, fleet returns to Massawa<br>- Ahmad Grag'n slaughters approximately 80 Portuguese at Massawa, Manuel da Gama commanding in absence of Estevão da Gama on Suez raid<br>- Portuguese army of 400 under Cristóvão da Gama lands, June, in Ethiopia; commences march against Ahmad Grag'n - December, army accompanied by Empress Sabla Vanggel, mother of Emperor Galawdewos<br>- Portuguese begin extensive exploration of Red Sea coast |
| 1542 | - February 2, Cristóvão da Gama's army captures Amba Sanayt; April 4, first major battle against Ahmad Grag'n; April 16, second battle; early August, third battle, Portuguese capture of Simien Mountains; August 28, fourth battle against Grag'n and death of Cristóvão da Gama<br>- Commencement of Portuguese arms trade with Japan<br>- Roman Inquisition established<br>- May, Padre Francis Xavier arrives in Goa |
| 1543 | - February 22, Battle of Waina Dega, Christian Highlanders and Portuguese against Muslims; death of Ahmad Grag'n, defeat of Muslim army, Christianity secured in Highlands<br>- Famine in Ethiopian Highlands |
| 1544 | - Minas ransomed; Empress Sabla Vanggel returns Ahmad Grag'n's captured son to his mother, Talwambara, at Gorgora |

# CHRONOLOGY

| | |
|---|---|
| 1545-1563 | - Council of Trent, the Counter-Reformation |
| 1546 | - Death of Martin Luther |
| 1547 | - Portuguese Inquisition promulgates first list of prohibited books |
| 1548 | - Padre Francis Xavier returns to Goa from Malay archipelago and establishes school for instruction of native priests and catechists in diocese of Goa, stretching from the Cape of Good Hope to China |
| 1550 | - First Portuguese contact with Macau |
| 1552 | - Death of Padre Francis Xavier in China |
| 1554 | - Turks occupy Massawa<br>- João Nunes Barreto named Roman Catholic prelate of Ethiopia; André de Oviedo appointed his bishop |
| 1555 | - Jesuits take over pedagogical control of Colleges of the Arts at Universities of Coimbra and Évora<br>- March, envoys of Rome and Lisbon, Diogo Dias and Padre Gonçalo Rodrigues, arrive at Debaroa, now in Eritrea; May, received by Emperor Galawdewos who denies Roman Catholic Church |
| 1556 | - Seventeen Spanish ships arriving from South America, provide Emperor Charles V with three million ducats, the first significant monetary transfer from the Americas<br>- Emperor Charles V abdicates, dies 1558<br>- Death of Ignatius Loyola<br>- September, Jesuit prelate João Nunes Barreto, and his bishop and successor, André de Oviedo, arrive in Goa |
| 1557 | - June, André de Oviedo arrives at Ethiopian court of Emperor Galawdewos in Waj accompanied by five other Jesuits: António Fernandes, Manuel Fernandes, Gonçalo Cardoso, Gonçalo Gualdames and Francisco Lopes<br>- Emperor Galawdewos sends army north to prevent invasion by Turks, but these latter succeed in occupying Massawa, from which they manage to control the Red Sea coastline until 1875 when they are replaced by the Egyptians, aided by the British, the Suez Canal having opened six years previously<br>- Death of Dom João III, King of Portugal |
| 1557-1578 | - Dom Sebastião, King of Portugal |
| 1558 | - Diogo do Couto estimates only 400 sailors available for service at Goa<br>- Death of Charles V, Holy Roman Emperor |
| 1559 | - March, attack by Nur-ibn-Mujahid crushes forces of Emperor Galawdewos<br>- Death of Galawdewos, Emperor of Ethiopia<br>- March, decree in Lisbon promulgating forcible conversion of "heathen" Hindu orphans in India, *"Pai dos Christões"*<br>- Persecution of Roman Catholics by Emperor Minas<br>- André de Oviedo publishes his manifesto forbidding close association between Roman Catholics and Ethiopian Orthodox |
| 1559-1563 | - Minas, Emperor of Ethiopia |
| 1560 | - Establishment of the Inquisition at Goa - *autos-da-fé*<br>- Ethiopian nobles take up arms against Emperor Minas under Azmach Yeshaq, governor of Tigray; André de Oviedo encourages Portuguese soldiers to support revolt |

| | |
|---|---|
| 1561 | - Ethiopian emperor defeats rebel noblemen, but rebel leader Yeshaq escapes; Minas confiscates Portuguese property, suspends their privileges; holds André de Oviedo under guard |
| 1562 | - André de Oviedo tries to send Gonçalo Gualdames as messenger to Goa, seeking arms to impose Roman Catholicism; Gualdames caught by Turks at Massawa, executed<br>- Yeshaq, governor of Tigray, forms alliance with Turks of Massawa, defeats Emperor Minas at Battle of Adigorro, gives shelter to André de Oviedo and other Jesuits at Mai Gwa Gwa, also known as Fremona, near Adwa, which becomes fixed centre of missionary activities<br>- December, Jesuit prelate João Nunes Barreto dies at Goa, succeeded by André de Oviedo |
| 1563 | - Death of Minas, Emperor of Ethiopia |
| 1563-1596 | - Sartsa Dengal, Emperor of Ethiopia<br>- André de Oviedo continues support of Yeshaq and Turks against new emperor |
| 1565 | - Jesuits gain full control over Colégio das Artes at Coimbra<br>- Emperor Sartsa Dengal gains control over rebellious nobles |
| 1566 | - Neither Portugal nor Rome prepared to support imposition of Roman Catholicism in Ethiopia by force; André de Oviedo advised by pope and Portuguese regent to leave Ethiopia, to go instead to China; he refuses |
| 1567 | - Famine in Ethiopian Highlands |
| 1568 | - Yeshaq abandons André de Oviedo, makes peace with Emperor Sartsa Dengal and is permitted to retain governorship of Tigray; Captain Francisco Jacomo, representing Portuguese and their descendants, makes peace with emperor<br>- Dutch rebel against rule of King Filipe II of Spain, later King Filipe I of Portugal |
| 1569 | - Plague in Lisbon kills 60,000 |
| 1571 | - October, Battle of Lepanto. Ottoman Turks driven from eastern Mediterranean by Don John of Austria |
| 1572 | - Publication of Luís Vaz de Camões' epic poem, *Os Lusíadas* |
| 1573 | - Venetians surrender Cyprus to Turks |
| 1575 | - Most confiscated Portuguese property in Ethiopian Highlands returned to their descendants |
| 1577 | - André de Oviedo dies in Ethiopia |
| 1578 | - Battle of Alcáçer Quibir and death of Dom Sebastião, King of Portugal |
| 1578-1580 | - Dom Henrique, King of Portugal |
| 1579 | - Yeshaq again forms alliance with Turks, defies Emperor Sartsa Dengal |
| 1580 | - Death of Dom Henrique, King of Portugal<br>- Death of Luís Vaz de Camões<br>- December, Yeshaq of Tigray finally defeated and killed, Turks driven back to Massawa |
| 1580-1598 | - King Filipe I, House of Castile, on throne of Portugal |
| 1583 | - Death of Portuguese adventurer/writer, Fernão Mendes Pinto |
| 1587 | - Emperor Sartsa Dengal storms Gusan, mountain stronghold of Falasha of Simien |
| 1588-1589 | - February, Jesuit Padres Pêro Páez and António de Monserrate leave Goa for Ethiopia, captured 1589; ransomed, returned to India, 1595 |
| 1589 | - Turks again defeated on coast of Tigray by Ethiopian army |
| 1595-1610 | - Attempted union of Egyptian Coptic Church with the Church of Rome |

| | |
|---|---|
| 1596 | - Famine in Portugal<br>- Franciscans expelled from Japan<br>- Castle of Guzara commenced, thought to be prototype of Gondar castles<br>- Death of Sartsa Dengal, Emperor of Ethiopia |
| 1596-1603 | - Ya'qob, Emperor of Ethiopia |
| 1597 | - Death of Francisco Lopes, last of André de Oviedo's companions<br>- Sussenyos, great grandson of Emperor Lebna Dengal, opens revolt – first against Emperor Ya'qob, later against Emperor Za Dengal |
| 1598 | - Death of King Filipe I of Castile and Portugal<br>- Dutch attack Príncipe and São Tomé |
| 1598-1621 | - King Filipe II, House of Castile, on throne of Portugal |
| 1602 | - Founding of Dutch East India Company |
| 1603 | - March, Padre Pêro Páez again leaves for Ethiopia; arrives Massawa, April<br>- Emperor Ya'qob dethroned |
| 1603-1604 | - Za Dengal, Emperor of Ethiopia |
| 1604 | - June, Emperor Za Dengal permits Padre Pêro Páez to preach to both Roman Catholics and Orthodox<br>- Emperor Za Dengal, favouring Roman Catholicism, issues unpopular proclamation forbidding observance of Saturday, the Orthodox Sabbath, as a religious holiday<br>- Death of Za Dengal, Emperor of Ethiopia in October |
| 1604-1607 | - Ya'qob, Emperor of Ethiopia for the second time<br>- Continuous fighting against Sussenyos; Emperor Ya'qob, promising Padre Pêro Páez he would convert to Roman Catholicism, requests Portuguese soldiers, but message never gets through |
| 1605 | - Dutch wrest Spice Islands (Moluccas) from Portugal; Portuguese re-establish at Macassar (South Celebes) to continue trade in Indonesian products, mainly sandalwood and cloves |
| 1607 | - Dutch fail in attempt to capture Mozambique Island<br>- Death of Ya'qob, Emperor of Ethiopia |
| 1607-1632 | - Sussenyos, Emperor of Ethiopia |
| 1608 | - Dutch fail for the second time to capture Mozambique Island, which ultimately leads to the founding of their own settlement at the Cape of Good Hope in 1652<br>- Galla forces enter Gojjam; Emperor Sussenyos requests Portuguese troops which never arrive |
| 1609 | - Emperor Sussenyos puts down rebellion in Tigray |
| 1611 | - Famine in Ethiopian Highlands<br>- Orthodox-Roman Catholic discussions at Emperor Sussenyos' court concerning human and divine natures of Christ<br>- King Filipe II promises troops to Emperor Sussenyos, but fails to honour his commitment |
| 1612 | - Dutch establish at Mouri (Fort Nassau), Gold Coast, securing majority of gold trade from Portuguese<br>- Sela Cristos, younger brother to Emperor Sussenyos, is converted to Roman Catholicism and given the governorship of Gojjam and Damot<br>- Jesuits establish missions at Collala and Sarca in Gojjam<br>- Pope promises military assistance to Emperor Sussenyos to back conversion of Ethiopia to Roman Catholicism, but the promise is not kept<br>- Epidemic forces the re-establishment of the Ethiopian court at Gorgora |

| | |
|---|---|
| 1612 (cont'd) | - Emperor Sussenyos issues edict forbidding Orthodox instruction of perfect unity of human and divine natures of Christ<br>- Orthodox Abun Simon excommunicates all adherents to Roman Catholic doctrine of the two natures of Christ |
| 1613 | - Major Orthodox ecclesiastical disputes; Sela Cristos, nominated as chief minister, acts on behalf of his brother<br>- March, Jesuit António Fernandes leaves Collala in an attempt to reach the East African coast at Malindi, there to arrange letters from Emperor Sussenyos to be carried to the king in Portugal and the pope in Rome summoning diplomatic, ecclesiastical and military assistance; the mission fails |
| 1614 | - Orthodox revolt in Begemdir<br>- Padre Pêro Páez commences construction of the palace of Emperor Sussenyos and Maryam Gemb church at Gorgora<br>- Publication of Fernão Mendes Pinto's well-known travel documentary, *Peregrinação* |
| 1616 | - Emperor Sussenyos' brother, Sela Cristos, appointed Prime Minister |
| 1617 | - Rebellions of Orthodox supporters against Emperor Sussenyos fail; Abun Simon killed; Padre Pêro Páez assures emperor he is God's chosen instrument for change |
| 1618 | - Jesuit mission opened at Atqhana, Aringo (?) |
| 1618-1619 | - Synod of Dort defines the Protestant canons of the Reformed Church of the Netherlands, names the Church of Rome "The Great Whore of Babylon," headed by the "Antichrist" pope |
| 1619 | - Dutch establish headquarters of Dutch East India Company at Batavia (Jakarta) |
| 1620 | - Emperor Sussenyos again issues proclamation condemning Orthodox doctrine, forbidding religious observance on Saturdays<br>- October, governor of Begemdir again rebels against Emperor Sussenyos; uprising in Gojjam |
| 1621 | - Death of King Filipe II of Castile and Portugal<br>- Famine in Portugal<br>- Both Begemdir and Gojjam rebellions sternly put down, large number of Orthodox being killed in Gojjam<br>- Influx of Roman Catholic missionaries throughout decade; emphasis now placed on converting the people, rather than the court<br>- Many Latin religious texts translated into Ge'ez |
| 1621-1640 | - Filipe III, House of Castile, on throne of Portugal |
| 1622 | - Publication of Padre Pêro Páez's work *História de Etiópia*<br>- March, Emperor Sussenyos converts to Roman Catholicism at Gorgora<br>- May, death of Padre Pêro Páez<br>- Afonso Mendes (1579-1659) appointed by Rome as Jesuit prelate of Ethiopia<br>- June, Dutch fail in their attack against Macau<br>- Persians capture Ormuz from Portuguese<br>- Portuguese builder Manuel Magro brought to Ethiopia by Manuel de Almeida; he is credited with introducing lime mortar to Highlands |
| 1623 | - Famine in Ethiopian Highlands |
| 1624 | - Dutch launch first attack against Brazil<br>- Orthodox liturgy revised and amended to bring it into line with Church of Rome; divorce made illegal, circumcision prohibited; Coptic calendar substituted by Gregorian calendar<br>- Emperor Sussenyos reaffirms faith in Roman Catholic Church, makes declaration of his faith and declares leaders of Ethiopian Orthodox Church are unfit for spiritual leadership |

| | |
|---|---|
| 1624 (cont'd) | - Opposition to central authority in Ethiopia gathers momentum<br>- Rebellion in Begemdir<br>- Afonso Mendes, Jesuit prelate, arrives in Ethiopia |
| 1625 | - Famine in Ethiopian Highlands<br>- Dutch fail to capture São Jorge da Mina<br>- December, Jesuit prelate Afonso Mendes arrives at Ethiopian court, accompanied by five other Jesuits, João de Velasco, Jerónimo Lobo, Francisco Marques, Manuel Luís and João Martins<br>- Emperor Sussenyos and Crown Prince Fasiladas pledge obedience to Church of Rome |
| 1626 | - February, Emperor Sussenyos declares Ethiopia to be Roman Catholic; his son, Fasiladas, consolidates control over Orthodox partisans<br>- Afonso Mendes, Jesuit prelate, received in solemn ceremony by Emperor Sussenyos<br>- Roman Catholic seminaries opened in Tigray, Dambea, Gojjam |
| 1627 | - Estimated 100,000 Roman Catholic converts in Ethiopia |
| 1628 | - Uprising in Tigray |
| 1630 | - Dutch capture Pernambuco |
| 1631 | - Uprising in Gojjam |
| 1632 | - June, restoration of Ethiopian Orthodox Church<br>- Abdication of Emperor Sussenyos; dies September<br>- Jesuits exiled first to Collala in Gojjam, later to Fremona in Tigray |
| 1632-1667 | - Fasiladas, Emperor of Ethiopia |
| 1632-1855 | - "Gondar Ethiopia" - national capital at Gondar |
| 1633 | - Famine in Ethiopian Highlands |
| 1634 | - Jesuits expelled from Ethiopia; widespread persecution and massacres<br>- Afonso Mendes, Jesuit prelate, expelled, captured by Turks |
| 1635 | - Afonso Mendes, Jesuit prelate, ransomed, arrives in Goa |
| 1635-1636 | - Famine in Ethiopian Highlands<br>- Apollinaris de Almeida, assistant bishop to Afonso Mendes, and seven other Jesuits refusing to leave Ethiopia, are caught; two are executed immediately; Apollinaris and remainder later hanged in public<br>- Death of King Filipe III of Castile and Portugal |
| 1656 | - Afonso Mendes, Jesuit prelate, dies in Goa aged 76 |

## Glossary

| | |
|---|---|
| Abobada – | (Portuguese) brick/stone dome, *cupola* |
| Abobadilha – | (Portuguese) brick/stone vaulted ceiling |
| Abrigo – | (Portuguese) shelter, refuge |
| Alizar – | (Portuguese) door/window casing, panel often in tile at the base of a wall |
| Amba – | (Amharic) literally a village, but in context of this work a mountain-top redoubt |
| Atalaia – | (Portuguese) look-out tower |
| Auto(s)-da-fè – | (Portuguese) "act(s) of faith" – punishment by the Inquisition, usually burning at the stake |
| Azmach – | (Amharic) senior political rank |
| Azuleijo – | (Portuguese) decorated glazed wall tile; blue, *azul*, being predominant colour |
| Bairro da lata – | (Portuguese) "tin quarter" or slum |
| Caixilho – | (Portuguese) door/window frame, usually in stone |
| Caminho – | (Portuguese) road |
| Carimbo – | (Portuguese) stamp of identification |
| Cupola – | (Portuguese) brick/stone dome, *abobada* |
| Desit – | (Amharic) island |
| Dom – | (Portuguese) honourific usually reserved for kings, princes, senior nobility or churchmen |
| Injera – | (Amharic) crêpe-like bread, staple throughout Ethiopia |
| Laje – | (Portuguese) flagstone |
| Mak'das – | (originating from the Ge'ez, now fully adopted into Amharic) the Holy of Holies usually in the centre of an Ethiopian Orthodox church where the tabot and church regalia are stored, strictly reserved for priests |
| Mestre – | (Portuguese) master, antiquated low honourific |
| Mestre-da-obra – | (Portuguese) literally "master of the work," expert or work supervisor, usually a master stonemason |
| Monte – | (Portuguese) country farm, usually in southern Portugal, where the farmhouse stands on a rise overlooking surrounding pastures |

| | |
|---|---|
| Património – | (Portuguese) heritage, property of the state |
| Pedreiro – | (Portuguese) stonemason |
| Ponte Romano – | (Portuguese) Roman bridge, or bridge built in Roman style |
| Praça – | (Portuguese) town square |
| Quinta – | (Portuguese) farm, but often simply country residence |
| Ras – | (Amharic) prince |
| Reboco – | (Portuguese) rendering on a wall, interior or exterior |
| Sala – | (Portuguese) drawing or reception room |
| Sebastianismo – | (Portuguese) anxious anticipation of the return of Dom Sebastião, killed during the Battle of Alcáçer Quibir; this is closely allied with the word *saudades* and is a commentary on hopelessness and yearning, the acceptance of an inevitable fate |
| Solar – | (Portuguese) country estate more usually in northern Portugal |
| Tabot (tabotat) – | (originating from the Ge'ez, now fully adopted into Amharic) the stones of the Ten Commandments, replicas of which are to be found in all consecrated Ethiopian Orthodox churches |
| Talha-mar – | (Portuguese) cutwater, that part of a bridge's piers or pontoons facing upstream and shaped like the prow of a ship |
| Tasca – | (Portuguese) wine bar |
| Tef – | (Amharic) endemic cereal used in the making of *injera* |
| Terra – | (Portuguese) literally it means earth, but used in the context of this work it would refer to origins or roots, one's village |
| Unhas – | (Portuguese) literally fingernails, in context here a simple devise used by *pedreiros* to ensure *reboco* will adhere to wood portion of a wall |
| UNESCO – | United Nations Educational, Scientific and Cultural Organization |
| Xisto – | (Portuguese) schist or slate |

# Index

Abay River (see Blue Nile River), 7
Abay Wenz, 156
Abba Gish Fasil, 155-157, 163
Abobada, 119, 121, 122, 138, 194
Abobadilha, 94, 138, 194
Abraha, King, 81
Abraham, Rabbi of Beja, 40, 185
Abrigo, 64, 131, 194
Abun (see Patriarch), 12, 42, 51, 58, 192
Abyssinia, 39, 47, 134, 180, 182
Adal, 45, 172
Addis Ababa, 24, 63, 66, 78, 139, 179, 181
Addis Ababa University, 13, 16, 79, 112
Adegada, 163
Aden, 39, 40, 44, 48, 66, 185-188
Adigorro, Battle of, 190
Adigrat, 8
Adwa, 54, 157, 190
Aedesius, 42
Afar Depression, 25
Af-mekurabia (see Pigpen), 116
Afonso V, Dom, 5, 33, 183, 184
Afonso, Jorge, 178
Afonso, Prince (Heir to João II), 185
Africa, 12, 22, 23, 25, 31, 33-35, 38-40, 47, 48, 68, 80, 129, 157, 170, 173, 180-185
Ahmad Ibn Ibrahim El Ghazi, the Left-Handed (see Grag'n), 12, 45-47, 51, 53, 57, 59, 82, 90, 91, 101, 103, 146, 172, 173, 180, 187-188
Ahmar Mountains, 67
Alata Bridge, 91-93, 162
Alata Falls (see Tis'isat), 91, 92
Albuquerque, Afonso de, 44, 119, 186
Alcáçer Quibir, Battle of, 23, 31, 53, 190, 195
Alcáçovas, Treaty of, 184
Alentejo, 63, 64, 93, 119, 122, 125, 130, 131, 158
Alexandria, 12, 26, 42, 51, 52
Alfonso V of Aragon, Dom, 26, 33
Alizar, 129, 194
Almeida, Apollinaris de, 193
Almeida, Francisco de, 186
Almeida, Manuel de, 13, 192
Álvares, Padre Francisco, 12, 23, 35, 43, 49, 180, 185, 187, 188
Amba (Detention Camp), 160
Amba Geshan, Battle of, 45, 188
Amba Sanayt, Battle of, 51, 173, 188
Amba Wehni, 160, 161
Amhara, 57, 104
Amharic, 20, 21, 34, 56, 112, 176, 194, 195
Anatolia, 37
Andalusia, 38
Angreb River, 126, 147
Ankober, 35, 65-68
Antichrist, 38, 192
Apse, 110
Arabia, 37, 47, 185, 187, 188
Arabian Peninsula, 25
Arabic, 34, 56
Arbués, Pedro de, 184
Architecture, 13, 16, 21, 22, 37, 48, 64, 77, 80, 85, 86, 89, 93, 113, 129, 134, 168, 170, 171, 175
Aringo, 116-118, 143, 163, 192
Ark of the Covenant, 25, 98, 101, 103, 112
Arkana, 163
Arkiko, 8, 35, 45, 48, 59
Armenia, 37, 90
Arms Trade with Japan, 188
Ashlar, 81, 83, 86, 144
Asia Minor, 37
Atalaia, 107
Athanasius, Bishop, 42
Atnatewos, 56
Atqhana, 118, 163, 192
Atsbaha, King, 81
Australian Eucalyptus, 68
Autos-da-fé, 189
Awash Valley, 67, 68
Axum, 26, 42, 80, 84, 85, 98, 103, 112, 132, 134, 168
Axumite Empire, 12, 41, 42, 84, 132
Ayba, 161
Azezo, 123-125
Azmach, 53, 189, 194
Azores, 183
Azuleijo, 194

Bab el Mandeb, Strait of, 39
Baeda Maryam, 183, 184
Baffin Island, 184
Bahir Dar, 19, 92, 94-98, 101, 103, 104, 106, 110-113, 115, 153, 156, 159, 165, 168, 169
Bahir Dar University, 14, 15, 17, 112, 166, 168, 203
Bairro da Lata, 129, 194
Bakafa, 135, 177
Bakafa's Castle (Palace), 133, 139
Balkans, 37
Baltic, 37
Barata, Martins, 171
Barcelos, Pedro de, 185
Barradas, Manuel, 13
Barrancos, 91, 93, 158
Barrel Vault(ed), 94, 122, 136
Barreto, Prelate João Nunes, 51, 52, 54, 55, 189, 190
Basilica, 143-145
Batavia (Jakarta), 192
Begemdir, 58, 60, 118, 161, 192, 193
Beira, 40
Beja, Duke of (see Manuel I, Dom), 33, 183
Beke, Charles, 89, 90, 180
Bell, 96
Benin, 39, 40, 184
Bermudez, João, 23, 49-53, 188
Bet Maryam Church, 133
Bhary Gemb, 67, 121-123
Bibi Giamberi, 131, 149
Bisan, 8
Black Jews, 25
Blue Nile River (see Abay River), 7, 42, 92, 93, 155, 175
Bombay, 186
Bosnia, 37
Boxer, C.R., 34, 36, 180, 181
Bragança, Duke of, 184

Brancaleone, Niccoló, 26
Brazier, 118
Brazil, 22, 27, 43, 181, 185, 192
Bristol, 185
Britain, 37, 59, 174, 178, 203
Bruce, Sir James of Kinnaird, 43, 155, 180, 186
Bruni, Padre Bruno, 84
Buddhism, 188
Burton, Sir Richard, 128
Byzantine Emperors, 38
Byzantium, 183

Cabo de Boa Esperança (see Cape of Good Hope), 6
Cabot, John, 185
Cabral, Pedro Álvares, 43, 185
Cairo, 34, 35, 39, 40, 185
Caixilho, 144, 194
Calicut, 6, 41, 43, 44, 119, 185, 186
Camarão Island, 187
Caminho, 86, 194
Camões, Luís Vaz de, 69, 174, 180, 187, 190
Campbell, Ian L., 78-80
Canada, 18-20, 166, 185
Canadian Arctic, 184
Cannanore, 6, 44, 119
Canary Islands, 183, 184
Canton, 187
Cão, Diogo, 184
Cape Bojador, 6
Cape Breton, 185
Cape Guardafui, 186
Cape of Bojador, 183
Cape of Good Hope (see Cabo de Boa Esperança), 32, 40, 43, 185, 186, 189, 191
Cape Verde Islands, 183
Carangolos, 44
Cardoso, Gonçalo, 189
Carimbo, 144, 169
Carreira da Índia, 187
Casa da Índia, 186
Casa dos Escravos, 184
Castanhoso, Miguel de, 46, 180
Castile, 33, 56, 184, 190-193
Castle Bridges, 133
Ceuta, 6, 183
Chad, 38

Charles V (see Holy Roman Emperor), 185, 187-189
Cheesman, R.E., Explorer, 180
Chicken House, 125
China, 31, 37, 47, 54, 187, 189, 190
Chojnacki, Dr. Stanislaw, 17, 78, 112
Christ, Jesus, 81, 98, 177
Christian I, King of Denmark, 184
Christianity, 12, 34, 37, 38, 41, 42, 46, 49, 51, 55, 98, 103, 137, 172, 173, 176, 181, 188
Christians, 12, 26, 34, 37, 42, 45, 46, 48, 49, 53, 55, 57, 70, 84, 146, 173, 183, 184, 186
Christie's, 178
Church of Rome, 23, 52, 54, 56-59, 70, 84, 98, 190, 192, 193
Cistern, 108, 109, 119, 145, 158
Cobblestone(s), 159
Cochin, 6, 44, 187
Codfish (see Grand Banks), 185
Coimbra, 179, 189, 190
Collala, 58, 105, 163, 191, 192, 193
Colonialism, 31, 36, 169
Columbus, Christopher, 171, 184, 185
Commander of the Cavalry, 133
Congo, 186
Congo River, 184, 187
Constantinople, 37
Copt, 12
Coptic Church, 42, 190
Córdoba, 184
Corte Real, Gaspar, 185
Corte Real, João Vaz, 184, 185
Corte Real, Miguel, 184
Corte Real, Vasco, 184
Council of India, 52
Council of Trent (Counter-Reformation), 189
Couto, Diogo do, 189
Covilhã, 32, 33

Covilhã, Pêro da, 16, 27, 31-45, 49, 66, 67, 77, 84-86, 90, 121, 166, 169, 172-175, 180, 183-187
Crenellation, 108
Cross of Malta (Cross of the Order of Christ), 144
Crusades, The, 38
Cupola, 119, 122, 123, 194
Cushitic, 25
Cyprus, 190

Daga Estefanos Monastery, 124
Daga Estefanos Island, 98, 99, 101-103
Dambea, 193
Damot, 58, 191
Dangila, 156
Dawit Choir & Music Room, 133
Dawit I, Emperor, 177
Dawit III, Emperor, 135
Debark, 8, 157
Debaroa, 163, 189
Debarwa, 163
Debre Birhan, 67, 68, 75
Debre Birhan Selassie Church, 89, 101
Debre Libanos, 8, 20, 78
Debre Libanos Monastery, 124
Debre Mai, 106, 108, 109
Debre Markos, 8, 163
Debre Maryam Church, Gorgora, 59
Debre Sina, 76
Debre Sina Church, Gorgora, 59
Debre Tabor, 97, 113, 115, 116, 143, 163
Debsan, 163
Debtors' Court, 26, 47
Defeche, 126
Defeche Kidane Mehret, 99, 149
Dejan, 8
Dek Island, 99
Delftware, 175
Denqaz, 13, 86, 124, 142-146, 163
Depesan, 163
Dervish Invasion, 124
Desit, 150, 194
Desit Giorghis, 150, 151

Dias, Bartolomeu, 40, 43, 185
Dias, Diogo, 52, 55, 189
Diet of Speyer, 188
Dinquinesh (see Lucy), 25
Discoveries, The, 34, 36, 181
Diu, 44, 186
Djibouti, 7, 66
Dog Leg, 93, 126
Dome, 119, 153, 194
Dominican, 39
Durão Ferreira, Fernanda, 17, 119, 180
Dutch, 36, 175, 190-193
Dutch East India Company, 191, 192

Eanes, Gonçalo, 39, 185
Eanes de Zurara, Gomes, 184
East Africa, 40, 173, 180, 185
Eastern Orthodox Church, 12, 55
Egg Mortar, 65, 79
Egypt, 12, 37-39, 44, 143, 167, 177, 187
Egyptian Pharaohs, 25
Egyptian-Gujarati Fleet, 44, 186, 187
El Cano, Sebastián de, 187
Eleni, Dowager Empress, 35, 37, 41-45, 66, 67, 81, 82, 84, 86, 91, 172, 174, 186, 187
Emfraz, 119
Endalamaw Sahilu, 17, 135
Enderta, Battle of, 54
Enlightenment, 25
Entos Eyesu Monastery, 97
Eritrea, 7, 25, 67, 163, 189
Eskendar, Emperor, 5, 26, 41, 66, 77, 184, 185
Ethiopian Highlands, 16, 21-23, 26, 28, 31, 33, 34, 41, 44, 57, 86, 93, 119, 137, 176, 188, 190-193
Ethiopian Orthodox Church, 25, 41, 45, 49-52, 55, 58, 60, 84, 94, 108, 112, 117, 167, 178, 192-194
Ethiopian Religious Art, 112
Europe, 12, 14, 15, 25, 26, 31, 36-39, 47, 55, 63, 85, 88, 124, 158, 170, 188
European Union, 176
Évora, Pêro da, 39, 185
Ezana, King of Axum, 42

Falashas, 25
Famine, 34, 47, 184, 187, 188, 190-193
Far East Trade, 13, 26, 176
Fasil Bridge, 126, 147
Fasiladas, Emperor, 5, 12, 13, 59, 60, 84, 86, 92, 93, 96-98, 101, 104, 119, 120, 124, 128, 132, 135, 141, 193
Fasil's Bath, 136, 141
Fasil's Castle, 133, 136, 138, 139
Fasil's Little Palace, 133
Fasil's Pool, 133
Ferdinand & Isabella, King & Queen of Spain, 184
Fernandes, António, 186, 189, 192
Fernandes, João, 185
Fernandes, Manuel, 189
Fernandes, Tomás, 119
Fernando, Infante Dom, 184
Fez, 33, 180, 184
"Fides, Religio, Moresque Aethiopum", 55, 188
Filipe I of Castile, 5, 190, 191
Filipe II of Castile, 5, 191, 192
Filipe III of Castile, 5, 192, 193
Filuk, 186
Fite Mikael Church, 133
France, 33, 37, 70, 184
Franciscans, 191
Fremona (see Mai Gwa Gwa), 54, 56, 57, 157, 158, 190, 193
Fresco, 146
Frumentius, 42

Gabarma, 163
Galawdewos Church, near Hamusit, 161, 163
Galawdewos, Emperor, 5, 45-47, 51-53, 59, 82, 163, 173, 188, 189
Galla, 46, 57, 191
Galvão, Duarte, 12, 187
Gama, Cristóvão da, 12, 23, 37, 46, 49-51, 101, 119, 173, 180, 188
Gama, Estêvão da, 46, 50, 188
Gama, Manuel da, 50, 51, 188

Gama, Vasco da, 31-33, 41, 44, 173, 174, 180, 183, 185, 187
Garden of Eden, 31, 39
Garden of Jesus (see Geneta Yesus & Winter Palace), 124
Ge'ez, 21, 56, 90, 192, 194, 195
Gemb Giorghis, 58, 108-110, 163
Gemb Kidane Mehret, 105, 106, 163
Gemb Maryam, 108
Geneta Yesus (see Garden of Jesus & Winter Palace), 124
Germany, 17, 37, 184
Getnet Yigsaw, 17, 146
Ghenghis Khan, 39
Gibraltar, Strait of, 38
Gish Abay, 155
Goa, 35, 40, 43-45, 50-52, 54, 56, 57, 59, 60, 79-81, 86, 119, 120, 172, 186-190, 193
Gobatit Bridge, 147, 148
Gois, Damião de, 55, 188
Gojjam, 22, 35, 42, 56-58, 66, 67, 78, 81, 82, 84, 92, 100, 132, 156, 161, 163, 169, 175, 191-193
Gomes, João, 186
Gondar, 13, 15, 17, 22, 63, 67, 77, 85, 86, 92, 97, 99-101, 113, 115, 119, 123, 125, 126, 128, 129, 131-139, 141, 143, 146, 157, 160, 161, 163, 169, 180, 191, 193
Gondarine, 21, 63, 64, 77, 89, 93, 99, 114, 121, 133, 134, 165, 166, 168, 169
Gorgora, 13, 17, 58, 59, 97, 115, 128, 131, 150, 161, 188, 191, 192
Goze, 75-77
Grag'n, Ahmad (see Ahmad Ibn Ibrahim El Ghazi, the Left-Handed), 12, 45-47, 51, 53, 57, 59, 82, 90, 91, 101, 103, 146, 172, 173, 180, 187-188
Grand Banks (see Codfish), 185
Great Rift Valley, 76, 77

Great Whore of Babylon, The, 192
Greece, Greek, 25, 26, 47, 69, 90
Greenland, 184
Gregorian Calendar, 192
Guadiana River, 136, 138, 160
Guinea Coast, 47
Gujarat, 81, 180
Gulf of Aden, 66
Gulf of Persia, 40
Gult, 42
Gumara River, 7
Gur River, 78
Guzara, 17, 86, 107, 118-120, 156, 163, 191
Guzmán Family, 33

Hadasha, 163
Hamelin, Pied Piper of, 109
Hamusit, 163
Hebrew, 38
Henrique, Dom, 5, 54, 190
Henry the Navigator, Prince, 33, 182-184
Henze, Paul, 89, 90, 181
Heresy, 55
Herzbruch, Kurt, 78
Hieroglyphs, 25
Highlands (Ethiopian Highlands), 16, 21-23, 26, 28, 31, 33, 34, 41, 44, 57, 86, 93, 119, 137, 176, 188, 190-193
Hindu, 44, 188, 189
"História de Etiópia", 192
"History of Rasselas, Prince of Abissinia, The", 175, 181
Holland, 17, 59
Holmes, Richard Rivington, 178
Holy Church of Saint Mary of Zion, 112
Holy Roman Emperor (See Charles V), 185, 187-189
Holy Roman Emperors, 38
Horn of Africa, 129

Iberia, 34, 37, 57, 93, 118, 129, 134, 158, 175
Inda Selassie (see Shire), 8, 157

India, 31-35, 38-41, 43-48, 52-54, 56, 86, 134, 136, 137, 143, 172, 180, 185-192
Indian Ocean, 23, 26, 31, 38, 40, 43, 44, 47, 48, 172-175, 185
Indonesia, 38
Industrial Revolution, 25
Injera, 156, 194
Inquisitor General, 184, 185
Inquisitor of Aragón, 184
Inquisitor of Seville, 184
Institute of Ethiopian Studies, 13, 16, 112, 181, 182, 203
Isabel (Daughter of Manuel I of Portugal), 187
Islam, 23, 37, 38, 44-46, 49-51, 55, 146, 167, 172, 173, 183, 186, 188
Islamic Invasions, 42
Islamic Threat, 34
Israel, 12
Italy, 37, 61, 70
Iyasu I, Emperor, 135, 177
Iyasu I Castle, 133
Iyasu II, Emperor, 135, 141, 177
Iyoas II, Emperor, 135

Jacomo, Francisco, 190
Japan, 31, 47, 188, 191
Javanese, 186
Jeddah, 6, 187
Jerusalem, 12, 25, 34, 37, 38, 98, 177
Jerusalem Talmud, 25
Jesuits (see Society of Jesus), 12, 13, 26, 36, 52-55, 58, 60, 80, 84, 86, 88, 92, 98, 106, 108, 124, 135, 137, 150, 157, 167, 175, 180, 182, 188-191, 193
Jewish Sacrificial Stones (see Talmud), Tana Kirkos, 104
Jewry, 55
João II, Dom, 5, 33-35, 184, 185
João III, Dom, 5, 50, 51, 187, 189
John of Austria, Don, 190
Johnson, Samuel, 181
Jordanus, 39
Joseph, 98

Karakorum, 39
Kebra Nagast, 178, 180
Kebran Gabriel, 95-97, 101
Kebran Gabriel Monastery, 95
Keep, 108, 152, 153
Kenya, 7, 58
Kiflewahd, 56
Kilwa, 6, 48
Korata Bridge, 148
Kusquaum, 136, 141
Kwer'ata Re'esu, 177-179

Labrador, 184, 185
Laje(s), 128, 136, 139, 160, 161, 194
Lake Tana, 13, 17, 46, 57-59, 63, 90, 95, 97, 98, 100, 104, 107, 111, 115, 116, 118, 124, 132, 143, 144, 150, 152, 156, 160, 163, 169, 173, 180
Lalibela, 80, 85, 132, 134, 168
Lamego, José de, 40-41
Latin, 55, 192
Lebna Dengal, Emperor, 5, 43-45, 50, 51, 57, 67, 82, 121, 172, 173, 186-188, 191
Ledje Negus, 163
Lefkowitz, Mary, 168, 170, 181
Lepanto, Battle of, 183, 190
Liblibo Church, near Zege, 97
Lima, Rodrigo de, 12, 35, 43, 45, 172, 187
Lime Mortar, 88, 192
Lion House, 133
Lisboa, António de, 34, 185
Lisbon, 24, 31-34, 37, 38, 40, 41, 43, 44, 50-53, 57, 58, 119, 149, 171, 176, 180-190
Lisbon Earthquake (1531), 188
Lisbon Earthquake (1755), 176
Little Abay, 156
Little Abay River, 7
Lobo, Jerónimo, 193
London, 179-182
Lopes, Francisco, 189, 191
Lopez, António, 186
Louis XI, King, 33, 184
Louvain, 55
Lowlands, 37, 44, 46, 118, 173
Loyola, Padre Ignatius, 12, 52, 188, 189
Lucy (see Dinquinesh), 25
Luís, Manuel, 193

Lusitania, 57, 69, 176
Luther, Martin, 184, 187, 189

Macassar (see South Celebes), 191
Macau, 189, 192
Madagascar (see São Lourenço), 186
Magalhães, Fernão de (see Magellan, Fernando), 171, 187
Magech River, 7
Magellan, Fernando (see Magalhães, Fernão de), 171, 187
Maghreb, 38, 134, 175
Magro, Manuel, 88, 192
Mahdists, 149
Mai Gwa Gwa (see Fremona), 54, 56, 57, 157, 158, 190, 193
Mak'das, 194
Makisegrit, 142, 143
Malabar Coast, 79
Malacca, 47, 119, 186
Malay Archipelago, 189
Malindi, 58, 59, 186, 192
Mamluk (Invasion of Nubia), 42
Mamo Getahun, 135
Mandapa, 150
Manuel I, Dom (see Beja, Duke of), 33, 183
Manueline Architecture, 21
Manz, 75
Maqdala, Battle of (1868), 177-178
Maraba, 163
Mariam Gemb Church, Gemb Giorghis (see St. Mary's Roman Catholic Church, Gemb Giorghis), 108-110
Mariam Gemb Church (and Sussenyos Palace), Gorgora, 7, 150, 152, 153
Marques, Francisco, 193
Martins Homem, Álvaro, 184
Martins, João, 193
Mary, 98
Massawa, 35, 46, 48, 50, 54-56, 59, 119, 135, 172, 173, 187-191
Matthew the Armenian, 186-187

Mauritania, 38
Mecca, 6, 35, 40, 185
Medina, 6, 35, 40, 185
Médina-Sidonia, Duke of, 33, 183
Mediterranean Sea, 37, 39, 190
Mekele, 8
Mendes, Prelate Afonso, 23, 59, 60, 84, 143, 172, 182, 190, 192, 193
Menelik (son of Solomon & Sheba), 25
Mentuabe, Empress, 135, 141
Mentuabe's & Iyasu's Castle, 133
Merid Wolde Aregay, 16, 181
Mertule Maryam, 15, 42, 49, 67, 81-87, 89-91, 101, 106, 137
Mestre (da Obra), 122, 194
Middle Ages, 37
Mikael Sehul, Ras, 135, 137
Mimesis, 63, 80, 113, 114, 129, 169
Minas, Emperor, 5, 47, 53, 54, 188-190
Minho, 63, 113
Mocha, 56
Mogadishu, 6, 48
Moinho do Gato, 138, 161
Moluccas (see Spice Islands), 191
Mombassa, 48, 59, 188
Monastery [-ies], 22, 45, 63, 81, 89, 95, 97-99, 101-104, 111, 124, 150, 169
Monserrate, António de, 190
Montaroyo, Pedro de, 34, 185
Monte, 194
Moor(ish), 57, 64, 135, 136, 171
Moors, 33, 134, 136, 138, 183, 184
Morocco, 23, 31, 134
Mos Majorum, 129
Moses, 111, 112
Mota, 8, 106, 162
Mount Sinai, 111
Mouri, 191
Mozambique, 6, 35, 40, 186
Mozambique Island, 48, 186, 191
Murtiga River, 93

Museum(s), Church, 24, 90, 91, 95-96, 101-102, 104, 128
Muslim, 12, 37-39, 42-46, 48, 50, 51, 77, 82, 101, 112, 131, 135, 146, 172, 173, 186-188
Mussolini Tunnel (see T'armaber Pass), 75

Nafasha, 163
Naming A Child, 63
Nanina, 163
Naod, Emperor, 5, 41, 185, 186
Napier, General Robert, 177, 178
Narga Selassie Monastery, 98-101
Nave, 110, 144, 153
Nestorians, 37
New Christians, 34, 183, 184, 186
Newfoundland, 185
Ninety-Five Theses (see Protestant Reformation), 187
Nogueira, António & Jorge, 119
Nogueira, Francisco, 119
Noronha, Garcia de, 188
North Africa, 33, 38, 183
North America, 184, 203
Norway, 184
"Not Out of Africa", 80, 170, 181
Noudar Castle, 93, 138
Nubia, 26, 37, 39, 42, 180
Nur-ibn-Mujahid, 189

"O Estilo Gondar", 17, 180
Ogané, 39, 184
Old Testament, 25
Oman, 56
Olive Grove, 145
Ormuz, 6, 35, 40, 119, 185, 186, 192
Oromo, 82
"Os Lusíadas", 69, 174, 180, 190
Oviedo, André de, 23, 51-55, 189, 190

Páez House, 94-96

Páez, Padre Pêro, 12, 23, 56-60, 84, 86, 88, 94, 143, 155, 190-192
Paiva, Afonso de, 34, 35, 39, 40, 185
Pakenham, Thomas, 160, 182
Palestine, 37
Pankhurst, Richard, 12, 16, 177, 180-182
Paradise, 26, 47, 48, 50, 69, 175
Patriarch (see Abun), 12, 42, 51, 58, 192
Património, 179, 195
Pedreiro, 170, 195
"Peregrinação", 182, 192
Pernambuco, 193
Persia, 31, 38-40, 185
Pigmentation, 70, 129, 130, 171
Pigpen (see Af-mekurabia), 116
Pied Piper of Hamelin, 109
Pining, Didrik, 184
Pinto, Fernão Mendes, 172, 182, 190
Pipa Bridge, 91
Plague, 47, 80, 183, 187, 190
Plasencia, 33
Policy of Secrecy, 186
Ponte Romano (see Roman Bridge), 93, 195
Pope, 50, 51, 55, 59, 188, 190-192
Paul III, Pope, 50
Polo, Marco, 39, 183
Portugal, 5, 12, 15-17, 19, 21-23, 27, 31-35, 37, 38, 40, 42-44, 47-55, 57, 59, 61, 64-66, 69, 80, 85, 89, 91, 93, 94, 99, 107, 112, 113, 116, 121, 122, 129, 136-139, 141, 144, 147, 158-160, 168-177, 179, 181-195
Portuguese Army under Cristovão da Gama, 101
Portuguese Bridge (Gur River), 78, 80 (Blue Nile River), 92, 192
Portuguese India, 46, 54, 86, 188
Portuguese Inquisition, 189
Portuguese Revolution (1974), 176

Pothorst, Hans, 184
Praça, 32, 195
Pre-Columbian, 36
Prester John, 12, 31, 34, 35, 38-42, 46, 47, 55, 66, 112, 134, 172, 175, 180, 182, 184-187
Príncipe, 191
Priorado do Rosário, 119, 120
Protestant Reformation (see Ninety-Five Theses), 187
Punt, 25

Qaha River, 148
Quadra, Gregório de, 187
Quarry (see Selassie Gemb (Washa)), 100, 161, 162
Quinta, 195
Qundy Mountain, 67-68

Racism, 36
Ras, 106, 135, 137, 195
Ras Mikael Sehul's Castle, 133
Reb River, 7, 163
Rebellion, 12, 53, 54, 56-58, 187, 191, 193
Reboco, 87, 94, 95, 136, 145, 160, 195
Red Sea, 12, 13, 25, 35, 38-42, 44, 46, 48, 50, 51, 56, 59, 122, 172, 180, 182, 185-189
Reform Churches, 55
Reid, Martin, 179
Reis Santos, Isabel, 179
Reis Santos, Prof. Luís, 179
Renaissance, 21, 26, 34-36, 39, 47-49, 61, 170
Rhodes, 6, 39
Rodrigues, Padre Gonçalo, 52, 55, 189
Roman Bridge (see Ponte Romano), 93, 195
Roman Catholic Church, 12, 25, 41, 48, 56, 61, 106, 108, 143, 189, 192
Roman Inquisition, 188
Rome, 12, 23, 26, 51, 52, 54-59, 70, 84, 98, 187, 189, 190, 192, 193
Rotary Club of Bahir Dar, 162
Russia, 37

Sabaean, 25

Sabara Dildiy, 90, 161, 162
Sabla Vanggel, Queen Mother, 163, 173, 188
Sack of Rome, 187
Saga Zaab, 50, 55, 187, 188
Sala, 160, 195
Saladin, 38
Saloio, 94
Sana'a, 37
Sanches, João, 186
São Jerónimos, 31
São Jorge da Mina, 39, 193
São Lourenço (see Madagascar), 186
São Tomé, 191
Sarca, 58, 163, 191
Sartsa Dengal, Emperor, 5, 20, 54-57, 119, 190, 191
Scandinavia, 37
Sebastianismo, 31, 195
Sebastião, Dom, 5, 23, 31, 53, 54, 189, 190, 195
Sek'ela, 155, 156
Sela Cristos, Ras, 58, 106, 191, 192
Selassie Gemb (Washa) (see Quarry), 17, 100, 161
Semitic, 20, 25
Sequeira, Diogo de, 45, 186, 187
Serra da Estrela, 32, 33
Sheba, Queen, 12, 25, 81
Shembra Kuré, Battle of, 45, 188
Shimbet Mikael, 96, 110-112, 169
Shimelash Bequele, 17, 111, 112
Shire (see Inda Selassie), 8, 157
Shoa, 26, 35, 41, 42, 57, 66, 67, 78, 85, 177, 186
Shoarobit, 75, 76
Sid Mohammed, 186
Simien Mountains, 8, 163, 188
Simon, Abun, 58, 192
Sinai, 39, 111
Sintra, 94, 141, 203
Sixtus IV, Pope, 184
Skulason, Jon, 184
Slate (see Xisto), 158, 195
Slave Trade, 185
Soares, Lopo, 187

Society of Jesus (see Jesuits), 12, 52, 188
Socotra, 6, 48, 186
Sodré, Vincente, 186
Sofala, 6, 35, 40, 186
Solar, 195
Solomon, King, 12, 25
Somalia, 7
Somaliland, 41, 66
South America, 189
South Celebes (see Macassar), 191
South China Sea, 187
Southeast Asia, 38
Spain, 18, 23, 33, 52, 59, 70, 80, 129, 147, 170, 185-187, 190
Spanish America, 185
Spanish Inquisition, 184
Spice Islands (see Moluccas), 23, 48, 191
Squinch, 100
St. Giorghis Church, 94, 95
St. Luke, 177
St. Mark, 12
St. Mary's Roman Catholic Church, Gemb Giorghis (see Mariam Gemb Church, Gemb Giorghis), 110
St. Peter, 12
Suakin, 39
Sudan, 7, 13, 37, 149
Suez, 50, 188, 189
Summerhouse, 133
Suriano, Francesco, 184
Sussenyos, Emperor, 5, 12, 13, 57-60, 84, 106, 124, 143-145, 150-152, 161, 180, 191-193
Sussenyos' Palace (and Mariam Gemb Church), Gorgora, 150-152
Synod of Dort, 192
Syria, 12, 37, 38, 44, 187

Tabot (Tabotat), 111, 194, 195
Tadele Fentahun, 156
Talha Mar, 93, 195
Talmud (see Jewish Sacrificial Stones, Tana Kirkos), 104
Talwambara, 188
Tana Kirkos Monastery, 98, 99, 101, 103-105
Tangiers, 33, 183

Tartar Lands, 37, 39
T'armaber Pass (see Mussolini Tunnel), 75
Tasca, 128, 195
Tef, 156, 195
Tekeze River, 143
Teklahaimanot Church, 123
Teklahaimanot, Emperor, 135, 177
Ten Commandments, 111, 195
Ternate, 186
Terra, 69, 195
Terra Cotta, 175
Tewedros II, Emperor, 177
The Four Indies, 38
"The Mountains of Rasselas", 160, 182
The Philippines, 47
Tigray, 22, 51-57, 63, 67, 80, 132, 157, 168, 189-191, 193
Tigrinha, 21
Tigris River, 38
Timbuktu, 39, 185
Tis'isat (see Alata Falls), 91-92
Tlemcen, 184
Toilet, 125, 145
Toledo, 183
Tôr, 39
Tordesillas, Treaty of, 52, 185
Toro, Battle of, 33, 184
Torquemada, Tomás de, 184, 185
Trás-os-Montes, 113
"Travels to Discover the Source of the Nile in the Years 1768, 1769, 1770, 1771, 1772, and 1773", 155, 180, 186
Trinity, 49, 55
Tsegaye Kebede, 75
Tucurol, 39, 185
Tumha, 163
Turk, 186
Turk Uprising, 186
Turkey, 37
Turkish Baths, 133

UNESCO, 13, 195
Unhas, 195
University College of Addis Ababa (see Addis Ababa University), 78
University of Coimbra, 179

University of Évora, 16, 17, 203
Ure Kidane Mehret Church, Zege, 7, 97

Vatican, 24, 37
Velasco, João de, 193
Venice, 34, 183
Victoria, Queen, 178

Waina Dega, Battle of, 46, 142, 146, 173, 188
Waj, 189
Wedding House, 133
Welega, 67
Whitewash(ing), 129, 130
Wimbledon, 179
Windsor Castle, 178
Winter Palace (see Garden of Jesus & Geneta Yesus), 124
Worms, Edict of, 187

Xavier, Padre Francis, 52, 186, 188, 189
Xisto (see Slate), 158, 195

Ya'qob, Emperor, 5, 41, 56, 57, 191
Yekuno Amlak, King of Shoa, 85
Yemen, 37, 56, 122
Yeshaq, Governor of Tigray Azmach, 53-55, 189, 190
Yewezazert, 106
Yibaba, 58, 106-108, 163
Yohannes I, Emperor, 135, 177
Yohannes IV, Emperor, 178
Yohannes' Chancellery, 133
Yohannes' Library, 133
Yosab, Abun, 51

Za Dengal, Emperor, 5, 12, 56, 58, 191
Zanzibar, 6, 48
Zara Wangel, Abun, 58
Zaragoza, 184
Zege Peninsula, 95
Zega River, 78
Zeila, 35, 40, 48, 66, 67, 185
Zobel, Tomb of, 136, 141

## About the Author

John Jeremy Hespeler-Boultbee was born at Vancouver, Canada, in 1935. His education started in Australia, continuing in the United States, Canada and Great Britain. As soldier and journalist he travelled widely throughout Africa, the Middle and Far East and North America.

He studied architectural history in Great Britain, returning to Canada in 1956 to work as a journalist. At the University of Victoria he studied classical history and anthropology, living for a winter among the people of the Nass and Skeena Rivers on British Columbia's Pacific Northwest coast. He earned his degree in history in art, three-dimensional design and ceramic sculpture.

As a journalist, he covered the Captain's Revolution in Portugal in 1974, the following year accepting a post as lecturer at the University of Lisbon. Simultaneously, and for twelve years, he re-designed and restored old Portuguese homes in the Sintra hills and the Alentejo. Through hands-on experience he absorbed the local secrets of traditional indigenous construction and stonemasonry, an apprenticeship-cum-expertise which stood him in excellent stead when he came to consider the subject of this book.

He lived for twenty-five years in Portugal, during that time making several forays into the Ethiopian Highlands on behalf of the Department of History and CIDEHUS *(Centro de Investigação e Desenvolvimento em Ciências Humanas e Sociais)*, the research and development institute at the University of Évora. He is an associate of the Institute of Ethiopian Studies, Addis Ababa University. For the two year period, 2007-2009, he lived in and conducted research from Bahir Dar on Lake Tana, Ethiopia, during which time he found his historical conclusions were at considerable variance with colleagues in the History Department at Bahir Dar University - disagreements which have prompted the revisions leading to this current updated and revised edition of *A Story in Stones*.

Hespeler-Boultbee currently makes his home in Victoria, B.C., Canada. Apart from his writing and his artwork he spends his time raising funds for a variety of Ethiopian projects.

www.ingramcontent.com/pod-product-compliance
Lightning Source LLC
Chambersburg PA
CBHW040910020526
44116CB00026B/20